BP 300

☼

An Annotated Bibliography of the Publications of The Borgo Press

1976-1998

by

Robert Reginald

and

Mary Wickizer Burgess

The Borgo Press
An Imprint of Wildside Press

MMVII

Borgo Literary Guides
ISSN 0891-9623
Number Ten

Library of Congress Cataloging in Publication Data for the first edition, *BP 250*:

Reginald, R.
        BP 250 : an annotated bibliography of the first 250 publications of the Borgo
Press, 1976-1996 / by Robert Reginald and Mary Wickizer Burgess.
        p. cm. — (Borgo Literary Guides, ISSN 0891-9623 ; no.10)
        Includes bibliographical references and index.
        1. Borgo Press—History—Bibliography—Catalogs. 2. Publishers and publish-
ing—United States—History—20th century—Bibliography—Catalogs. 3. Borgo
Press—Catalogs. 4. Catalogers, Publishers'—United States. 5. United States—
Imprints—Catalogs. I. Burgess, Mary Wickizer, 1938- . II. Title. III. Series.
Z473.B674R44 1996   96-1744
016.0705—dc20   CIP

SECOND EDITION

CONTENTS

DEDICATION

To the Memory of

Ted Dikty
(1920-1991)

and

Alfred Saunders
(1929-1997)

And to a Fevre Dream
Yclept The Borgo Press

(Somewhere Out Near Castle Dracula)

INTRODUCTION

WHAT WE DID IN OUR "SPARE TIME"

In the spring of 1975 I received my first large royalty check from Gale Research Company for *Cumulative Paperback Index, 1939-1959,* my second book, which had been published in 1973. I realized that the sum would have to be reinvested by the end of the year, or I would lose a significant portion to taxes. Thus Borgo Press was born.

I had been doing editorial work for Nectar Press and Newcastle Publishing Co., Inc., since 1970, and I approached Alfred and Joseph Saunders, the publishers, with an idea for a new line of author and music critiques, plus some fiction titles for the expanding science fiction field. In early 1975 they agreed to distribute the books to the trade.

In June I met my future wife, Mary A. Wickizer, and she soon became a sounding board for my ideas. By the fall of 1975 we had established the basis for the business and had begun acquiring manuscripts. Our first two books were released in April 1976. We actually tied the knot about the time our second list appeared.

Borgo split with Newcastle in 1980, moving away from the trade exclusively into the library market. Simultaneously, we acquired distribution rights to the entire Newcastle line, rebinding their books in cloth for the library market; this formed the basis for similar agreements we signed later with other publishers. At one time we handled over a thousand distributed titles from thirty-five outside houses.

Our own interests in literature and history formed the focal point for our proprietary publications. From the beginning we concentrated primarily on critiques and bibliographies, particularly of genre literature and authors, for we perceived that little had been published on those subjects at that time; and we later moved into publishing books on history, political science, and current affairs.

In 1989 we issued our 100th title. In 1991 we acquired several smaller lines—Brownstone Books, St. Willbrord's Press, and Sidewinder Press—and maintained them as separate imprints. Also in 1991 we pur-

BP 300, by Robert Reginald & Mary Wickizer Burgess

chased a small series on contemporary writers from Starmont House, and later acquired 100 other titles from that company when they went out of business in February 1993. We published our 200th proprietary book in 1994. We also added to our list the imprints Burgess & Wickizer, Emeritus Enterprises, and Unicorn & Son to reflect specific programs or interests.

We were fortunate over the years to encounter and publish a remarkable number of works by such well-known professionals as Piers Anthony, Mike Ashley, Reginald Bretnor, Algis Budrys, Max Allan Collins, D. G. Compton, L. Sprague de Camp, Jack Dann, Harlan Ellison, Raymond Z. Gallun, James Gunn, R. A. Lafferty, Ursula K. Le Guin, Robert W. "Doc" Lowndes, Ross Macdonald, Henry Miller, Robert Nathan, William F. Nolan, Pamela Sargent, Brian Stableford, William F. Temple, Geoffrey Wagner, Leonard Wibberley, Colin Wilson, and George Zebrowski, among many others. We were assisted in our efforts by a fine editorial and business staff, including: Scott Alan Burgess, Al Charlton, John Hansen Gurley, Daryl F. Mallett, Barbara A. Quarton, M. Louise Reynnells, Richard A. Rogers, Paul-David Seldis, and Yvonne P. Tevis. The quality of our publications over the years was enhanced by our outside editors, including: Allan Adrian, Barbara Dikty, Jeffrey M. Elliot, Nathan Kravetz, Bishop Karl Pruter, Dale Salwak, Roger C. Schlobin, William L. Slout, and Guy M. Townsend.

Along with the others mentioned previously, Douglas A. Menville and Barry R. Levin were there at the beginning; their unconditional friendship, support, and encouragement over the years made the path we chose a little less lonely; and Thaddeus E. "Ted" Dikty shared hopes and fears and dreams with us—he was a decent man and a dear friend—and we miss him, even after all these years.

In the end, however, 300 titles proved to be enough. By early 1999 we were tired and burned out. We decided to shut the press down in the spring of that year, and we closed our doors finally in August, paying off our vendors and authors, and returning all literary rights to the books to their original owners. It was a sad but a necessary time. Borgo had never made any money. In order to begin the process of reaching towards retirement, in order to free ourselves from the burden that Borgo Press had finally become, in order to find more writing time for ourselves, we did the sane thing and put *finis* to the old beastie.

I remember feeling as if a close family member had suddenly died. But as with other deaths, one moves on. In retrospect, we had a very good time publishing these books. We met some interesting people

BP 300, by Robert Reginald & Mary Wickizer Burgess

and produced a few works that will stand the test of time. And I regret none of it, even the closure. All things come to an end.

Then I was approached early in 2003 by John Betancourt of Wildside Press. John wanted to acquire the remnants of Borgo Press for his own house. Well, of course, there wasn't much left beyond the unsold stock of limited titles, and the books that Mary and I had penned ourselves. We sold the lot to Wildside for the grand sum of $1.

John immediately offered me a role as Advisory Editor for Wildside Press. He wanted to continue the imprint, to reprint old Borgo Press books where possible, and to do new books under the Borgo Press label. As it happened, we had had a number of projects left unfinished when we shut down the press in 1999. I was just beginning to contact prospective authors and to issue contracts for new and old books alike, when I was laid low by a close encounter with the Grim Reaper on July 30, 2003.

Somehow I survived the blow, albeit with serious and long-term heart damage. It took me a year to gather enough energy to pick up the pieces of Borgo Press. John was always very understanding about my situation, and simply said to bide my time until I could do the work again. And so it happened.

The Borgo Press has now been resurrected as an imprint of Wildside Press, and this final bibliography of the publications engendered by Robert Reginald (Prof. Michael Burgess) and Mary Wickizer Burgess is being produced by Wildside as one of the first batch of the new titles being issued in 2005.

Others will ultimately judge whether what we did in our "spare time" was worthy of publication. We cannot. We did the best we could with limited resources, limited help, and limited time. We learned a great deal along the way, and we had our fair share of trials, tribulations, and fun. But now we want to look to the future of Borgo Press, not to the past. We want to see what Wildside Press will do as it explores the edges of the publishing universe. As our dear friend, Le Duc d'Alver, might say,

"Vive le Borgeau!"

—Robert Reginald
Mary Wickizer Burgess
11 February 1996 & 31 August 2004

ABOUT THE FORMAT

We've employed here the format that we developed for the various bibliographies that Borgo Press published during its existence. Each section is arranged in descending chronological order by publication date. A typical entry includes: item number, title (bold-faced italics), author, series and series numbers (when appropriate, in small caps), page count, LC number, OCLC number, ISBN(s) with format(s) and price(s), cover description, and month and year of publication. All additional printings are recorded in chronological order under the first edition. This is followed by a brief description of the book, plus a detailed list of its contents, and other notes of interest. The Series Index simply gives series name, series number, title, and author. The other indexes, by author and title, are keyed to item number. It should be noted that the list of Starmont House books only reflects those titles actually acquired by Borgo Press for distribution and/or republication, and not every item that Starmont and FAX Collector's Editions actually published.

A.

BORGO PRESS BOOKS
1976-1998

A1. ***Robert A. Heinlein: Stranger in His Own Land***, by George Edgar Slusser. THE MILFORD SERIES: POPULAR WRITERS OF TODAY, Volume 1. ii+60 p. LC 76-6104. OCLC #2089497. Newcastle ISBN 0-87877-201-4 (later assigned Borgo ISBN 0-89370-201-3) paper $1.95. Cover: standard series design, probably by Jacqueline Thibaud, red ink on gold background. First Edition, March 1976.

A critique of American science fiction writer, Robert A. Heinlein (1907-1988).
CONTENTS: Introduction (p. i-ii); 1. Twins and Doubles: *Time for the Stars* and *Double Star* (p. 1-16); 2. The Two Smiths: *Stranger in a Strange Land* and *I Will Fear No Evil* (p. 17-37); 3. The Deification of Lazarus Long: *Time Enough for Love* and *Methuselah's Children* (p. 38-50); 4. Heinlein in His Own Land: *Have Space Suit—Will Travel* (p. 51-55); Afterword (p. 56); Biography & Bibliography (p. 57-60).
See also the Second Edition (**A10**), which is completely rewritten. All of these early Borgo Press books were saddle-stitched (i.e., stapled) through the spine. Backcover copy shows publisher as Newcastle/ Borgo Press with Newcastle's address. The early Borgo Press covers are uncredited.

A2. ***The Beach Boys: Southern California Pastoral***, by Bruce Golden. THE WOODSTOCK SERIES: POPULAR MUSIC OF TODAY, Volume 1. 59 p. LC 76-5902. OCLC #2089472. Newcastle ISBN 0-87877-202-2 (later assigned Borgo ISBN 0-89730-202-1) paper $1.95. Cover: standard series design, probably by

Jacqueline Thibaud, orange and yellow ink on black background. First Edition, March 1976.

b. Later reprinted in cloth on a single-copy basis via xerography, with ISBN 0-89370-102-5.

A critique of the modern American pop group, The Beach Boys.
CONTENTS: Preface and Acknowledgments (p. 3); 1. Introduction (p. 7-12); 2. "Surfin'" to *All Summer Long* (1962-1964) (p. 13-22); 3. *Beach Boys Today* to *Beach Boys Party* (1965) (p. 23-26); 4. *Pet Sounds* to *Holland* (1966-1973) (p. 27-39); Discography (p. 40-52); Bibliography (p. 53-56); Notes (p. 57-59).
See also the Revised Edition (**A120**).

A3. ***The Attempted Assassination of John F. Kennedy: A Political Fantasy***, by Lucas Webb. 47 p. LC 76-40282. OCLC #2424932. Newcastle ISBN 0-87877-204-9 (later assigned Borgo ISBN 0-89370-204-8) paper $1.95. Cover painting (four-color) on white background by Mike Bennett, depicting an aged John F. Kennedy. First Edition, September 1976.

b. Later rebound in cloth (beginning February 1979) with ISBN 0-89370-104-1.

The author Michael Burgess, writing under his one-time pseudonym Lucas Webb (a name drawn, like "Boden Clarke," from a *San Bernardino Sun* marriage column in which someone named Lucas was marrying someone named Webb), here postulates an alternate history in which the old-world monarchies were never displaced, and in which Kennedy was never assassinated, but survived to serve a second term in office.
See also the rewritten version, *If J.F.K. Had Lived* (**A49**). Note: the author did not write the novels *Eli's Road* (Doubleday, 1971) or *Stribling* (Doubleday, 1973), written by another pseudonymous Lucas Webb.

A4. ***The Farthest Shores of Ursula K. Le Guin***, by George Edgar Slusser. THE MILFORD SERIES: POPULAR WRITERS OF TODAY, Volume 2. 60 p. LC 76-41929. OCLC #2423766. Newcastle ISBN 0-87877-205-7 (later assigned Borgo ISBN 0-89370-205-

6) paper $1.95. Cover: standard series design, probably by Judy Cloyd, dark blue and black ink on light blue background. First Edition, September 1976.

b.   Later rebound in cloth (beginning February 1979) with ISBN 0-89370-105-X).

A critique of modern American writer, Ursula K. Le Guin (1929-).
     CONTENTS: Introduction (p. 3-4); The Early Hainish Novels (p. 5-16); *The Left Hand of Darkness* (p. 17-31); The Earthsea Trilogy (p. 31-46); *The Dispossessed* (p. 46-56); Conclusion (p. 57-58); Biography & Bibliography (p. 59-60).

A5.   *Alistair MacLean: The Key Is Fear*, by Robert A. Lee, anonymously edited and rewritten by Robert Reginald. THE MILFORD SERIES: POPULAR WRITERS OF TODAY, Volume 3. 60 p. LC 76-29047. OCLC #2401713. Newcastle ISBN 0-87877-203-0 (later assigned Borgo ISBN 0-89370-203-X) paper $1.95. Cover: standard series design, probably by Judy Cloyd, silver and black ink on dark red background. First Edition, October 1976.

b.   Later rebound in cloth (beginning February 1979) with ISBN 0-89370-103-3.

A critique of the late British suspense writer, Alistair MacLean (1922-1987).
     CONTENTS: Introduction (p. 3); The War Novels (p. 5-18); The Secret Agents (p. 19-29); Transitions (p. 30-38); Renaissance (p. 39-47); The Search for Something New (p. 48-57); Conclusion (p. 58); Biography & Bibliography (p. 59-60).

A6.   *Up Your Asteroid! A Science Fiction Farce*, by C. Everett Cooper. 47 p. LC 77-866. OCLC #2798670. ISBN 0-89370-206-4 paper $1.95. Cover painting (four colors, purple predominating) by Tony Yamada. First Edition, April 1977.

b.   Later rebound in cloth (beginning February 1979) with ISBN 0-89370-106-8.

BP 300, by Robert Reginald & Mary Wickizer Burgess

This was the first book to bear a Borgo Press ISBN number, the first to be typeset and designed by Borgo Press on its own equipment (as were all books thereafter), and the first to feature four-color cover art. This short novel is both a parody of *Star Trek* and an attempt to satirize contemporary politics and social mores.

A7.   *The Bradbury Chronicles*, by George Edgar Slusser. THE MILFORD SERIES: POPULAR WRITERS OF TODAY, Volume 4. 63 p. LC 77-774. OCLC #2798946. ISBN 0-89370-207-2 paper $1.95. Cover: standard series design, probably by Judy Cloyd, dark green and white ink on light green background. First Edition, April 1977.

   b.   Later rebound in cloth (beginning February 1979) with ISBN 0-89370-107-6.

A critique of the modern American writer, Ray Bradbury (1920-).
   CONTENTS: [Introduction] (p. [3]-10); *The October Country* (p. 10-26); *The Vintage Bradbury* (p. 26-43); *The Machineries of Joy* (p. 43-52); *Fahrenheit 451* (p. 52-54); *Dandelion Wine & The Martian Chronicles* (p. 54-59); Conclusion (p. 60); [Biography & Bibliography] (p. 61-63).

A8.   *John D. MacDonald and the Colorful World of Travis McGee*, by Frank D. Campbell, Jr., anonymously edited by Robert Reginald. THE MILFORD SERIES: POPULAR WRITERS OF TODAY, Volume 5. 63 p. LC 77-773. OCLC #2798947. ISBN 0-89370-208-0 paper $1.95. Cover: standard series design, probably by Judy Cloyd, blue and green ink on a light green background. First Edition, April 1977.

   b.   Later rebound in cloth (beginning February 1979) with ISBN 0-89370-108-4.

A critique of the late American writer, John D. MacDonald (1916-1986).
   CONTENTS: Foreword (p. 3); Blue (p. 4-6); Pink (p. 6-9); Purple (p. 9-12); Red (p. 12-16); Gold (p. 16-20); Orange (p. 20-23); Amber (p. 23-27); Yellow (p. 27-30); Gray (p. 30-34); Brown (p. 34-38); Indigo (p. 38-41); Lavender (p. 41-45); Tan (p. 45-49);

Scarlet (p. 49-52); Turquoise (p. 52-56); Lemon (p. 57-62); [Biography & Bibliography] (p. 63).

A9. ***Harlan Ellison: Unrepentant Harlequin***, by George Edgar Slusser. THE MILFORD SERIES: POPULAR WRITERS OF TODAY, Volume 6. 63 p. LC 77-768. OCLC #2798953. ISBN 0-89370-209-9 paper $1.95. Cover: standard series design, probably by Judy Cloyd, black and bright pink ink on light pink background. First Edition, April 1977.

   b.   Later rebound in cloth (beginning February 1979) with the ISBN 0-89370-109-2.

A critique of modern American writer, Harlan Ellison (1934-).
   CONTENTS: Introduction (p. 3-8); Journalism (p. 8-23); Fantasy (p. 23-42); Myth (p. 42-59); Conclusion (p. 59-61); [Biography & Bibliography] (p. 62-63).

A10. ***Robert A. Heinlein: Stranger in His Own Land, Second Edition***, by George Edgar Slusser. THE MILFORD SERIES: POPULAR WRITERS OF TODAY, Volume 1. 64 p. LC 77-5657. OCLC #2910839. ISBN 0-89370-210-2 paper $1.95. Cover: standard series design, probably by Judy Cloyd, gold and white ink on black background. Second Edition, July 1977.

   b.   Later rebound in cloth (beginning February 1979) with ISBN 0-89370-110-6.

A study of the late American writer Robert A. Heinlein (1907-1988), completely rewritten from the First Edition (see **A1**).
   CONTENTS: Introduction (p. 3-8); Twins and Doubles (p. 9-23); The Two Smiths (p. 23-48); The Deification of Lazarus Long (p. 48-61); Afterword (p. 61-62); Biography (p. 62); Bibliography (p. 63-63).

A11. ***Kurt Vonnegut: the Gospel from Outer Space; (or, Yes We Have No Nirvanas)***, by Clark Mayo. THE MILFORD SERIES: POPULAR WRITERS OF TODAY, Volume 7. 64 p. LC 77-24460. OCLC #3167190. ISBN 0-89370-211-0 paper $1.95. Cover: standard series design by Judy Cloyd, brown and ocre ink on light brown background. First Edition, October 1977.

b. Later rebound in cloth (beginning February 1979) with ISBN 0-89370-111-4.

A critique of the modern American writer, Kurt Vonnegut (1922-).
CONTENTS: Introduction: The Naive Vision (p. 3-8); *Player Piano*; or, Stay Close to the Edge (p. 9-15); *The Sirens of Titan*; or, What Is, Is; and What Isn't, Isn't (p. 15-23); *Mother Night*; or, Be Careful What You Pretend to Be (p. 23-27); *Cat's Cradle*; or, Live by Harmless Untruths (p. 28-34); *God Bless You, Mr. Rosewater*; or, False Pearls Before Real Swine (p. 34-41); The Short Stories and Plays; or, No Pain (p. 41-45); *Slaughterhouse-Five*; or, Wonderful New Lies (p. 45-52); *Breakfast of Champions*; or, Adapting to Chaos (p. 52-58); *Slapstick*; or, Life as a Turkey Trot (p. 58-63); Conclusion; or, Reaching Equilibrium (p. 63); Biography and Bibliography (p. 64).

A12. ***Aldiss Unbound: The Science Fiction of Brian W. Aldiss***, by Richard Mathews. THE MILFORD SERIES: POPULAR WRITERS OF TODAY, Volume 9. 64 p. LC 77-24582. OCLC #3186622. ISBN 0-89370-213-7 paper $1.95. Cover: standard series design by Judy Cloyd, white ink on a particolored purple and magenta background. First Edition, October 1977.

b. Later rebound in cloth (beginning February 1979) with ISBN 0-89370-113-0.

A critique of the modern British writer, Brian W. Aldiss (1925-).
CONTENTS: Wherein Proteus Meets Prometheus (p. 3-4); Singing in a New Universe (p. 4-7); Short and Sweet (p. 8-11); The Communion of Laughter (p. 11-18); Heat, Cold, and Other Dichotomies (p. 18-23); A Grey and Beautiful World (p. 23-34); Head Waters (p. 34-48); Flashback (p. 48-50); What Rough Beast (p. 50-56); Repairing the Fabric (p. 56-61); Biography & Bibliography (p. 62-64).

A13. ***Piers Anthony's Hasan***, by Piers Anthony. 190 p. LC 77-24589. OCLC #3186611. ISBN 0-89370-215-3 paper $3.95. Cover painting (a striking wraparound cover of Hasan and a bird-girl) and four interior drawings by George Barr. Afterword by Richard Mathews. First Edition, October 1977.

b. Later rebound in cloth (beginning February 1979) with ISBN 0-89370-115-7.

Hasan, a simple lad from medieval Bassorah, travels to fantastic Serendip, where he makes friends with an ifrit, finds romance, and battles for the restoration of the rightful Queen.

This was the longest Borgo Press book published to this date, the first to be perfect bound (not saddle-stitched), and the first full-length novel in the line. Reprint editions were later sold to Dell Books and Tor Books.

A14. *The Classic Years of Robert A. Heinlein*, by George Edgar Slusser. THE MILFORD SERIES: POPULAR WRITERS OF TODAY, Volume 11. 63 p. LC 77-24626. OCLC #3186521. ISBN 0-89370-216-1 paper $1.95. Cover: standard series design by Judy Cloyd, black and brown ink on brown background. First Edition, October 1977.

b. Later rebound in cloth (beginning February 1979) with ISBN 0-89370-116-5.

A critique of the late American writer, Robert A. Heinlein (1907-1988), and a companion volume to **A10**.

CONTENTS: The Classic Years (p. 3-9); Stories (p. 9-24); Novellas (p. 24-39); Two Novels of Intrigue (p. 39-49); A Heinlein Masterpiece (p. 49-57); Afterthoughts (p. 57-60); Biography and Bibliography (p. 61-63).

The original printing contained a defective page 6; this was replaced in most of the copies distributed.

A15. *The Delany Intersection: Samuel R. Delany Considered As a Writer of Semi-Precious Words*, by George Edgar Slusser. THE MILFORD SERIES: POPULAR WRITERS OF TODAY, Volume 10. 64 p. LC 77-24580. OCLC #3186626. ISBN 0-89370-214-5 paper $1.95. Cover: standard series design by Judy Cloyd, black and white and red ink on an orange-red background. First Edition, December 1977.

b. Later rebound in cloth (beginning February 1979) with ISBN 0-89370-114-9.

A critique of the modern African-American writer, Samuel R. Delany (1942-).
CONTENTS: The Delany Intersections (p. 3-12); The Fall of the Towers (p. 12-29); From *Babel-17* to *Nova* (p. 29-60); From *The Tides of Lust* to *Triton*: Old Patterns, New Directions (p. 60-63); Biography and Bibliography (p. 64).
Delayed from its announced publication date of October 1977.

A16. ***The Wings of Madness: A Novel of Charles Baudelaire***, by Geoffrey Wagner. 224 p. LC 78-1039. OCLC #3627161. ISBN 0-89370-220-X paper $3.95. Cover painting (wrap-around cover) of Charles Baudelaire and mistress by Mary Sherman, with blue background; frontispiece photo of Charles Baudelaire; afterword by Peter M. Briscoe. First Edition, April 1978.

b. Later rebound in cloth (beginning February 1979) with ISBN 0-89370-120-3.

A biographical novel of the life of French poet Charles Baudelaire (1821-1867), with numerous original translations of Baudelaire verse scattered throughout the novel.
This was the largest Borgo Press book published to this date.

A17. ***Worlds Beyond the World: The Fantastic Vision of William Morris***, by Richard Mathews. THE MILFORD SERIES: POPULAR WRITERS OF TODAY, Volume 13. 63 p. LC 78-247. OCLC #3650332. ISBN 0-89730-218-8 paper $2.45. Cover: standard series design by Judy Cloyd, dark purple ink on a lighter purple and white wallpaper background. First Edition, May 1978.

b. Later rebound in cloth (beginning February 1979) with ISBN 0-89370-118-1.

A critique of the fiction of the British Victorian writer, William Morris (1834-1896).
CONTENTS: Worlds Beyond the World (p. 3-4); 1. Into the Unknown (p. 4-18); 2. The Dream of a Better World (p. 18-34); 3.

Killing Time (p. 34-43); 4. Beyond the World (p. 43-61); 5. Some Closing Remarks (p. 61-62); Selected Critical Sources (p. 63).
This was the first Milford Series title to be perfect bound.

A18. *The Dream Quest of H.P. Lovecraft*, by Darrell Schweitzer. THE MILFORD SERIES: POPULAR WRITERS OF TODAY, Volume 12. 63 p. LC 78-891. OCLC #3627325. ISBN 0-89370-217-X paper $2.45. Cover: standard series design by Judy Cloyd, red and black ink on a gray background. First Edition, May 1978.

  b. Later rebound in cloth (beginning February 1979) with ISBN 0-89370-117-3.

A critique of the late American horror writer, H. P. Lovecraft (1890-1937).
    CONTENTS: Background (p. 3-5); Early Horror Tales (p. 5-11); Lovecraft and Lord Dunsany (p. 11-20); Hauntings and Horrors (p. 20-25); Nameless Hordes (p. 25-30); Lovecraft at His Best (p. 30-40); An Interlude with Disaster (p. 41-42); Final Renaissance (p. 43-47); Last Years (p. 47-51); The Revisions (p. 51-55); Lovecraft's Nonfiction (p. 55-57); Lovecraft's Poetry (p. 57-59); The "Collaborations" with August Derleth (p. 59); Conclusion (p. 59-61); Bibliography (p. 62-63).

A19. *The Space Odysseys of Arthur C. Clarke*, by George Edgar Slusser. THE MILFORD SERIES: POPULAR WRITERS OF TODAY, Volume 8. 64 p. LC 77-24438. OCLC #3167251. ISBN 0-89370-212-9 paper $1.95. Cover: standard series design by Judy Cloyd, purple and blue ink on a blue background. First Edition, July 1978.

  b. Later rebound in cloth (beginning February 1979) with ISBN 0-89370-112-2.

A critique of the modern British writer, Arthur C. Clarke (1917-).
    CONTENTS: The Odyssey Pattern: Progress and Clarke's Elegaic Humanism (p. 3-35); Six Odysseys (p. 35-64); Biography (p. 64).
    Delayed from its announced publication date of October 1977. This was the last of the Borgo saddle-stitched books.

A20. *Lightning from a Clear Sky: Tolkien, the Trilogy, and the Silmarillion*, by Richard Mathews. THE MILFORD SERIES: POPULAR WRITERS OF TODAY, Volume 15. 63 p. LC 78-922. OCLC #3669969. ISBN 0-89370-221-8 paper $2.45. Cover: standard series design by Judy Cloyd, blue and black ink on a light blue and white background. First Edition, July 1978.

 b. Later rebound in cloth (beginning February 1979) with ISBN 0-89370-121-1.

A critique of the late British writer, J. R. R. Tolkien (1892-1973).
CONTENTS: Preface (p. 3-4); I. J. R. R. Tolkien (p. 5-7); II. *The Hobbit* (p. 7-18); III. The Lord of the Rings (p. 18-56); IV. *The Silmarillion* (p. 57-59); V. Some Closing Remarks (p. 59-61); Selected Critical Sources (p. 62); Biography & Bibliography (p. 63).

A21. *Beware of the Mouse*, by Leonard Wibberley. 189+[iii] p. LC 78-14993. OCLC #4114592. ISBN 0-89370-226-9 paper $3.95; ISBN 0-89370-001-0 signed, limited cloth edition of 50 copies. Cover (four-color wraparound painting) plus ten interior illustrations by Cathy Hill; the cover depicts the battle between the French invaders and the Grand Fenwick defenders, with a gold background; afterword by Richard Mathews. First Borgo Edition, October 1978.

 b. Later rebound in cloth (beginning February 1979) with ISBN 0-89370-126-2.

The first book of the Mouse That Roared series is set in the year 1450, and features the humorous escapades of Sir Roger Fenwick, third Duke of the Duchy, as he attempts to repel French invaders.
This facsimile reprint of the 1958 Putnam edition includes ten new illustrations by Cathy Hill.

A22. *Conan's World and Robert E. Howard*, by Darrell Schweitzer. THE MILFORD SERIES: POPULAR WRITERS OF TODAY, Volume 17. 64 p. LC 78-14569. OCLC #4135546. ISBN 0-89370-223-4 paper $2.45. Cover: standard series design by Judy Cloyd, white ink on a purple and white landscape background. First Edition, November 1978.

b. Later rebound in cloth (beginning February 1979) with ISBN 0-89370-123-8.

A critique of the late American fantasy and adventure writer, Robert E. Howard (1906-1936).
    CONTENTS: Introduction (p. 3-5); The Conan Phenomenon (p. 5-10); Conan as Howard Wrote Him (p. 10-49); The Conan Series in the Order Written (p. 50-52); Conan's World (p. 52-56); Conclusion (p. 56-62); Summation (p. 62); Bibliography (p. 63-64).

A23. *A Usual Lunacy*, by D. G. Compton. 191 p. LC 78-14953. OCLC #4114652. ISBN 0-89370-225-0 paper $3.95; ISBN 0-89370-000-2 signed, limited cloth edition of 50 copies. Cover painting (four-color wraparound cover) and interior drawings by Mary Sherman, with portraits of the heads of a man and woman on a teal background. Afterword by George Edgar Slusser. First Edition, November 1978.

b. Later rebound in cloth (beginning February 1979) with ISBN 0-89370-125-4.

This original science-fiction novel is set in a near-future world where love is literally a disease.

A24. *Against Time's Arrow: The High Crusade of Poul Anderson*, by Sandra Miesel. THE MILFORD SERIES: POPULAR WRITERS OF TODAY, Volume 18. 64 p. LC 78-14913. OCLC #4114713. ISBN 0-89730-224-2 paper $2.45. Cover: standard series design by Judy Cloyd, purple ink on a mustard and white clock background. First Edition, December 1978.

b. Later rebound in cloth (beginning February 1979) with ISBN 0-89370-124-6.

A critique of the modern American writer, Poul Anderson (1926-2001).
    CONTENTS: Introduction (p. 3-7); The Ultimate Emptiness (p. 7-24); Fetters of Madness (p. 24-43); When the Sun Grows

BP 300, by Robert Reginald & Mary Wickizer Burgess

Cold (p. 43-59); Forging and Reforging the Shield (p. 59-61); [Biography and Bibliography] (p. 62-64).

A25. *The Clockwork Universe of Anthony Burgess*, by Richard Mathews. THE MILFORD SERIES: POPULAR WRITERS OF TODAY, Volume 19. 63 p. LC 78-14552. OCLC #4135562. ISBN 0-89370-227-7 paper $2.45. Cover: standard series design by Judy Cloyd, orange ink on a black and white clockface background. First Edition, December 1978.

b. Later rebound in cloth (beginning February 1979) with ISBN 0-89370-127-0.

A critique of the late British writer, Anthony Burgess (1917-1993).
CONTENTS: Preface (p. 3-4); 1. *A Vision of Battlements* (p. 5-16); 2. *The Long Day Wanes* (p. 16-33); 3. *The Doctor Is Sick* (p. 33-36); 4. *A Clockwork Orange* (p. 36-43); 5. *The Wanting Seed* (p. 43-51); 6. *One Hand Clapping* (p. 51-60); 7. The Clockwork Ending (p. 60-61); Biography & Bibliography (p. 62-63).

A26. *Pretender: Science Fiction*, by Piers Anthony and Frances Hall. 159 p. LC 79-317. OCLC #4638182. ISBN 0-89370-130-0 cloth $10.95; ISBN 0-89370-230-7 paper $4.95; ISBN 0-89370-002-9 signed limited edition of 50 copies. Cover painting (four-color wraparound cover) and interior drawings by Larry Ortiz, depicting a bright blue spaceship above orange Babylonian structures. First Edition, April 1979.

This original science-fiction novel is set in Babylon in the sixth century B.C., and features a marooned alien who must learn to survive in a primitive Earth culture.

A27. *The Quest of Excalibur*, by Leonard Wibberley. 190 p. LC 79-192. OCLC #4591355. ISBN 0-89370-131-9 cloth $10.95; ISBN 0-89370-231-5 paper $4.95. Cover painting (four-color wraparound cover) and interior drawings by Cathy Hill, the cover featuring King Arthur driving a classic automobile. First Borgo Edition, April 1979.

BP 300, by Robert Reginald & Mary Wickizer Burgess

This facsimile reprint of the 1959 G. P. Putnam's Sons edition is a fantasy in which the legendary King Arthur returns to modern-day England and finds himself having to cope with the new-fangled gadgets of twentieth-century society.

A28. ***The Haunted Man: The Strange Genius of David Lindsay***, by Colin Wilson. THE MILFORD SERIES: POPULAR WRITERS OF TODAY, Volume 20. 63 p. LC 79-194. OCLC #4591353. ISBN 0-89370-128-9 cloth $8.95; ISBN 0-89370-228-5 paper $2.95; ISBN 0-89370-003-7 signed, limited cloth edition of 50 copies. Cover: standard series design by Judy Cloyd, black and white ink on a gold background, with image of a Victorian head. First Edition, May 1979.

A critique of the late British writer and philosopher, David Lindsay (1878-1945).
CONTENTS: The Haunted Man (p. 3-63); Biography & Bibliography (p. 63).

A29. ***Colin Wilson: The Outsider and Beyond***, by Clifford P. Bendau. THE MILFORD SERIES: POPULAR WRITERS OF TODAY, Volume 21. 63 p. LC 79-288. OCLC #4591281. ISBN 0-89370-129-7 cloth $8.95; ISBN 0-89370-229-3 paper $2.95. Cover: standard series design by Judy Cloyd, gold and black ink on a white background, with stylized drawing of a man. First Edition, May 1979.

A critique of the modern British writer, Colin Wilson (1931-).
CONTENTS: Introduction (p. 3-5); Chapter I: The New Existentialism (p. 5-11); Chapter II: Perception and Imagination (p. 11-16); Chapter III: Literature, Imagination, and Human Values (p. 16-23); Chapter IV: The Critics (p. 24-30); Chapter V: A Critical Chronology (p. 30-59); Chapter VI: Conclusion (p. 59-61); Bibliography (p. 62-63).

A30. ***A Poetry of Force and Darkness: The Fiction of John Hawkes***, by Eliot Berry. THE MILFORD SERIES: POPULAR WRITERS OF TODAY, Volume 22. 64 p. LC 79-282. OCLC #4591284. ISBN 0-89370-132-7 cloth $8.95; ISBN 0-89370-232-3 paper $2.95. Cover: standard series design by Judy Cloyd, dark blue ink on a pale green and white background. First Edition, May 1979.

BP 300, by Robert Reginald & Mary Wickizer Burgess

A critique of the modern American writer, John Hawkes (1925-).
CONTENTS: Perspective (p. 3-8); The Early Landscapes: Repression and Experimentation: *Charivari* (1949), *The Goose on the Grave, The Owl* (1954) (p. 8-18); The Sack of the Past: *The Cannibal* (1949) (p. 18-26); From Fishing Rod to Lighthouse: *The Beetle Leg* (1951) and *Second Skin* (1964) (p. 26-38); Words on Rock by Plebian: *The Lime Twig* (1961) (p. 38-49); The Iceberg Surfaces: *The Blood Oranges* (1971), *Death, Sleep and the Traveler* (1973), *Travesty* (1976) (p. 49-64); Biography & Bibliography (p. 64).

A31. ***Science Fiction Voices #1: Interviews with Science Fiction Writers***, conducted by Darrell Schweitzer. THE MILFORD SERIES: POPULAR WRITERS OF TODAY, Volume 23. 63 p. LC 82-640033. OCLC #4579150. ISBN 0-89370-133-5 cloth $8.95; ISBN 0-89370-233-1 paper $2.95. Cover: standard series design by Judy Cloyd, purple and blue ink on a pink background. First Edition, October 1979.

A collection of previously-published interviews with seven American science fiction writers.
CONTENTS: Introduction: Conversations in Print (p. 3); Theodore Sturgeon (p. 4-18); Alfred Bester (p. 18-25); Frederik Pohl (p. 26-32); James Gunn (p. 32-36); Fritz Leiber (p. 37-43); Hal Clement (p. 43-53); L. Sprague de Camp (p. 53-63).

A32. ***A Clash of Symbols: The Triumph of James Blish***, by Brian M. Stableford. THE MILFORD SERIES: POPULAR WRITERS OF TODAY, Volume 24. 62 p. LC 79-13067. OCLC #4933454. ISBN 0-89370-134-3 cloth $8.95; ISBN 0-89370-234-X paper $2.95; ISBN 0-89370-005-3 signed, limited edition of 50 copies. Cover: standard series design by Judy Cloyd, red ink on a pale orange background. First Edition, October 1979.

A critique of the late American science fiction writer, James Blish (1921-1975).
CONTENTS: Introduction (p. 3-7); 1. Foundation Stones (p. 7-15); 2. Tectogenesis and Pantropy (p. 15-22); 3. *Cities in Flight* (p. 22-28); 4. Experiments in Thought (p. 28-37); 5. Experiments in Adventure (p. 37-46); 6. Juveniles (p. 46-50); 7. *After Such*

Knowledge (p. 50-58); 8. Conclusion (p. 58-60); Biography & Bibliography (p. 61-62).

A33. ***Farewell, Earth's Bliss***, by D. G. Compton. 188 p. LC 79-12824. OCLC #4932853. ISBN 0-89370-135-1 cloth $10.95; ISBN 0-89370-235-8 paper $4.95. Cover painting (four-color wraparound cover) and frontispiece by Larry Ortiz, depicting a spaceship above the planet Mars. First Borgo Edition, October 1979.

Reprinted from the 1971 Ace Books edition, this science fiction novel tells of a future in which Mars is used as a prison planet by a repressive Earth government, which sends hardened criminals and political malcontents on a one-way trip to Hell.

A34. ***Sir Henry***, by Robert Nathan. 187 p. LC 79-12787. OCLC #4932943. ISBN 0-89370-136-X cloth $10.95; ISBN 0-89370-236-6 paper $4.95. Cover painting (four-color wrap-around cover) by Mary Sherman, depicting a knight and dragon in a dark green forest; frontispiece by Larry Ortiz. First Borgo Edition, October 1979.

In this fantasy novel, reprinted from the 1955 Alfred A. Knopf edition, Sir Henry of Brentwood goes on a dragon-hunting quest with his intrepid steed, Ponderer.

This was the last novel (of ten) published in Borgo's trade paperback science-fiction program. The eleventh book, Piers Anthony's novel *The Ring*, was scheduled for April 1980, and cover art commissioned, but was canceled when Borgo Press withdrew from its distribution agreement with Newcastle Publishing Co., Inc.

A35. ***Science Fiction Voices #2: Interviews with Science Fiction Writers***, conducted by Jeffrey M. Elliot. THE MILFORD SERIES: POPULAR WRITERS OF TODAY, Volume 25. 62 p. LC 82-640033. OCLC #4579150. ISBN 0-89370-137-8 cloth $10.95; ISBN 0-89370-237-4 paper $2.95. Introduction by Richard A. Lupoff. Cover: standard series design by Judy Cloyd, avocado and blue ink on a pale green background. First Edition, October 1979.

BP 300, by Robert Reginald & Mary Wickizer Burgess

A collection of previously published interviews with five American science fiction writers.

CONTENTS: Introduction, by Richard A. Lupoff (p. 3-7); Foreword (p. 8); Larry Niven: Science Fiction's Master World-Builder (p. 9-19); Ray Bradbury: Poet of Fantastic Fiction (p. 20-29); A. E. van Vogt: A Writer with a Winning Formula (p. 30-40); Poul Anderson: Seer of Far-Distant Futures (p. 41-50); Robert Silverberg: Next Stop—*Lord Valentine's Castle* (p. 51-62).

A36. *Earth Is the Alien Planet: J. G. Ballard's Four-Dimensional Nightmare*, by David Pringle. THE MILFORD SERIES: POPULAR WRITERS OF TODAY, Volume 26. 63 p. LC 79-13065. OCLC #4933455. ISBN 0-89370-138-6 cloth $10.95; ISBN 0-89370-238-2 paper $2.95. Cover: standard series design by Judy Cloyd, black ink on a mustard and white herringbone background. First Edition, October 1979.

A critique of the modern British writer, J. G. Ballard (1930-).

CONTENTS: I. Introduction (p. 3-15); II. The Fourfold Symbolism (p. 15-36); III. The Lamia, the Jester and the King: Ballard's Characters (p. 37-51); IV. Imprisonment and Flight: Ballard's Themes (p. 51-61); Bibliography of J. G. Ballard's Novels and Short Story Collections (p. 62); Bibliography of Criticism and Secondary Sources (p. 63).

This was the last book regularly produced and distributed to the trade by Newcastle Publishing Co., Inc., except for several special arrangements (e.g., Harlan Ellison's *Sleepless Nights in the Procrustean Bed*). The Spring (April) 1980 list, which had already been announced, was published later, except for a reprint of Piers Anthony's novel, *The Ring*, which was later canceled.

A37. *The Rainbow Quest of Thomas Pynchon*, by Douglas A. Mackey. THE MILFORD SERIES: POPULAR WRITERS OF TODAY, Volume 28. 63 p. LC 80-11219. OCLC #6043075. ISBN 0-89370-142-4 cloth $8.95; ISBN 0-89370-242-0 paper $2.95. Cover: standard series design by Judy Cloyd, red and orange ink on a white background, with ribbon design. First Edition, June 1980.

b. Second Printing, 1985 (?). Specific printing information is not listed in book, although the original imprint date on the title page is deleted, as is the "First Edition" statement at the bottom of the copyright page.

c. Third Printing, September 1989. 68 p. Includes a new four-page index.

A critique of the modern American writer, Thomas Pynchon (1937-).

CONTENTS: Chapter One: From Here to Entropy (p. 3-12); Chapter Two: Cherchez la Femme (p. 12-26); Chapter Three: A Woman in the Wasteland (p. 26-36); Chapter Four: The Locus of Transformation (p. 36-59); Chapter Five: The Road of Excess (p. 59-61); Bibliography (p. 62-63); [Index (p. 64-68)—in Third Printing only].

A38. ***Still Worlds Collide: Philip Wylie and the End of the American Dream*,** by Clifford P. Bendau. THE MILFORD SERIES: POPULAR WRITERS OF TODAY, Volume 30. 63 p. LC 80-10756. OCLC #6016489. ISBN 0-89370-144-0 cloth $10.95; ISBN 0-89370-244-7 paper $2.95. Cover: standard series design by Judy Cloyd, blue and red ink on a white background with American flag design. First Edition, August 1980.

b. Second Printing, August 1981.

A critique of the late American writer, Philip Wylie (1902-1971).

CONTENTS: I. Philip Wylie—The Reappearance (p. 3-8); II. The Early Achievements (p. 8-23); III. The Philosophical Works (p. 23-41); IV. The Atomic Age (p. 41-55); V. *The End of the Dream* (p. 55-61); Selected Bibliography (p. 62-63).

A39. ***Literary Voices #1*,** by Jeffrey M. Elliot. THE MILFORD SERIES: POPULAR WRITERS OF TODAY, Volume 27. 64 p. LC 80-12768. OCLC #6144048. ISBN 0-89370-139-4 cloth $8.95; ISBN 0-89370-239-0 paper $2.95. Introduction by Alex Haley; illustrated with photographs of the authors. Cover: standard series design by Judy Cloyd, white and orange ink on a black background. First Edition, October 1980.

A collection of previously-published interviews with five modern American writers.

BP 300, by Robert Reginald & Mary Wickizer Burgess

CONTENTS: Introduction, by Alex Haley (p. 3-4); Alex Haley: The Man Behind *Roots* (p. 5-15); Christopher Isherwood: Through the Looking Glass (p. 16-24); Jessica Mitford: Pioneer Spirit of Investigative Journalism (p. 26-34); Richard Armour: Humor Is Shield, Satire Is His Spear (p. 35-49); Robert Anton Wilson: Searching for Cosmic Intelligence (p. 50-64).

A40. *Science Fiction Voices #3: Interviews with Science Fiction Writers*, conducted by Jeffrey M. Elliot. THE MILFORD SERIES: POPULAR WRITERS OF TODAY, Volume 29. 64 p. LC 82-640033. OCLC #4579150. ISBN 0-89370-143-2 cloth $8.95; ISBN 0-83970-243-9 paper $2.95. Introduction by A. E. van Vogt; illustrated with photographs of the authors. Cover: standard series design by Judy Cloyd, purple and blue ink on a pale blue background. First Edition, November 1980.

A collection of previously-published interviews with five American science fiction writers.
CONTENTS: Introduction, by A. E. van Vogt (p. 3-7); Preface (p. 8); Harlan Ellison: Outspoken, Outrageous, Outstanding! (p. 9-18); David Gerrold: His *Star Trek* Continues (p. 19-32); Richard Lupoff: On the Verge... (p. 33-43); Gregory Benford: A Scientist Looks at Science Fiction (p. 44-52); Jerry Pournelle: From Space Program to Space Opera (p. 53-64).
The recession year of 1980 featured the fewest Borgo Press books ever published, with just four titles.

A41. *Science Fiction & Fantasy Awards*, by R. Reginald. THE BORGO REFERENCE LIBRARY, Volume II. 64 p. LC 80-10788. OCLC #6042800. ISBN 0-89370-806-2 cloth $8.95; ISBN 0-89370-906-9 paper $2.95. First Edition, December 1981. Cover design by Michael Pastucha, red ink on white background.

A comprehensive guide to the awards given in the science fiction, fantasy, and horror fields.
This was one of only two books actually published in this aborted series, which was later renamed Borgo Reference Guides. See also the second edition (**A132**). The time interval between this book and its predecessor was the longest production lapse to occur between books in the history of The Borgo Press, lasting some thirteen months.

A42. *Anti-Sartre, with an Essay on Camus*, by Colin Wilson. THE MILFORD SERIES: POPULAR WRITERS OF TODAY, Volume 34. 63 p. LC 80-24098. OCLC #6580237. ISBN 0-89370-149-1 cloth $8.95; ISBN 0-89370-249-8 paper $2.95; ISBN 0-89370-006-1 signed, limited cloth edition of 50 copies $25.00. Cover: standard series design by Michael Pastucha, black ink on pale green background. First Edition, December 1981.

A collection of previously-published essays on the late French writers and philosophers, Jean-Paul Sartre (1905-1980) and Albert Camus (1913-1960).
    CONTENTS: Anti-Sartre (p. 3-44); Sartre Obituary (p. 45-47); An Essay on Albert Camus (p. 48-63).

A43. *The Future of the Space Program; Large Corporations & Society: Discussions with 22 Science-Fiction Writers*, conducted by Jeffrey M. Elliot. GREAT ISSUES OF THE DAY #1. 64 p. LC 80-17954. OCLC #6581630. ISBN 0-89370-140-8 cloth $8.95; ISBN 0-89370-240-4 paper $2.95. Cover design by Michael Pastucha, black ink on tan background. First Edition, December 1981.

A compilation of previously-published articles with the responses of twenty-two science fiction writers to two questions posed to them by the compiler. Authors responding included: Poul Anderson, Mildred Downey Broxon, Octavia E. Butler, C. J. Cherryh, Gordon R. Dickson, Raymond Z. Gallun, James E. Gunn, Isidore Haiblum, James P. Hogan, Robert A. W. "Doc" Lowndes, Richard A. Lupoff, Larry Niven, Charles Sheffield, Robert Silverberg, Jack Vance, A. E. van Vogt, John Varley, Joan D. Vinge, Jack Williamson, Robert Anton Wilson, Chelsea Quinn Yarbro, Roger Zelazny.
    CONTENTS: Foreword (p. 3-4); What Explains the Present Lack of Citizen Interest in and Support for the U.S. Space Program? (p. 5-28); What Role Can and Should Science Fiction Writers Play in Working with America's Major Corporations in Planning for Society's Future? (p. 29-55); Contributors (p. 56-64).

A44. *Masters of Science Fiction: Essays on Six Science Fiction Authors*, by Brian M. Stableford. THE MILFORD SERIES:

BP 300, by Robert Reginald & Mary Wickizer Burgess

POPULAR WRITERS OF TODAY, Volume 32. 64 p. LC 80-24116. OCLC #6580286. ISBN 0-89370-147-5 cloth $8.95; ISBN 0-89370-247-1 paper $2.95. Cover: standard series design by Michael Pastucha, black ink on blue background. First Edition, December 1981.

A collection of previously-published essays on science fiction authors.
  CONTENTS: Introduction (p. 3-5); Edmond Hamilton and Leigh Brackett: An Appreciation (p. 6-14); Locked in the Slaughterhouse: The Novels of Kurt Vonnegut (p. 15-23); Insoluble Problems: Foot-Notes to Barry Malzberg's Career in Science Fiction (p. 24-31); The Metamorphosis of Robert Silverberg (p. 32-42); Utopia—And Afterwards: Socioeconomic Speculation in the SF of Mack Reynolds (p. 43-64).
  See also the Second Edition (**A233**).

A45. *Science Fiction Voices #5: Interviews with American Science Fiction Writers of the Golden Age*, conducted by Darrell Schweitzer. THE MILFORD SERIES: POPULAR WRITERS OF TODAY, Volume 35. 64 p. LC 82-640033. OCLC #4579150. ISBN 0-89370-151-3 cloth $8.95; ISBN 0-89370-251-X paper $2.95. Cover: standard series design by Michael Pastucha, black ink on gold background. First Edition, December 1981.

A collection of previously-published interviews with nine American science fiction writers.
  CONTENTS: Introduction (p. 5-6); Isaac Asimov (p. 7-14); Lin Carter (p. 14-26); Lester del Rey (p. 26-35); Edmond Hamilton and Leigh Brackett (p. 35-41); Frank Belknap Long (p. 41-48); Clifford D. Simak (p. 48-55); Wilson Tucker (p. 55-60); Jack Williamson (p. 60-64).

A46. *Fantasy Voices: Interviews with American Fantasy Writers*, conducted by Jeffrey M. Elliot. THE MILFORD SERIES: POPULAR WRITERS OF TODAY, Volume 31. 64 p. LC 80-22575. OCLC #6762077. ISBN 0-89370-146-7 cloth $8.95; ISBN 0-89370-246-3 paper $2.95. Illustrated with photographs of the authors; introduction by William F. Nolan. Cover: standard series design by Michael Pastucha, black ink on pink background, with photograph of author on the back cover. First Edition, January 1982.

A collection of previously-published interviews with four American fantasy writers.
CONTENTS: Introduction, by William F. Nolan (p. 3-5); Manly Wade Wellman: Better Things Waiting (p. 5-18); John Norman: The Chronicles of Gor (p. 18-30); Hugh B. Cave: Master of Vintage Horror (p. 31-44); Katherine Kurtz: Tapestries of Medieval Wonder (p. 44-64).

A47. *Science Fiction Voices #4: Interviews with Modern Science Fiction Authors*, conducted by Jeffrey M. Elliot. THE MILFORD SERIES: POPULAR WRITERS OF TODAY, Volume 33. 63 p. LC 82-640033. OCLC #4579150. ISBN 0-89370-148-3 cloth $8.95; ISBN 0-89370-248-X paper $2.95. Illustrated with photographs of the authors; introduction by Raymond Z. Gallun. Cover: standard series design by Michael Pastucha, black ink on orange background. First Edition, January 1982.

A collection of previously-published interviews with four American and British science fiction writers.
CONTENTS: Preface (p. 5); Introduction, by Raymond Z. Gallun (p. 6-10); Charles D. Hornig: A Question of Conscience (p. 11-25); Bob Shaw: Preserving Science Fiction Traditions (p. 26-37); Frank Kelly Freas: Portrait of an Artist (p. 38-50); Brian M. Stableford: An Academic Looks at Science Fiction (p. 51-63).

A48. *Wilderness Visions: Science Fiction Westerns, Volume One*, by David Mogen. I.O. EVANS STUDIES IN THE PHILOSOPHY & CRITICISM OF LITERATURE, Number 1. 64 p. LC 80-8673. OCLC #6982261. ISBN 0-89370-152-1 cloth $8.95; ISBN 0-89370-252-8 paper $2.95. Cover design by Michael Pastucha, brown ink on white background. First Edition, February 1982.

A critique focusing on the western theme in modern science fiction.
CONTENTS: Introduction (p. 3-4); Science Fiction "Westerns" and American Literature (p. 5-15); The Frontier Metaphor in American Culture (p. 16-26); The Frontier Metaphor as Prophecy (p. 27-33); Blazing Trails to Outer Space: Heinlein,

Asimov, and *The Space Merchants* (p. 34-62); Bibliography of Works Cited in *Wilderness Visions* (p. 63-64).
See also the Second Edition (**A170**).

A49. *If J.F.K. Had Lived: A Political Scenario*, by R. Reginald and Jeffrey M. Elliot. BORGO POLITICAL SCENARIOS, Number 1. 64 p. LC 81-19516. OCLC #8032078. ISBN 0-89370-155-6 cloth $9.95; ISBN 0-89370-255-2 paper $3.95. Cover and title design by Michael Pastucha, with drawing of JFK coin on front cover, black ink on silver background. First Edition, April 1982.

This revision of **A3** is alternative scenario in dialogue form of a world in which the monarchies of Europe were never displaced, and Kennedy was never assassinated.

A50. *Candle for Poland: 469 Days of Solidarity*, by Dr. Leszek Szymanski, edited by R. Reginald. STOKVIS STUDIES IN HISTORICAL CHRONOLOGY AND THOUGHT, Number Two. 128 p. LC 82-1231. OCLC #8195954. ISBN 0-89370-166-1 cloth $10.95; ISBN 0-89370-266-8 paper $4.95. Cover design of burning candle by Michael Pastucha, black and red ink on white background, and photo of author on back cover. First Edition, June 1982.

An account of the Solidarity Crisis of 1980-81.
CONTENTS: Introduction, by Jeffrey M. Elliot (p. 5-7); Chapter 1: The Struggle for Bread and Freedom: The *Magna Carta* in the Soviet Empire (p. 9-27); Chapter 2: Triumph: More Freedom Than Bread (p. 28-59); Chapter 3: What Is to Be Done? The Burden of the Past and the Threat of the Future (p. 60-76); Appendix A: "On the Present Methods of Prosecution of Illegal Anti-Socialist Activity" (p. 79-87); Appendix B: "An Open Letter to Shipyard Workers and All Coastal Workers," by Jacek Kuron (p. 88-91); Appendix C: "The Gdansk Accord" (p. 92-99); Appendix D: *The Constitution of the Independent, Self-Governing Trade Union Solidarity* [excerpts] (p. 100-103); Appendix E: "Government's Report on the Economy and a Program of Reform, August, 1981" (p. 104-106); Appendix F: "Who Are the Anti-Socialists?" (p. 107-109); Appendix G: "The Program of ISTU Solidarity" (p. 110-115); Appendix H: "The Radom Declaration" (p. 116-117); Appendix I: Members of the Presidium of the

National Commission of Solidarity (p. 118); Bibliography (p. 119); Biographical Notes (p. 120-121); Glossary (p. 122-125); Index (p. 125-128).

A51. *From Here to Absurdity: The Moral Battlefields of Joseph Heller*, by Stephen W. Potts. THE MILFORD SERIES: POPULAR WRITERS OF TODAY, Volume 36. 64 p. LC 81-21602. OCLC #8034757. ISBN 0-89370-156-4 cloth $9.95; ISBN 0-89370-256-0 paper $3.95. Cover: standard series design by Michael Pastucha, black ink on mustard background, with picture of bomber dropping bombs. First Edition, September 1982.

A critique on the modern American writer, Joseph Heller (1923-1999).
CONTENTS: Introduction (p. 3-4); I: *Catch-22* (p. 5-19); II: The Plays (p. 20-31); III: *Something Happened* (p. 32-46); IV: *Good as Gold* (p. 47-60); Conclusion (p. 61-63); Bibliographical Notes (p. 64).
See also the Second Edition (**A230**).

A52. *The House of the Burgesses*, by M. R. Burgess. BORGO FAMILY HISTORIES, Number 1. xii+155 p. LC 80-10759. OCLC #6016498. ISBN 0-89370-801-1 cloth $14.95; ISBN 0-89370-901-8 paper $6.95. Illustrated with a chart and photographs. Cover design by Michael Pastucha, cover and title page photo of Joseph Fields Burgess mansion in Scott County, Kentucky, black ink on tan background. First Edition, February 1983.

A genealogical history of the descendants of William Burges(s) (d. 1712) of Richmond (later King George) Co., Virginia.
CONTENTS: Family Chart; Pictures; Introduction; The House of the Burgesses; Burgess Name Index; Burgess Spouses Index; Afterword.
See also the Second Edition (**A184**).

A53. *The Wickizer Annals: Wickizer, Wickiser, Wickkiser, Wickkizer, Wickheiser*, by Mary Wickizer Burgess with M. R. Burgess. BORGO FAMILY HISTORIES, Number 2. xviii+126 p. LC 80-11075. OCLC #6042975. ISBN 0-89370-802-X cloth $12.95; ISBN 0-89370-902-6 paper $6.95. Illustrated with charts and photographs. Cover design by Michael Pastucha, with a photo of

BP 300, by Robert Reginald & Mary Wickizer Burgess

Wickizer family members, black ink on pale blue background. First Edition, February 1983.

A genealogical history of the descendants of Conrad Wickizer (d. 1802) of Luzerne Co., Pennsylvania.
CONTENTS: Dedications; Charts; Introduction; Pictures; The Wickizer Annals; Wickizer Name Index; Spouses Index; Afterword; Pictures.

A54. *Pulp Voices; or, Science Fiction Voices #6: Interviews with Pulp Magazine Writers and Editors*, conducted by Jeffrey M. Elliot. THE MILFORD SERIES: POPULAR WRITERS OF TODAY, Volume 37. 64 p. LC 81-21632. OCLC #8052189. ISBN 0-89370-157-2 cloth $9.95; ISBN 0-89370-257-9 paper $3.95. Illustrated with photographs of the authors; introduction by Poul Anderson. Cover: standard series design by Michael Pastucha, black ink on red background. First Edition, March 1983.

A collection of previously-published interviews with five science fiction editors and writers from the pulp magazine period.
CONTENTS: Foreword (p. 3-4); Introduction, by Poul Anderson (p. 5-8); Jack Williamson: In at the Creation (p. 9-24); Horace L. Gold: *Galaxy*'s Pioneering Editor (p. 25-31); Stanton A. Coblentz: "I Pant for the Music Which Is Divine" (p. 32-44); C. L. Moore: Poet of Far-Distant Futures (p. 45-51); Raymond Z. Gallun: Seeker of Tomorrow (p. 52-63); photographs (p. 64).

A55. *Deathman Pass Me By: Two Years on Death Row*, by Philip Brasfield with Jeffrey M. Elliot. BORGO BIOVIEWS, Number 3. 96 p. LC 82-4126. OCLC #8220997. ISBN 0-89370-164-5 cloth $10.95; ISBN 0-89370-264-1 paper $4.95. Illustrated with four photographs by Doug Magee. Cover design by Michael Pastucha, showing a photo of a prison cell, black ink on white background. First Edition, April 1983.

b. Second Printing, 1985 (?). The imprint date on the title page and "First Edition" statement on the copyright page have been removed, but the printing is not otherwise indicated. The book is one centimeter taller than the first edition.
c. Third Printing, 1986 (?). The imprint date on the title page and "First Edition" statement on the copyright page have been

removed, but the printing is not otherwise indicated. The book is one centimeter taller than the first edition.

An account of the trial and conviction of Philip Brasfield for murder in Wichita County, Texas, and his subsequent two-year stay on Death Row. His autobiographical memoir is a testimonial against capital punishment.

CONTENTS: Acknowledgments (p. 6); Chapter One (p. 7-12); Chapter Two (p. 13-17); Chapter Three (p. 18-26); Chapter Four (p. 27-36); Chapter Five (p. 37-43); Chapter Six (p. 44-53); Chapter Seven (p. 54-63); Chapter Eight (p. 64-71); Chapter Nine (p. 72-76); Chapter Ten (p. 77-84); Chapter Eleven (p. 85-89); Chapter Twelve (p. 90-96).

The book was selected for sale by a Methodist organization book club, and reprinted twice in much longer print runs from another printer, as noted above, the second printer's presses having a slightly larger trim size.

A56. *The Pulp Western: A Popular History of the Western Fiction Magazine in America*, by John A. Dinan. I.O. EVANS STUDIES IN THE PHILOSOPHY & CRITICISM OF LITERATURE, Number 2. 128 p. LC 81-21697. OCLC #8112699. ISBN 0-89370-161-0 cloth $11.95; ISBN 0-89370-261-7 paper $5.95. Illustrated with reproductions of cover art. Cover design by Michael Pastucha using a drawing from one of the Western pulps, black ink on brown background. First Edition, August 1983.

A history of and guide to the western pulp magazine in America.

CONTENTS: Acknowledgments (p. 4); Foreword (p. 5-8); I. In the Beginning: The Dime Novels (p. 9-12); II. Ghost Writers in the Sky: 1. The Pulp Western (p. 13-16); "I Remember *Wild West Weekly*," by Redd Boggs (p. 17-33); 2. The Romance Westerns (p. 34-35); 3. The Hero Westerns (p. 36-46); 4. Further Variations (p. 47-50); III. The Western Pulp Story (p. 51-53); "Plotting the Western Story," by Walker A. Tompkins (p. 54-60); Other Writing Techniques (p. 61-64); IV. The Men Behind the Masks: The Editors (p. 65); "Letter from the Editor," by Michael Tilden (p. 66-72); V. Hacking Them Out by the Dozens: The Writers (p. 73-84); "Another View," by Elmer Kelton (p. 85-92); "Autobiographical Letter," by B. M. Bower (p. 93-104); VI. To "B" or Not to "B": The Pulps and the Movies (p. 105-108); VII.

BP 300, by Robert Reginald & Mary Wickizer Burgess

Beneath a Pastel Sun: The Artists (p. 109-114); VIII. The End of the Trail: The Demise of the Pulp Western (p. 115); "The *Western* Story in Europe," by Finn Arnesen (p. 116-120); Bibliography (p. 121-124); Index (p. 125-128).

A57. *Tempest in a Teapot: The Falkland Islands War*, by R. Reginald & Jeffrey M. Elliot. Research Assistants: Renata Parrino and Mary A. Burgess. STOKVIS STUDIES IN HISTORICAL CHRONOLOGY AND THOUGHT, Number 3. 176 p. LC 83-8807. OCLC #9557957. ISBN 0-89370-167-X cloth $12.95; ISBN 0-89370-267-6 paper $6.95. Illustrated with charts and maps. Cover drawing of stylized teapot by Tim Kirk, cover design by Michael Pastucha, black and gray ink on light blue background. First Edition, August 1983.

A history of the 1982 Falkland Islands War between Argentina and Great Britain.

CONTENTS: Introduction (p. 5-6); Chronology (p. 7-12); I. Invitation to a Tea Party: 1. The Falkland Islands/Las Islas Malvinas (p. 13-15); 2. Colonial Land Claims (p. 15-23); 3. The British Occupation of the Islands (p. 23-32); II. A Simmering Brew: 1. The Argentine Government (p. 33-37); 2. A Period of Negotiations (p. 37-42); 3. Impasse (p. 42-46); III. The Pot Boils Over: 1. Ominous Mutterings (p. 47-59); 2. The Argentine Invasion (p. 59-68); 3. War! (p. 68-97); IV. Pekoe and Pekoe: Two Views on the Falklands: 1. Background to the Interviews (p. 98-99); 2. The Official British Position (p. 99-117); 3. The Official Argentine Position (p. 117-128); V. Reading the Tea Leaves: 1. Claims and Blames (p. 129-131); 2. To the Last Dregs (p. 131-136); 3. Prognostications (p. 136-139); Appendix A: Governors of the Falkland Islands (p. 140-142); Appendix B: Chart of Forces and Losses (p. 143); Appendix C: Selected Documents (p. 144-162); Notes (p. 163-165); Bibliography (p. 166-169); Index (p. 169-173); Maps (p. 174-176).

A58. *Interviews with Britain's Angry Young Men: Literary Voices #2*, conducted by Dale Salwak. THE MILFORD SERIES: POPULAR WRITERS OF TODAY, Volume 39. 96 p. LC 81-21686. OCLC #8112683. ISBN 0-89370-159-9 cloth $11.95; ISBN 0-89370-259-5 paper $4.95. Illustrated with photographs of the authors; introduction by Colin Wilson. Cover: standard series design by

BP 300, by Robert Reginald & Mary Wickizer Burgess

Michael Pastucha, with photos of the interviewees on cover, white ink on pink background. First Edition, May 1984.

A collection of previously-published interviews with five modern British writers of the "Angry Young Men" Movement of the 1950s.
    CONTENTS: Introduction, by Colin Wilson (p. 5-11); I. Kingsley Amis: Mimic and Moralist (p. 13-40); II. John Braine: The Man at the Top (p. 41-59); III. Bill Hopkins: Looking for the Revolutionary (p. 61-66); IV. John Wain: Man of Letters (p. 67-81); V. Colin Wilson: The Man Behind *The Outsider* (p. 82-93); Index (p. 94-96).

A59. *Sleepless Nights in the Procrustean Bed: Essays*, by Harlan Ellison, edited by Marty Clark. I.O. EVANS STUDIES IN THE PHILOSOPHY & CRITICISM OF LITERATURE, Number 5. 192 p. LC 83-27543. OCLC #10322376. ISBN 0-89370-170-X cloth $14.95; ISBN 0-89370-270-6 paper $7.95. Illustrated with photographs of the author. Cover design by David Reneric, gold and black ink on teal blue background, with a photo of the author and editor on the back cover. First Edition, July 1984.

b.   Signed, Limited Edition of 200 copies; ISBN 0-89370-007-X sewn cloth $30.00, July 1984.
c.   Second Printing, August 1990. Cover colors were changed for this and subsequent printings (black and blue ink on white background), and the cover type slightly reworked.
d.   Third Printing, August 1992.
e.   Fourth Printing, June 1995. The cover was reworked to include EAN Bookland Bar Codes on the rear panel and to rearrange the spine copy; the front matter was reworked; black and blue ink on cream background.

A collection of previously-published literary essays and autobiographical pieces. It won the 1984 (1985) *Locus* Award for Best Nonfiction Book of the Year.
    CONTENTS: Editor's Introduction (p. 11-17); You Don't Know Me, I Don't Know You (p. 19-32); Stealing Tomorrow (p. 33-35); Down the Rabbit-Hole to TV-Land (p. 36-44); Revealed at Last! What Killed the Dinosaurs! And You Don't Look So Terrific Yourself (p. 45-55); Epiphany (p. 56-59); Rolling Dat Ole

BP 300, by Robert Reginald & Mary Wickizer Burgess

Debbil Electronic Stone (p. 60-66); A Love Song to Jerry Falwell (p. 67-72); Science Fiction: Turning Reality Inside-Out (p. 73-80); Defeating the Green Slime (p. 81-86); How You Stupidly Blew $15 Million a Week, Avoided Having an Adenoid-Shaped Swimming Pool in Your Back Yard, Missed the Opportunity to Have a Mutually Destructive Love Affair with Clint Eastwood and/or Raquel Welch, and Otherwise Pissed Me Off (p. 87-98); Fear Not Your Enemies (p. 99-103); Face-Down in Gloria Swanson's Swimming Pool (p. 104-108); From Albany, with Hate (p. 109-120); Leiber: A Few Too Few Words (p. 121-123); Serita Rosenthal Ellison: A Eulogy (p. 124-132); Centerpunching (p. 133-145); Voe Doe Dee Oh Doe (p. 146-154); Robert Silverberg: An Appreciation (p. 155-157); Cheap Thrills on the Road to Hell (p. 158-161); True Love: Groping for the Holy Grail (p. 162-182); Notes (p. 183-185); Index (p. 187-192).

A60. *A Guide to Science Fiction & Fantasy in the Library of Congress Classification Scheme*, by Michael Burgess. BORGO REFERENCE LIBRARY, Volume VIII. 86 p., 8.5 x 11". LC 80-11418. OCLC #6092531. ISBN 0-89370-807-0 cloth $19.95; ISBN 0-89370-907-7 spiral-bound paper $9.95. Cover design by Michael Pastucha, using brown ink on ecru vellum paper in spiral binding (later offprints side-stitched). First Edition, August 1984.

A guide to LC cataloging practice for science fiction and fantasy authors and books.
CONTENTS: Introduction (p. 3); Subject Headings (p. 4-13); Author Main Entries and Literature Numbers (p. 14-66); Artist Main Entries and Artist Numbers (p. 67-68); Motion Picture and Television Entries (p. 69); Classification Numbers (p. 70-80); Index (p. 80-86).
See also the second edition (**A87**).

A61. *The Magic Labyrinth of Philip José Farmer*, by Edgar L. Chapman. THE MILFORD SERIES: POPULAR WRITERS OF TODAY, Volume 38. 96 p. LC 81-21603. OCLC #8034758. ISBN 0-89370-158-0 cloth $11.95; ISBN 0-89370-258-7 paper $4.95. Cover: standard series design by Michael Pastucha, blue ink on white background with maze design. First Edition, December 1984.

36

BP 300, by Robert Reginald & Mary Wickizer Burgess

A critique on the modern American science fiction writer, Philip José Farmer (1918-).

CONTENTS: Introduction (p. 3-8); I. The Romantic Rebel (p. 9-20); II. The Speculative Iconoclast (p. 21-34); III. Trickster Heroes and Primitive Worlds (p. 35-43); IV. The Tarzan and Doc Savage Mythos (p. 44-58); V. The Virtuoso Artist (p. 59-68); VI. The Fabulous Riverworld (p. 69-83); VII. Against the Sun's Darkness: A Conclusion (p. 84-90); Selected Bibliography (p. 91-93); Index (p. 94-96).

A62. *The Work of Jeffrey M. Elliot: An Annotated Bibliography & Guide*, by Boden Clarke. BIBLIOGRAPHIES OF MODERN AUTHORS, Number 2. 50 p. LC 84-21745. OCLC #11316036. ISBN 0-89370-381-8 cloth $19.95; ISBN 0-89370-481-4 paper $9.95. Cover: standard series design by Michael Pastucha, with photo of the author by Mark Lee, black ink with brick red frame on white background. First Edition, December 1984.

A bibliography and literary guide to the works of the modern American political scientist, Dr. Jeffrey M. Elliot (1947-).

CONTENTS: Introduction (p. 3-4); A. Books (p. 5-13); B. Articles (p. 14-21); C. Book Reviews (p. 22-25); D. Letters to the Editor (p. 26); E. Speeches and Papers (p. 27-31); F. Television Productions and Appearances (p. 32); G. Radio Appearances (p. 33); H. Other Media (p. 34); J. Honors and Awards (p. 35-36); K. About the Author (p. 37-39); L. Unpublished Material (p. 40); Quoth the Critics (p. 41); Index (p. 43-50).

A63. *The Work of R. Reginald: An Annotated Bibliography & Guide*, by Michael Burgess with Jeffrey M. Elliot. BIBLIOGRAPHIES OF MODERN AUTHORS, Number 5. 48 p. LC 84-21672. OCLC #11260185. ISBN 0-89730-384-2 cloth $19.95; ISBN 0-89370-484-9 paper $9.95. Cover: standard series design by Michael Pastucha, with photo of the author by Louise Rogers, green ink on cream background. First Edition, January 1985.

A bibliography and literary guide to the works of the modern American librarian, publisher, and author, Robert Reginald (1948-).

BP 300, by Robert Reginald & Mary Wickizer Burgess

CONTENTS: "I Fear the Greeks...": An Introduction to the Life and Work of Robert Reginald (p. 3-10); A. Books (p. 11-23); B. Articles and Reviews (p. 24-29); C. Periodicals, Serials, and Publishing Companies (p. 30-37); D. Juvenilia (p. 38); E. Radio and Television Appearances (p. 39); F. About the Author (p. 40-41); G. Honors and Awards (p. 42); H. Unpublished Works (p. 43); J. Miscellanea (p. 44); Index (p. 45-48).

See also the second edition (**A137**).

A64. *The Work of Julian May: An Annotated Bibliography & Guide*, by Thaddeus Dikty and R. Reginald. BIBLIOGRAPHIES OF MODERN AUTHORS, Number 3. 66 p. LC 84-21705. OCLC #11290834. ISBN 0-89370-382-6 cloth $19.95; ISBN 0-89370-482-2 paper $9.95. Cover: standard series design by Michael Pastucha, with photo of author by Thaddeus Dikty, black ink with purple frame on white background. First Edition, March 1985.

A bibliography and literary guide to the works of the modern American writer, Julian May (1931-).

CONTENTS: Introduction (p. 3-7); Contents (p. 8); A. Books (p. 9-34); B. Articles (p. 35-36); C. Short Fiction (p. 37); D. Study Prints (p. 38-42); E. Lesson Plans (p. 43); F. Kits (p. 44); G. Audio Cassettes (p. 45-50); H. Audio Recordings (p. 51); I. Music (p. 52); J. Maps (p. 53); K. Media Productions (p. 54); L. About the Author (p. 55); M. Unpublished Works (p. 56-57); N. Miscellanea (p. 58); Title Index (p. 59-66).

A65. *Exploring Fantasy Worlds: Essays on Fantastic Literature*, edited by Darrell Schweitzer. I.O. EVANS STUDIES IN THE PHILOSOPHY & CRITICISM OF LITERATURE, Number 3. 112 p. LC 81-21657. OCLC #8112335. ISBN 0-89370-162-9 cloth $14.95; ISBN 0-89370-262-5 paper $6.95. Four-color cover painting (wraparound cover) of an eerie tree by Mary Cleland, cover design by Michael Pastucha. First Edition, April 1985.

An anthology of previously-published and original essays on fantasy.

CONTENTS: Introduction (p. 5-6); Aspects of Fantasy, by Michael Moorcock (p. 7-34); Dreams Within Dreams, by Sandra Miesel (p. 35-42); Prithee, Sirrah, What Dosttou Mean by Archaic

BP 300, by Robert Reginald & Mary Wickizer Burgess

Style in Fantasy? by Darrell Schweitzer (p. 43-51); Robert E. Howard's Fiction, by L. Sprague de Camp (p. 52-66); The Fantasy of Johannes V. Jensen, by Poul Anderson (p. 67-75); The Anima Archetype in Science Fiction, by Fritz Leiber (p. 76-82); *Titus Groan*: An Appreciation, by David H. Keller (p. 83-88); Portrait of Nathan, by Ben Indick (p. 89-93); A Robert Nathan Checklist, by Darrell Schweitzer (p. 94-96); Cabell: Fantasist of Reality, by Paul Spencer (p. 97-106); Contributors (p. 107-108); Index (p. 109-112).

A66. ***Lords Temporal & Lords Spiritual: A Chronological Checklist of the Popes, Patriarchs, Katholikoi, and Independent Archbishops and Metropolitans of the Monarchical Autocephalous Churches of the Christian East and West***, by Boden Clarke. STOKVIS STUDIES IN HISTORICAL CHRONOLOGY & THOUGHT, Number 1. 136 p. LC 80-10979. OCLC #6042926. ISBN 0-89370-800-3 cloth $19.95; ISBN 0-89370-900-X paper $9.95. Cover design by Michael Pastucha, featuring two bishops on a chessboard, black and white ink on green background. First Edition, May 1985.

A history of the Eastern Orthodox Churches, with checklists of their patriarchs.

CONTENTS: Introduction (p. 5-7); Abbreviations (p. 8); Aght'amar (p. 9); Albania (p. 10); Albania (Caucasian) (p. 11-12); Alexandria (Coptic) (p. 13-15); Alexandria (Coptic Catholic) (p. 16); Alexandria (Greek) (p. 17-18); America (various churches) (p. 19-22); Antioch (Greek) (p. 23-25); Antioch (Greek Melkite) (p. 26-28); Antioch (Maronite) (p. 29-30): Antioch (Syrian Catholic) (p. 31-33); Antioch (Syrian Jacobite) (p. 34-36); Armenia (p. 37-39); Assyria (p. 40-42); Babylon and Assyria (Chaldean) (p. 43-45); Belorussia (p. 46); Bulgaria (p. 47-49); Cilicia (Armenian Apostolic) (p. 50-51); Cilicia (Armenian Catholic) (p. 52); Constantinople (Armenian) (p. 53-54); Constantinople (Greek) (p. 55-59); Cyprus (p. 60-61); Czechoslovakia (p. 62); Estonia (p. 63); Ethiopia (p. 64-66); Georgia (p. 67-69); Greece (p. 70-71); Jerusalem (Armenian) (p. 72-73); Jerusalem (Greek) (p. 74-75); Latvia (p. 76); Macedonia and Ohrid (p. 77-78); Malabar and Malankara (p. 79-82); Poland (p. 83); Romania (p. 84); Rome (p. 85-89); Russia (p. 90-91); Serbia and Pec (p. 92-93); Sinai (p. 94-95); Turkey (p. 96);

Ukraine (p. 97-99); Selected Bibliography (p. 100-104); Comparative Name Tables (p. 105-111); Index (p. 112-136).
See also the Second Edition (**A232**).

A67. *The Work of Bruce McAllister: An Annotated Bibliography & Guide*, by David Ray Bourquin. BIBLIOGRAPHIES OF MODERN AUTHORS, Number 10. 30 p. LC 85-22400. OCLC #12583580. ISBN 0-89370-489-X paper $9.95; ISBN 0-89370-389-3 cloth $19.95. Cover: standard series design by Michael Pastucha, with photo of author, black ink on bright green. First Edition, December 1985.

A bibliography and literary guide to the works of the modern American writer, Bruce McAllister (1946-).
CONTENTS: Introduction (p. 3-4); A. Books (p. 5-6); B. Short Fiction (p. 7-12); C. Non-Fiction (p. 13); D. Poetry (p. 14-17); E. Graphic/Experimental Work (p. 18); F. Papers (p. 19); G. Editorial Posts (p. 20-21); H. Media Appearances (p. 22); I. Awards and Prizes (p. 23); J. About the Author (p. 24-25); Critical Comments (p. 26); Title Index (p. 27-30).
See also the revised edition (**A70**).

A68. *The Barstow Printer: A Personal Name and Subject Index to the Years 1910-1920*, by Buckley Barry Barrett. SAN BERNARDINO COUNTY STUDIES, Number 1. 79 p., 8.5 x 11". LC 84-14550. OCLC #10996277. ISBN 0-89370-840-2 cloth $19.95; ISBN 0-89370-940-9 spiral-bound paper $9.95. Cover design by Michael Pastucha, black ink on gray background in spiral binding (later offprints saddle-stitched). First Edition, December 1985.

A comprehensive index to persons and events listed in this Mojave Desert newspaper.
CONTENTS: The Newspaper (p. 3-4); About the Index (p. 4-5); Lost Issues (p. 5); Acknowledgments (p. 6); Subject-Name Index (p. 7-79).
Photocopied from the original; later copies of the paperbound edition were stapled through the spine. This series was renamed West Coast Studies with its second volume.

A69. *Survivors: A Personal Story of the Holocaust*, by Jacob Biber. STUDIES IN JUDAICA AND THE HOLOCAUST, Number 2. [viii]+200

p. LC 85-22415. OCLC #12583762. ISBN 0-89370-370-2 cloth $19.95; ISBN 0-89370-470-9 paper $9.95. Illustrated with a map. Cover design by Peter Richards adapted by Michael Pastucha and featuring a Star of David, red and black ink on white background. First Borgo Edition, March 1986.

b. Second Printing, with new four-page index and using the original, previously printed covers, December 1989. [viii]+204 p.
c. Third Printing, with four-page index and using the original, previously printed covers, September 1991. [viii]+204 p.
d. Fourth Printing, with four-page index and using the original, previously printed covers, August 1994. [viii]+204 p.
e. Fifth Printing, with four-page index and using the original, previously printed covers, August 1998. [viii]+204 p.

The story of Jacob and Eva Biber and their survival of the Holocaust in the Ukraine during World War II.

CONTENTS: Chapter One: Berka's Family (p. 1-28); Chapter Two: Under the Soviet Occupation (p. 29-40); Chapter Three: First Action (p. 41-51); Chapter Four: Four O'Clock (p. 52-64); Chapter Five: Back Home (p. 65-76); Chapter Six: Tsyganko (p. 77-89); Chapter Seven: The Advice of the Evangelist (p. 90-104); Chapter Eight: The Last Escape (p. 105-122); Chapter Nine: A New Profession (p. 123-156); Chapter Ten: With the Rebels (p. 157-175); Chapter Eleven: The Survivors in Matzeev (p. 176-188); Chapter Twelve: To Safety (p. 189-200); [Index (p. 201-204 in later printings)].

A reprint of the edition originally published by Star Publishers in 1984; extra covers were printed with the first Borgo edition, and then used for all subsequent printings. The Borgo version also has an errata list on page (vi), and later printings contain a specially-prepared index. This was the first published book in the Studies in Judaica and the Holocaust series. See also the sequel, *Risen from the Ashes* (see **A107**).

A70. *The Work of Bruce McAllister: An Annotated Bibliography & Guide, [Revised Edition]*, by David Ray Bourquin. BIBLIOGRAPHIES OF MODERN AUTHORS, Number 10. 32 p. LC 85-22400. OCLC #12583580. ISBN 0-89370-389-3 cloth $19.95; ISBN 0-89370-489-X paper $9.95. Cover: standard series design by Michael Pastucha, with photo of author, black ink on bright green. Revised Edition, May 1986.

A bibliography and literary guide to the works of the modern American writer, Bruce McAllister (1946-).

CONTENTS: Introduction (p. 3-4); A. Books (p. 5-6); B. Short Fiction (p. 7-12); C. Non-Fiction (p. 13); D. Poetry (p. 14-17); E. Graphic/Experimental Work (p. 18); F. Papers (p. 19); G. Editorial Posts (p. 20-22); H. Media Appearances (p. 23); I. Awards and Prizes (p. 24); J. About the Author (p. 25-26); Critical Comments (p. 27); Title Index (p. 29-32).

Updated and completely reset from the previous version (see **A67**). Half of the run was printed with blank covers in paperback for rebinding in cloth.

A71. ***The Work of Charles Beaumont: An Annotated Bibliography & Guide***, by William F. Nolan, edited by R. Reginald. BIB-LIOGRAPHIES OF MODERN AUTHORS, Number 6. 48 p. LC 85-460. OCLC #11754477. ISBN 0-89370-385-0 cloth $19.95; ISBN 0-89370-485-7 paper $9.95. Cover: standard series design by Michael Pastucha, with photo of author, black ink on yellow background. First Edition, May 1986.

b. Second Printing, January 1988.

A bibliography and literary guide to the works of the late American writer, Charles Beaumont (1929-1967).

CONTENTS: Introduction (p. 3-4); A. Books (p. 5-9); B. Short Fiction (p. 9-24); C. Non-Fiction (p. 25-29); D. Screenplays (p. 30-31); E. Teleplays (p. 32-35); F. Comics (p. 36); G. Letters (p. 37); H. Unpublished Stories (p. 38); I. Awards (p. 39); J. Artwork (p. 40); K. Editorial Posts (p. 41); L. About the Author (p. 42-44); Title Index (p. 45-48).

Half of the run was printed with blank yellow covers in paperback for rebinding in cloth. See also the Second Edition (**A116**).

A72. ***The Work of George Zebrowski: An Annotated Bibliography & Guide***, by Jeffrey M. Elliot and R. Reginald. BIBLIOGRAPHIES OF MODERN AUTHORS, Number 4. 54 p. LC 84-24239. OCLC #11346334. ISBN 0-89370-383-4 cloth $19.95; ISBN 0-89370-

483-0 paper $9.95. Cover: standard series design by Michael Pastucha, with photo of the author by Jay Kay Klein, black ink with blue frame on white background. First Edition, May 1986.

A bibliography and literary guide to the works of the modern American writer, George Zebrowski (1945-).
CONTENTS: Introduction (p. 3-6); A. Books (p. 7-13); B. Short Fiction (p. 13-22); C. Translations (p. 23); D. Articles and Reviews (p. 24-32); E. Journals and Publishing Series (p. 33-34); F. Juvenilia (p. 35-37); G. About the Author (p. 38-39); H. Honors and Awards (p. 40); I. Public Appearances (p. 41-43); J. Published Works (p. 44); K. Miscellanea (p. 45); Quoth the Critics (p. 46-50); Title Index (p. 51-54).
Half of the run was printed with blank blue covers in paperback for rebinding in cloth. See also the Second Edition (**A114**).

A73. ***Demon Prince: The Dissonant Worlds of Jack Vance***, by Jack Rawlins. THE MILFORD SERIES: POPULAR WRITERS OF TODAY, Volume 40. 104 p. LC 81-21600. OCLC #8034755. ISBN 0-89370-163-7 cloth $14.95; ISBN 0-89370-263-3 paper $6.95. Cover: standard series design by Michael Pastucha, black ink on red background, with stylized drawing of demon head. First Edition, June 1986.

A critique of the modern American writer, Jack Vance (1916-).
CONTENTS: Abbreviations (p. 3-4); Chronology (p. 5-8); I. About Jack Vance (p. 9-11); II. Vance's Works (p. 12-48); III. Vance's Words (p. 49-65); IV. Vance's Plots (p. 66-85); V. Afterword: New Directions (p. 86-87); VI. An Interview with Jack Vance (p. 88-96); VII. Selective Secondary Bibliography (p. 97-99); Index (p. 100-104).
Half of the run was printed with blank red covers for rebinding in cloth.

A74. ***The Holy Grail Revealed: The Real Secret of Rennes-le-Château***, by Patricia and Lionel Fanthorpe, edited with an Introduction by R. Reginald. 144 p. LC 82-4303. OCLC #8346240. ISBN 0-89370-660-4 cloth $19.95. Illustrated throughout with charts, drawings, and photographs, some by

BP 300, by Robert Reginald & Mary Wickizer Burgess

Patrick Kirby. Cover: printed with plain white covers. First Borgo Edition (labeled Second Printing), November 1986.

b. Third [i.e., Second] Printing, with new ten-page index, September 1989. 154 p., $22.95. Cover: printed with plain peach covers.

A look at the mystery surrounding Rennes-le-Château in France, intended as a response to Michael Baigent, Richard Leigh, and Henry Lincoln's bestselling book, *Holy Blood, Holy Grail*.
    CONTENTS: Foreword (p. 5); Introduction: Once Upon a Time, by R. Reginald (p. 9-16); 1. The Man (p. 17-22); 2. The Place (p. 23-28); 3. Treasures of Jerusalem and Rome (p. 29-34); 4. Franks, Merovingians, and Carolingians (p. 35-40); 5. The Cathars, or Albigensians (p. 41-46); 6. The Templars (p. 47-53); 7. The Priory of Sion (p. 54-61); 8. The Broken Tombstone (p. 62-68); 9. The Scrolls Behind the Altar (p. 69-74); 10. Rennes-le-Château and the Tarot (p. 75-78); 11. Poussin and Teniers (p. 79-85); 12. Sir Francis Bacon's Cipher (p. 86-93); 13. The Shugborough Hall Mystery (p. 94-99); 14. Victor Hugo (p. 100-103); 15. The Hapsburg Dimension (p. 104-110); 16. Henri Buthion's Story (p. 111-118); 17. Theories Old and New (p. 119-128); 18. The Grail Trail of Baigent, Leigh, and Lincoln (p. 129-137); 19. The Holy Grail Revealed: An Answer (p. 138-143); [Index (p. 145-154 in later printing)].
    Reprinted facsimile from the 1982 Newcastle edition; both printings were printed with blank covers in paperback for rebinding in cloth.

A75. ***Blond Barbarians & Noble Savages***, by L. Sprague de Camp. ESSAYS ON FANTASTIC LITERATURE, Number 2. 49 p. LC 85-28944. OCLC #12974804. ISBN 0-89370-545-4 cloth $15.95. Cover: printed in plain blue covers. First Borgo Edition, November 1986.

A critique of the fiction of Robert E. Howard (1906-1936) and H. P. Lovecraft (1890-1937), reprinted from the 1975 T-K Graphics edition with a new index.
    CONTENTS: Introduction (p. 5); Lovecraft and the Aryans (p. 6-20); Howard and the Celts (p. 21-33); The Heroic Barbarian (p. 34-46); Index (p. 47-49).

BP 300, by Robert Reginald & Mary Wickizer Burgess

Printed with blank covers in paperback for rebinding in cloth.

A76. *It's Down the Slippery Cellar Stairs*, by R. A. Lafferty. ESSAYS ON FANTASTIC LITERATURE, Number 1. 54 p. LC 85-29969. OCLC #12970324. ISBN 0-89370-543-8 cloth $15.95. Cover: printed in plain gray covers. First Borgo Edition, November 1986.

A collection of literary essays and speeches, reprinted from the 1984 Drumm Books edition with a new index.
CONTENTS: Acknowledgments (p. 3); The World's Narration (p. 5-7); The Ten Thousand Masks of the World (p. 8-10); Great Awkward Gold (p. 11-13); Something New Under the Black Sun (p. 14-17); More Worlds Than One? (p. 18-20); For a Little Bit of Gold (p. 21-22); Riddle-Writers of the Isthmus (p. 23-26); Through the Red Fire (p. 27-29); Tell It Funny, Og (p. 30-32); Rare Earths and Pig-Weeds (p. 33-35); The Gathering of the Tribes (p. 36-40); The Day After the World Ended (p. 41-47); It's Down the Slippery Cellar Stairs (p. 48-50); Index (p. 51-54).
Printed with blank covers in paperback for rebinding in cloth. See also the Second Edition (**A217**).

A77. *George Orwell's Guide Through Hell: A Psychological Study of Nineteen Eighty-Four*, by Robert Plank. THE MILFORD SERIES: POPULAR WRITERS OF TODAY, Volume 41. 123 p. LC 84-11075. OCLC #10799573. ISBN 0-89370-199-8 cloth $15.95; ISBN 0-89370-299-4 paper $7.95. With a photograph of the late author. Cover: standard series design by Judy Cloyd, black ink on pale yellow background. First Edition, December 1986.

A critique of the late British writer, George Orwell (1903-1950), and his seminal work, *Nineteen Eighty-Four*.
CONTENTS: Dedication (p. 4); Chronology (p. 5-6); Introduction (p. 7-10); I. Preparing to Descend into Hell (p. 11-14); II. Who Is Winston Smith? (p. 15-19); III. The Ghostly Bells of London (p. 20-28); IV. The Chestnut Tree Café (p. 29-35); V. The World in a Globe of Glass (p. 36-50); VI. The Inquisitor (p. 51-65); VII. Trust and Betrayal (p. 66-73); VIII. The Sanctity of the Word (p. 74-87); IX. Julia and the Rats (p. 88-94); X. Power and Paranoia (p. 95-106); The End of the Voyage Through Hell

(p. 107-110); Notes (p. 111-116); Bibliography (p. 117-118); Index (p. 119-123).
See also the Revised Edition (**A198**).

A78. ***Decisive Warfare: A Study in Military Theory***, by Reginald Bretnor. STOKVIS STUDIES IN HISTORICAL CHRONOLOGY AND THOUGHT, Number 5. [xxii]+9-192 p. LC 84-315. OCLC #10348392. ISBN 0-89370-320-6 cloth $19.95; ISBN 0-89370-420-2 paper $9.95. Cover: standard series design by Judy Cloyd Graphic Design, black ink on tan background. First Borgo Edition, December 1986.

A facsimile reprint of the 1969 Stackpole edition, with a new introduction by the author. Bretnor's treatise discusses the philosophy and practice of modern war.
CONTENTS: Prefatory Comment 1986 (p. [ix-xxii]); Preface (p. 9-13); Chapter 1: Vulnerability and the Equations of War (p. 14-43); Chapter 2: Destructive Force and the Equations of War (p. 44-71); Chapter 3: Time and the Equations of War (p. 72-99); Chapter 4: The Critical Imbalance (p. 100-151); Chapter 5: The Optimum Response (p. 152-188); Index (p. 189-192).
A first printing of this book was misprinted by the printer with the title page on the front cover, and scrapped.

A79. ***D.H. Lawrence: The Poet Who Was Not Wrong***, by Douglas A. Mackey. THE MILFORD SERIES: POPULAR WRITERS OF TODAY, Volume 42. 149 p. LC 84-291. OCLC #10349873. ISBN 0-89370-171-8 cloth $15.95; ISBN 0-89370-271-4 paper $7.95. Cover: standard series design by Judy Cloyd, black ink on orange background. First Edition, December 1986.

A critical guide to the poetry of British writer, D. H. Lawrence (1885-1930).
CONTENTS: Chronology (p. 5-6); I. The Fourth Dimension (p. 7-15); II. Kissing and Horrid Strife (p. 16-48); III. Pax (p. 49-81); IV. The Morning Star (p. 82-105); V. The Longest Journey (p. 106-139); VI. Bibliography (p. 140-142); Index of Poems (p. 143-146); General Index (p. 147-149).

A80. ***Science Fiction and Fantasy Research Index, Volume 7***, by Hal W. Hall and Jan Swanbeck. [ii]+197 p., 8.5 x 11". OCLC

BP 300, by Robert Reginald & Mary Wickizer Burgess

#24614822. ISBN 0-8095-6103-3 cloth $24.95. Cover design: printed with plain dark red covers. First Edition, 1987.

A continuing subject and author index to critical and bibliographical materials in the science fiction and fantasy genres.

Printed with blank covers in paperback for rebinding in cloth; later copies were reproduced via xerography.

A81. *The Sociology of Science Fiction*, by Brian M. Stableford. I.O. EVANS STUDIES IN THE PHILOSOPHY & CRITICISM OF LITERATURE, Number 4. 189 p. LC 81-21607. OCLC #8034762. ISBN 0-89370-165-3 cloth $19.95; ISBN 0-89370-265-X paper $9.95. Cover: standard series design by Judy Cloyd, black ink on peach background. First Edition, April 1987.

A reprint of the author's Ph.D. dissertation on the sociological aspects of modern science fiction literature, with updates and corrections.

CONTENTS: Acknowledgments (p. 4); Introduction (p. 5-8); I. Approaches to the Sociology of Literature (p. 9-30); II. The Analysis of Communicative Functions (p. 31-44); III. The Evolution of Science Fiction As a Publishing Category (p. 45-67); IV. The Expectations of the Science Fiction Reader (p. 68-95); V. Themes and Trends in Science Fiction (p. 96-143); VI. Conclusion: The Communicative Functions of Science Fiction (p. 144-157); Notes and References (p. 159-166); Bibliography (p. 166-172); Index (p. 173-188); About the Author (p. 189).

A82. *The Theatrical Rambles of Mr. and Mrs. John Greene*, by Charles Durang, ed. by William L. Slout. CLIPPER STUDIES IN THE AMERICAN THEATRE, Number 1. 142 p. LC 84-11165. OCLC #10851008. ISBN 0-89370-360-5 cloth $19.95; ISBN 0-89370-460-1 paper $9.95. Cover: standard series design by Judy Cloyd Graphic Design, black ink on pale green background. First Edition, April 1987.

The first book publication of a biography of two nineteenth-century American actors, Anne Nuskey Greene (1800-1862) and John Greene (d. 1860); the original was serialized in the *New York Clipper* in 1865.

BP 300, by Robert Reginald & Mary Wickizer Burgess

CONTENTS: Chronology (p. 4); Preface (p. 5-8); The Theatrical Rambles (p. 9-114); Notes (p. 115-126); Bibliography (p. 127-133); Index (p. 134-142).

A83. *Non-Literary Influences on Science Fiction,* by Algis Budrys. ESSAYS ON FANTASTIC LITERATURE, Number 4. 30 p. LC 85-31439. OCLC #13063948. ISBN 0-89370-542-X cloth $15.95. Cover: printed in plain orange covers. First Borgo Edition, December 1987.

An essay on science fiction by a well-known author and critic, reprinted from the 1983 Drumm Books edition with new index.
CONTENTS: Non-Literary Influences on Science Fiction: (An Essay) (p. 5-23); Notes (p. 24-27); Index (p. 28-30.
Printed with blank covers in paperback for rebinding in cloth.

A84. *Mystery and Detective Fiction in the Library of Congress Classification Scheme,* by Michael Burgess. BORGO CATALOGING GUIDES, Number 2. 184 p. LC 84-12344. OCLC #10913797. ISBN 0-89370-818-6 cloth $22.95; ISBN 0-89370-918-2 paper $12.95. Cover: standard series design by Highpoint Type & Graphics, black ink on red background. First Edition, December 1987.

A guide to Library of Congress cataloging practice regarding crime fiction.
CONTENTS: Introduction (p. 3-4); I. Subject Headings (p. 5-17); II. Classification Numbers (p. 18-26); Index to Classification Numbers (p. 27-30); III. Author Main Entries and Literature Numbers (p. 31-178); LC Literature Tables (p. 179-181); IV. Motion Picture Main Entries and Numbers (p. 182); V. Television Program Main Entries and Numbers (p. 183); VI. Comic Strip Main Entries and Numbers (p. 184).

A85. *Whaling Masters,* compiled by the Federal Writers Project of the Works Progress Administration of Massachusetts. STOKVIS STUDIES IN HISTORICAL CHRONOLOGY AND THOUGHT, Number 8. 314 p. LC 87-872. OCLC #15196983. ISBN 0-89370-833-X cloth $24.95; ISBN 0-89370-933-6 paper $14.95. Cover: standard series design by Judy Cloyd Graphic Design, black ink on blue background. Illustrated with photographs. First Borgo Edition, December 1987.

b. Second Printing, September 1989.
c. Third Printing, December 1991, with new pictorial cover and redesigned type by Highpoint Type & Graphics using a stylized whaling ship.

This facsimile reprint of the 1938 original edition of the Old Dartmouth Historical Society includes lists of whaling captains and ships who operated out of the ports of New Bedford, Nantucket, New London, and Cape Cod during the nineteenth century.
CONTENTS: Foreword (p. 7); Log of the Whaler (p. 9-19); "Thar She Blows!" (p. 20-25); Fin Out—But Not Finis (p. 26-27); Glossary (p. 28-30); A Few Books About Whaling (p. 31); Directory of American Whaling Masters (p. 33-314).
This was the largest Borgo Press book published to this date.

A86. *Science Fiction and Fantasy Research Index, Volume 8*, compiled by Hal W. Hall. iv+68 p., 8.5 x 11". OCLC #24614822. ISBN 0-8095-6111-5 cloth $22.95. First Edition, 1988.

A continuing subject and author index to critical and bibliographical materials in the science fiction and fantasy genres. Reproduced via xerography.

A87. *A Guide to Science Fiction and Fantasy in the Library of Congress Classification Scheme, Second Edition*, by Michael Burgess. BORGO CATALOGING GUIDES, Number 1. 168 p. LC 87-6308. OCLC #15283987. ISBN 0-89370-827-5 cloth $22.95; ISBN 0-89370-927-1 paper $12.95. Cover: standard series design by Highpoint Type & Graphics, black ink on gold background. Second Edition, February 1988.

A guide to LC cataloging practice for science fiction and fantasy authors and books.
CONTENTS: Introduction (p. 3-4); I. Subject Headings (p. 5-26); II. Classification Numbers (p. 27-48); Index to Classification Numbers (p. 49-57); III. Author Main Entries and Literature Numbers (p. 58-154); LC Literature Tables (p. 155-158); IV. Artist Main Entries and Artist Numbers (p. 159-161); V. Motion

Picture Main Entries and Numbers (p. 162-164); VI. Television & Radio Program Main Entries and Numbers (p. 165-166); VI. Comic Strip Main Entries and Numbers (p. 167); About the Author (p. 168).

An expanded version of **A60**.

A88. *Ah, Julian! A Memoir of Julian Brodetsky*, by Leonard Wibberley. BORGO BIOVIEWS, Number 3. [vi]+154 p. LC 84-307. OCLC #10375501. ISBN 0-89370-341-9 cloth $19.95. Frontispiece photo of Brodetsky by Dalton Creaser. Cover: printed with plain blue covers. First Borgo Edition, February 1988.

This reprint of the 1963 William Morrow edition is a poignant biography of well-known violinist, Julian Brodetsky (1893-1962), a friend and instructor of the author.

Printed with blank covers in paperback for rebinding in cloth. Originally announced in paper and cloth, but the paper version was canceled.

A89. *Hugo Gernsback, Father of Modern Science Fiction, with Essays on Frank Herbert and Bram Stoker*, by Mark Siegel. THE MILFORD SERIES: POPULAR WRITERS OF TODAY, Volume 45. 96 p. LC 84-318. OCLC #10375518. ISBN 0-89370-174-2 cloth $19.95; ISBN 0-89370-274-9 paper $9.95. Illustrated with a frontispiece photograph of Hugo Gernsback. Cover: standard series design by Judy Cloyd Graphic Design and Highpoint Type & Graphics, black ink on lime background. First Edition, March 1988.

b.   Second printing, December 1989.

A collection of critical essays on editor Hugo Gernsback (1884-1967) and writers Frank Herbert (1920-1986) and Bram Stoker (1847-1912).

CONTENTS: Acknowledgments (p. 6); Reactive Criticism: An Introduction to the Essays (p. 7-10); Hugo Gernsback Chronology (p. 11-12); I. Hugo Gernsback, Father of Modern Science Fiction: Introduction (p. 13-14); 1. The Man and His Times (p. 15-23); 2. The Science Fiction Writings of Hugo Gernsback (p. 24-36); 3. Hugo Gernsback, Editor and Publisher

(p. 37-47); 4. Gernsback's Influence (p. 48-56); Selected Bibliography (p. 57-61); Frank Herbert Chronology (p. 63-64); II. The Ecology of Politics and the Politics of Ecology in Frank Herbert's *Dune* (p. 65-74); Selected Bibliography (p. 75); Bram Stoker Chronology (p. 76-77); III. Carnal Knowledge: *Dracula* As Anti-Quest (p. 78-89); Selected Bibliography (p. 90-91); Index (p. 92-95); About the Author (p. 96).

A first printing was printed with several faint pages, but was scrapped.

A90. ***The Work of William F. Nolan: An Annotated Bibliography & Guide***, by Boden Clarke and James Hopkins. BIBLIOGRAPHIES OF MODERN AUTHORS, Number 14. 224 p. LC 87-6334. OCLC #15318087. ISBN 0-89370-393-1 cloth $22.95; ISBN 0-89370-493-8 paper $12.95. Illustrated with photographs of the author's books by Richard Cline. Cover: standard series design by Michael Pastucha, photo of author by Nobumitsu Kobaka, black ink on brown background. First Edition, October 1988.

A bibliography of and literary guide to the works of modern American writer, William F. Nolan (1928-).

CONTENTS: Introduction: "The Multi-Media Man," by Jeffrey M. Elliot (p. 5-9); William F. Nolan: A Chronology (p. 10-18); A. Books (p. 19-44); B. Short Fiction (p. 45-68); C. Verse (p. 69-71); D. Personality Profiles (p. 72-89); E. Reviews (p. 90-94); Selected Illustrations (p. 95-101); F. Other Nonfiction (p. 102-126); G. Screenplays (p. 127-128); H. Teleplays (p. 129-132); I. Film and Television Outlines (p. 133-137); J. Radio (p. 138); K. Stage (p. 139); L. Comics (p. 140-141); M. Letters (p. 142-146); N. Juvenilia (p. 147-153); O. Interviews (p. 154-156); P. Speeches and Public Appearances (p. 157-162); Q. Television and Radio Appearances (p. 163-166); R. Other Media (p. 167); S. Artwork (p. 168-174); T. Editorial Posts (p. 175); U. Honors and Awards (p. 176-177); V. About the Author (p. 178-185); W. Unpublished Works (p. 186-193); X. Miscellanea (p. 194-203); Quoth the Critics (p. 204-206); Index (p. 207-224).

A91. ***Western Fiction in the Library of Congress Classification Scheme***, by Michael Burgess and Beverly A. Ryan. BORGO CATALOGING GUIDES, Number 3. 48 p. LC 87-6309. OCLC #15283900. ISBN 0-89370-822-4 cloth $22.95; ISBN 0-89370-

BP 300, by Robert Reginald & Mary Wickizer Burgess

922-0 paper $12.95. Cover: standard series design by Highpoint Type & Graphics, black ink on tan background. First Edition, October 1988.

A guide to LC cataloging practice for Western fiction authors and books.
CONTENTS: Introduction (p. 5-6); I. Subject Headings (p. 7-8); II. Classification Numbers (p. 9-12); Index to Classification Numbers (p. 13); III. Author Main Entries and Literature Numbers (p. 14-39); LC Literature Tables (p. 40-44); IV. Motion Picture Main Entries and Numbers (p. 44-45); V. Television Program Main Entries and Numbers (p. 46-47); VI. Radio Program Main Entries and Numbers (p. 48).

A92. *California Ranchos: Patented Private Land Grants Listed by County*, by Burgess McK. Shumway, edited by Michael & Mary Burgess. STOKVIS STUDIES IN HISTORICAL CHRONOLOGY AND THOUGHT, Number 11. A Sidewinder Press Book. 144 p. LC 87-11696. OCLC #15628291. ISBN 0-89370-835-6 cloth $19.95; ISBN 0-89370-935-2 paper $9.95. Cover: standard series design by Judy Cloyd Graphic Design and Highpoint Type & Graphics, black ink on rose background. First Borgo Edition, October 1988.

b. Second Printing, with new back cover copy and laminated covers, April 1993.

This guide to the land grants given by the early Spanish and Mexican governors of California was extensively reworked and reset by the editors from a 1942 WPA project, *Ranchos of California*.
CONTENTS: Introduction: The Ranchos of California, by Michael Burgess (p. 5-6); Preface: California's Land Grants, by Robert G. Cowan (p. 7-9); Note (p. 10); Alameda County (p. 11-13); Amador County (p. 14); Butte County (p. 15-16); Calaveras County (p. 17); Colusa County (p. 18); Contra Costa County (p. 19-21); Fresno County (p. 22); Glenn County (p. 23); Kern County (p. 24); Kings County (p. 25); Lake County (p. 26); Los Angeles County (p. 27-37); Marin County (p. 38-40); Mariposa County (p. 41); Mendocino County (p. 42); Merced County (p. 43); Monterey County (p. 44-53); Napa County (p. 54-56);

Orange County (p. 57-60); Riverside County (p. 61-62); Sacramento County (p. 63-64); San Benito County (p. 65-67); San Bernardino County (p. 68-69); San Diego County (p. 70-74); San Francisco County (p. 75-76); San Joaquin County (p. 77); San Luis Obispo County (p. 78-82); San Mateo County (p. 83-86); Santa Barbara County (p. 87-92); Santa Clara County (p. 93-100); Santa Cruz County (p. 101-103); Shasta County (p. 104); Solano County (p. 105); Sonoma County (p. 106-109); Stanislaus County (p. 110); Sutter County (p. 111); Tehama County (p. 112-113); Ventura County (p. 114-116); Yolo County (p. 117); Yuba County (p. 118); Governors of Spanish and Mexican California (p. 119); Index of Governors and Other Grantors (p. 120); Index of Ranchos (p. 121-130); Index of Grantees (p. 131-144).

A93. *Black Paradise: The Rastafarian Movement*, by Peter B. Clarke. NEW RELIGIOUS MOVEMENTS SERIES, Number 1. 112 p. LC 86-18811. OCLC #28798194. ISBN 0-8095-7021-1 cloth $22.95. Illustrated with photographs and maps. Cover: printed with plain gray covers. First Borgo Edition, November 1988.

b.   Second Printing, November 1989. Printed with plain white covers.
c.   Third Printing, August 1992. Printed with plain gray covers.

This facsimile reprint of the 1986 Aquarian Press (Thorsons Publishers) edition is a popular history of the Rastafarian movement.
CONTENTS: Series Editor's Preface (p. 7); Acknowledgements (p. 9); Introduction: The Rastafarian Movement and New Religions in Britain (p. 11-16); 1. The African Diaspora (p. 17-26); 2. The Back-to-Africa Movement and the Rise of Ethiopianism (p. 27-35); 3. Marcus Garvey: Black Moses and Prophet of God in Ethiopia (p. 36-44); 4. Babylon: The Rise and Development of the Rastafarian Movement in Jamaica and Britain (p. 45-62); 5. Beliefs (p. 63-78); 6. Rastafarian Lifestyle and Rituals (p. 79-94); 7. From Self-Awareness to the Brotherhood of Man (p. 95-100); Notes (p. 101-107); Select Bibliography (p. 109-110); Index (p. 111-112).
The book was printed with blank covers in paperback for rebinding in cloth. See also the Revised Edition (**A179**).

A94. *My Sweet Lord: The Hare Krishna Movement*, by Kim Knott. NEW RELIGIOUS MOVEMENTS SERIES, Number 2. 112 p. LC 86-18810. OCLC #14001837. ISBN 0-8095-7023-8 cloth $22.95. Illustrated with photographs. Cover: printed with plain white covers. First Borgo Edition, November 1988.

This facsimile reprint of the 1986 Aquarian Press (Thorsons Publishers) edition is a popular history of the Hare Krishna movement.

CONTENTS: Series Editor's Preface (p. 9); Acknowledgements (p. 11-12); Introduction (p. 13-17); 1. Hinduism and the West: The Rise of Krishna Consciousness (p. 19-43); 2. The Hare Krishna Devotees: Continuity and Change (p. 44-58); 3. The Beliefs and Practices of Krishna Consciousness (p. 59-74); 4. Hare Krishna from the Outside (p. 75-84); 5. The Hare Krishna Movement in Perspective (p. 85-91); Notes (p. 93-100); Select Bibliography (p. 101-103); Glossary (p. 105-110); Index (p. 111-112).

The book was printed with blank covers in paperback for rebinding in cloth.

A95. *The Way of the Heart: The Rajneesh Movement*, by Judith Thompson and Paul Heelas. NEW RELIGIOUS MOVEMENTS SERIES, Number 3. 142 p. LC 87-29792. OCLC #17209736. ISBN 0-8095-7038-6 cloth $22.95. Illustrated with photographs. Cover: printed with plain yellow covers. First Borgo Edition, November 1988.

This facsimile reprint of the 1986 Aquarian Press (Thorsons Publishers) edition is a popular history of the Rajneesh movement.

CONTENTS: Acknowledgement (p. 6); Series Editor's Preface (p. 7-8); Introduction (p. 9-11); 1. Bhagwan's Path: 'The Unfolding Vision' (p. 13-32); 2. The Teaching: 'Off with Your Heads' (p. 33-50); 3. Techniques of Transformation: 'Waking the Buddhas' (p. 51-70); 4. The Quality of Life: 'Coming Closer' (p. 71-86); 5. Daily Life in the Communal Buddhafield: 'An Experiment to Provoke God' (p. 87-110); 6. The Rule of Freedom or the Freedom to Rule: 'A Master of Contradiction' (p. 111-118); 7. The Case of Bhagwan Shree Rajneesh: 'A Good Way of Being?' (p. 119-131); Notes (p. p. 133-139); Index (p. 141-142).

The book was printed with blank covers in paperback for rebinding in cloth.

A96. *The Work of Colin Wilson: An Annotated Bibliography & Guide*, by Colin Stanley, edited by Boden Clarke. BIBLIOGRAPHIES OF MODERN AUTHORS, Number 1. 312 p. LC 84-11181. OCLC #10799641. ISBN 0-89370-817-8 cloth $29.95; ISBN 0-89370-917-4 paper $19.95; ISBN 0-89370-010-X signed, limited cloth edition of 80 copies $49.95. Cover: standard series design by Highpoint Type and Graphics, using photo of Colin Wilson by Anna de Courcy; black ink on gray background. First Edition, September 1989.

b. Second Printing 1990, with printing information not noted internally.

A bibliography of and literary guide to the works of modern British writer, Colin Wilson (1931-).

CONTENTS: Acknowledgment and Note (p. 4); Introduction: The Quest for Colin Wilson (p. 5-9); A Colin Wilson Chronology (p. 10-14); A. Books (p. 15-125); B. Short Fiction (p. 126-127); C. Nonfiction (p. 128-182); D. Introductions and Afterwords (p. 183-189); E. Book Reviews (p. 190-201); F. Other Media (p. 202-203); G. Editorial Credits (p. 204-205); H. About the Author: Monographs (p. 206-219); I. About the Author: Critiques, Profiles, Interviews (p. 220-228); J. About the Author: Short Bio-Bibliographies (p. 229-240); K. About the Author: Other Materials (p. 241-242); L. Miscellanea (p. 243-246); Quoth the Critics (p. 247-253); Afterword: Inside Outside, by Colin Wilson (p. 254-265); About Colin Stanley (p. 266); Title Index to Colin Wilson's Works (p. 267-279); Subject Index with Author/Title Index (p. 280-312).

The signed, limited edition consisted of only about twenty signed and numbered copies that were actually bound.

A97. *Existentially Speaking: Essays on the Philosophy of Literature*, by Colin Wilson, introduction by Colin Stanley. I.O. EVANS STUDIES IN THE PHILOSOPHY AND CRITICISM OF LITERATURE, Number 7. 144 p. LC 84-272. OCLC #10349867. ISBN 0-89370-301-X cloth $19.95; ISBN 0-89370-401-6 paper $9.95; ISBN 0-89370-008-8 signed, limited cloth edition of 80 copies

BP 300, by Robert Reginald & Mary Wickizer Burgess

$39.95. Cover: standard series design by Judy Cloyd Graphic Design and Highpoint Type & Graphics, black ink on tan background. First Edition, September 1989.

b.   Second Printing 1990, with printing information not noted internally.

A collection of previously-published essays on literature and philosophy.
        CONTENTS: Preface: Colin Wilson, Literary High Flyer, by Colin Stanley (p. 5-8); Introduction: Affirmations of Faith (p. 9-16); 1. Science Fiction and Existentialism: A Personal View (p. 17-32); 2. An Integrity Born of Hope: Notes on Christopher Isherwood (p. 33-52); 3. Michel Foucault (p. 53-59); 4. Arthur Koestler (p. 60-70); 5. Husserl and Evolution (p. 71-82); 6. Wyndham Lewis: A Refracted Talent? (p. 83-104); 7. Robert Musil, the Man Without Qualities (p. 105-110); 8. The Decline and Fall of Existentialism (p. 111-127); Index (p. 129-143); About the Author (p. 144).
        The signed, limited edition consisted of only about twenty signed and numbered copies that were actually bound.

A98.   *The Monumental Inscriptions in the Churches and Churchyards of the Island of Barbados, British West Indies*, by Vere Langford Oliver. STOKVIS STUDIES IN HISTORICAL CHRONOLOGY AND THOUGHT, Number 13. San Bernardino, CA: The Borgo Press; Glendale, CA: The Sidewinder Press. viii+224 p. LC 88-34120. OCLC #18909432. ISBN 0-89370-329-X cloth $24.95; ISBN 0-89370-429-6 paper $14.95. Illustrated with maps. Cover: standard series design by Judy Cloyd Graphic Design and Highpoint Type & Graphics, black ink on red background. First Borgo Edition, September 1989.

This facsimile reprint of the 1915 Mitchell Hughes and Clarke edition is a compilation of headstone readings from the British colony of Barbados copied in 1913-14 by the author.
        CONTENTS: Preface (p. v-vii); [New] Introduction: A Monumental Work, by Michael Burgess (p. viii); Monumental Inscriptions in Barbados (p. 1-208); Index Nominum (p. 209-223); Abbreviations (p. [224]).
        See also the retitled edition (**A209**).

A99. *The Poison Maiden & the Great Bitch: Female Stereotypes in Marvel Superhero Comics*, by Susan Wood. ESSAYS ON FANTASTIC LITERATURE, Number 5. 27 p. LC 86-2268. OCLC #13123351. ISBN 0-89370-537-3 cloth $15.95. Cover: printed in plain green covers. First Borgo Edition, September 1989.

An essay on the depiction of women in Marvel comic books, reset from the 1974 T-K Graphics edition, with a new index.
CONTENTS: Introduction: About Susan Wood, by Robert Reginald (p. 3-4); The Poison Maiden & the Great Bitch (p. 5-19); Notes (p. 20-22); Index (p. 23-27).
Printed with blank covers in paperback for rebinding in cloth. This was the shortest Borgo Press book ever published.

A100. *Ray Bradbury: Dramatist*, by Ben P. Indick. ESSAYS ON FANTASTIC LITERATURE, Number 3. 47 p. LC 88-34666. OCLC #18908726. ISBN 0-89370-540-3 cloth $15.95. Cover: printed with blank yellow covers in paperback for rebinding in cloth. First Edition, September 1989.

   b. [Second Printing, August 1990]. ISBN 0-89370-540-3 cloth $17.95; ISBN 0-89370-559-4 paper $7.95. Includes a newly designed paperbound cover with standard series design by Highpoint Type & Graphics, black ink on gray background. Scrapped due to an incorrect edition statement (September 1989) by the printer.
   c. Second Printing [i.e., Third Printing], September 1990. This replaced the invalid second printing.

A critique on the plays of modern American writer, Ray Bradbury (1920-), rewritten from the author's earlier work, *The Drama of Ray Bradbury* (T-K Graphics, 1977).
CONTENTS: Acknowledgments (p. 4); Introduction (p. 5-7); 1. Radio Plays (p. 9-10); 2. Teleplays (p. 11-12); 3. Screenplays (p. 13-21); 4. Stage Plays (p. 22-35); 5. The Future of the Theatre (p. 36); Notes (p. 37-40); Selected Bibliography (p. 41); Index (p. 42-46); About the Author (p. 47).

A101. *The Work of Chad Oliver: An Annotated Bibliography & Guide*, by Hal W. Hall, edited by Boden Clarke. BIBLIOGRAPHIES OF

57

BP 300, by Robert Reginald & Mary Wickizer Burgess

MODERN AUTHORS, Number 12. 88 p. LC 86-2288. OCLC #13123413. ISBN 0-89370-391-5 cloth $19.95; ISBN 0-89370-491-1 paper $9.95. Cover: standard series design by Highpoint Type & Graphics, using photo of author, black ink on mauve background. First Edition, October 1989.

A bibliography of and literary guide to the works of the late American writer, Chad Oliver (1928-1993).

CONTENTS: Acknowledgments (p. 4); Introduction, by Howard Waldrop (p. 5-7); A Chad Oliver Chronology (p. 9-12); A. Books (p. 13-23); B. Short Fiction (p. 24-38); C. Nonfiction (p. 39-41); D. Letters (p. 42-45); E. Other Media (p. 46); F. Unpublished Works (p. 47); G. About the Author: Monographs, Profiles, Critiques (p. 48-55); H. About the Author: News Releases (p. 56-57); I. Honors and Awards (p. 58); J. Miscellanea (p. 59-60); An Interview with Chad Oliver, Conducted by Hal W. Hall and Richard D. Boldt (p. 61-78); Second Thoughts, by Chad Oliver (p. 79-81); About Hal W. Hall (p. 82); Index (p. 83-88).

A102. *Pioneer Tales of San Bernardino County*, compiled by the WPA Writers' Program. WEST COAST STUDIES, Number 2. Hollywood, CA: A Sidewinder Book. 60 p. LC 88-34119. OCLC #18909427. ISBN 0-89370-836-4 cloth $17.95; ISBN 0-89370-936-0 paper $7.95. Illustrated with woodcuts. Cover design by Highpoint Type & Graphics, adapting one of the woodcuts from the text, brown ink on tan background. First Borgo Edition, November 1989.

This facsimile reprint of the 1940 WPA project originally published by the Sun Co. includes stories about early life in San Bernardino County, California, the San Bernardino Mountains, and the Mojave Desert. The book includes a new index.

CONTENTS: Preface, by Leon Dorais (p. 3); Introduction, by Jerome B. Kavanaugh (p. 5); Frontier Days in Old San Bernardino (p. 9-14); Life in Calico (p. 15-20); The Mojave Desert (p. 21-26); Redskins, Scouts, and Muzzle Loaders (p. 27-34); Leaves from a Frontier Scrapbook (p. 35-40); Frontier Names and Places (p. 41-46); Tall Tales (p. 47-48); Bear Stories (p. 49-53); [New] Index (p. 54-60).

A103. *The Work of Ian Watson: An Annotated Bibliography & Guide*, by Douglas A. Mackey, edited by Boden Clarke. BIBLIOGRAPHIES OF MODERN AUTHORS, Number 18. 148 p. LC 88-36646. OCLC #18981817. ISBN 0-8095-0512-6 cloth $22.95; ISBN 0-8095-1512-1 paper $12.95. Cover: standard series design by Highpoint Type & Graphics, photo of author by Matjaz Sekoranja, black ink on fuchsia background. First Edition, December 1989.

A bibliography of and literary guide to the modern British author, Ian Watson (1943-).

CONTENTS: About Douglas A. Mackey (p. 4); Introduction: Elementary Watson (p. 5-9); An Ian Watson Chronology (p. 11-14); A. Books (p. 15-42); B. Short Fiction (p. 43-83); C. Nonfiction (p. 84-97); D. Letters (p. 98-100); E. Poetry (p. 101); F. Campaign Literature (p. 102); G. Other Media (p. 103-104); H. Unpublished Manuscripts (p. 105-106); I. Awards (p. 107); J. Editorial Posts (p. 108-109); K. Public Appearances (p. 110-111); L. Interviews (p. 112-115); M. About the Author (p. 116-118); N. Miscellanea (p. 119-120); Quoth the Critics (p. 121-128); Afterword: Dancing on a Tightrope, by Ian Watson (p. 129-134); Index (p. 135-148).

A104. *The Work of Reginald Bretnor: An Annotated Bibliography & Guide*, by Scott Alan Burgess, edited by Boden Clarke. BIBLIOGRAPHIES OF MODERN AUTHORS, Number 8. 122 p. LC 85-31405. OCLC #13008816. ISBN 0-89370-387-7 cloth $19.95; ISBN 0-89370-487-3 paper $9.95. Cover: standard series design by Highpoint Type & Graphics, using photo of author, black ink on pale mustard. First Edition, December 1989.

A bibliography of and literary guide to the late American writer, Reginald Bretnor (1911-1992).

CONTENTS: Introduction: The Ghosts We Share, by Judith Merril (p. 5-8); A Reginald Bretnor Chronology (p. 9-12); A. Books (p. 13-26); B. Short Fiction (p. 27-40); C. Nonfiction (p. 41-53); D. Feghoots (p. 54-87); E. Verse (p. 88); F. Editorial Credits (p. 89); G. Unpublished Works (p. 90); H. Honors and Awards (p. 91); I. About the Author (p. 92-94); J. Miscellanea (p. 95-96); Quoth the Critics (p. 97-103); From Reginald Bretnor: Through Time and Space with Ferdinand Feghoot #118 (p. 104);

BP 300, by Robert Reginald & Mary Wickizer Burgess

On the Proper Perpetration of Feghoots (p. 105-106); Through Time and Space with Ferdinand Feghoot #119 (p. 107); Afterword: Debts and Acknowledgments (p. 108-113); About Scott Alan Burgess (p. 114); Index (p. 115-122).

A105. *Chronology of the Death Valley Region in California, 1849-1949; and, Place Names of the Death Valley Region in California and Nevada, 1845-1947: An Index of the Events, Persons, and Publications Connected with Its History*, by T. S. Palmer. WEST COAST STUDIES, Number 3. Hollywood, CA: Sidewinder, distributed by The Borgo Press. [ii]+22+5-80 p. LC 88-34098. OCLC #18909279. ISBN 0-89370-837-2 cloth $19.95; ISBN 0-89370-937-9 paper $9.95. Cover design by Highpoint Type & Graphics, adapting a woodcut, black ink on beige background. First Borgo Edition, December 1989.

This facsimile reprint of the 1952 and 1948 editions combines into one version two publications on the Death Valley region of California and Nevada. Each section of the book is separately paginated.

A106. *The Work of Ross Rocklynne: An Annotated Bibliography & Guide*, by Douglas Menville, edited by Boden Clarke. BIBLIOGRAPHIES OF MODERN AUTHORS, Number 17. 70 p. LC 88-34360. OCLC #18907332. ISBN 0-8095-0511-8 cloth $19.95; ISBN 0-8095-1511-3 paper $9.95. Cover: standard series design by Highpoint Type & Graphics, photo of author by Keith Rocklin, black in on dark blue. This first printing was scrapped due to printer's errors. First Edition, December 1989.

    b.   [Second Printing, January 1990], black ink on light blue cover. Most of the first print run was stripped and subsumed into this printing. Only about ten copies with the original dark blue covers survive.

A bibliography of and literary guide to the late American writer, Ross Rocklynne (1913-1988).
    CONTENTS: Introduction: "A Man for All Magazines," by Arthur Jean Cox (p. 5-13); A Ross Rocklynne Chronology (p. 14-18); A. Books (p. 19-20); B. Short Fiction (p. 21-39); C. Nonfiction (p. 40-42); D. Fanzine Contributions (p. 43-45); E.

Radio Productions (p. 46); F. Juvenilia (p. 47); G. About the Author (p. 48-51): H. Unpublished Works (p. 52-57); I. Miscellanea (p. 58-60); Quoth the Critics (p. 61-63); Index (p. 64-69); About Douglas Menville (p. 70).

A107. *Risen from the Ashes: A Story of the Jewish Displaced Persons in the Aftermath of World War II, Being a Sequel to Survivors*, by Jacob Biber, edited by Mary A. Burgess. STUDIES IN JUDAICA AND THE HOLOCAUST, Number 5. 170 p. LC 87-851. OCLC #15196929. ISBN 0-89370-372-9 cloth $28; ISBN 0-89370-472-5 paper $18. Cover: standard series design by Highpoint Type & Graphics adapted from the cover by Peter Richards for *Survivors*, brown ink on cream background. First Edition, January 1990.

In this sequel to *Survivors* (see **A69**), Biber tells of his experiences in a displaced persons camp in the aftermath of World War II, and his subsequent coming to America.

    CONTENTS: Introduction: Against Indifference, by Elie Wiesel (p. 5); Part One: Föhrenwald. 1. A Reason for Living (p. 9-29); 2. A New Life (p. 30-48); 3. Achievements of the Homeless (p. 49-65); 4. Guests (p. 66-71); 5. Fear (p. 72-88); 6. The Desire to Leave (p. 89-93); 7. Zionism (p. 94-99); Part Two: Preston. 8. Out of the Desert (p. 103-114); 9. Farming on New Soil (p. 115-131); 10. Family (p. 132-134); 11. From Israel (p. 135-159); Notes (p. 161-162); Index (p. 163-170).

A108. *T'ai-Chi Ch'uan, Its Effects & Practical Application*, by Chen Yen-Lin. vi+184+[xx] p. LC 80-19810. OCLC #6603222. ISBN 0-89370-643-4 cloth $24.95; ISBN 0-89370-995-6 paper $12.95. Illustrated with charts, drawings, and diagrams. Cover design of a stylized kickboxer by Riley K. Smith, adapted for the Borgo edition by Highpoint Type & Graphics; brown ink on yellow background. First Borgo Edition, January 1990.

  b. Second Printing, January 1993. This version is eight pages shorter than the first printing, the book having been reorganized and several blank pages removed. Cover: black ink on yellow background.

***BP 300*,** by Robert Reginald & Mary Wickizer Burgess

This facsimile reprint of the 1979 Newcastle edition includes cover work adapted from the original.

CONTENTS: Preface (p. [iii]); Part I. Introduction (p. 1-4); Simple Explanation of the Grand Terminus Diagrams (p. 5-6); Preliminary Knowledge (p. 7-9); Some Effects of the Practice of T'ai-Chi Chüan (p. 10-12); T'ai-Chi Chüan as Related to Physiology (p. 13-14); T'ai-Chi Chüan as Related to Dynamics (p. 15-21); T'ai-Chi Chüan as Related to Psychology (p. 22-24); T'ai-Chi Chüan as Related to Moral Life (p. 25-26); Part II. Attention (p. 27-30); Preliminary Exercises (p. 31-49); Part III. Explanation of the Graphs (p. 50); T'ai-Chi Chüan (p. 51-128); Applications (p. 129-154); Part IV. Joint Hand Operations with Fixed Steps (p. 155-165); Joint Hand Operations with Active Steps (p. 166-168); Part V. Ta Lü (p. 169-182); Index (p. 183-184).

A109. ***The Work of Pamela Sargent: An Annotated Bibliography & Guide***, by Jeffrey M. Elliot, edited by Boden Clarke. BIBLIOGRAPHIES OF MODERN AUTHORS, Number 13. 80 p. LC 88-34361. OCLC #18907341. ISBN 0-89370-394-X cloth $19.95; ISBN 0-89370-494-6 paper $9.95. Cover: standard series design by Highpoint Type & Graphics, photo by George Zebrowski, black ink on pink background. First Edition, January 1990.

A bibliography of and literary guide to the modern American writer, Pamela Sargent (1948-).

CONTENTS: Introduction: "Let the Rest Take Care of Itself" (p. 5-9); A Pamela Sargent Chronology (p. 10-12); A. Books (p. 13-31); B. Short Fiction (p. 32-43); C. Nonfiction (p. 44-50); D. Unpublished Works (p. 51); E. Editorial Credits (p. 52-53); F. Other Media (p. 54); G. Juvenilia (p. 55); H. Public Appearances (p. 56-58); I. Honors and Awards (p. 59); J. About the Author (p. 60-63); K. Miscellanea (p. 64-65); Quoth the Critics (p. 66-73); Afterword: "Through the Looking Glass," by Pamela Sargent (p. 74-75); About Jeffrey M. Elliot (p. 76); Index (p. 77-80).

See also the Second Edition (**A250**).

A110. ***You Are What You Eat***, by Victor H. Lindlahr. 128 p. LC 80-19722. OCLC #6555330. ISBN 0-89370-604-3 cloth $22.95; ISBN 0-89370-990-5 paper $10.95. Illustrated with charts, drawings, and diagrams. Cover design of a fruit basket by Mary Sherman Hair, adapted for the Borgo edition by Highpoint Type

BP 300, by Robert Reginald & Mary Wickizer Burgess

& Graphics; green ink on a pale green background. First Borgo Edition, January 1990.

b. Second Printing, August 1992. Cover: black ink on pale green background.
c. Third Printing, with redesigned back cover copy featuring EAN Bookland bar codes, June 1994. Cover: black ink on bright green background, with shaded cover illustration.
d. Fourth Printing, December 1996 (January 1997).

This facsimile reprint from the 1971 Newcastle edition includes cover work adapted from the original.

CONTENTS: Foreword (p. 3); Part I. 1. What Foods Can Do for You (p. 7-10); 2. Different Foods Do Different Things (p. 11-13); 3. Foods That Stick to Your Ribs (p. 14-15); 4. "Dust Thou Art..." (p. 16-18); 5. The Wonderful Vitamins (p. 19-22); 6. A Root Cause of Digestive Diseases (p. 23-26); 7. Constipation—An Insidious Evil (p. 27-31); 8. How to Balance Your Diet (p. 32-35); 9. Get Your Vitamins and Minerals from Foods (p. 36-39); 10. How Cooking May Harm Foods (p. 40-43); Part II. Vitamin Tables (p. 44-45); Vegetables and Fruits Highest in Vitamins (p. 46); Caloric Value of Vegetables and Fruits (p. 47); Mineral Tables (p. 48); Vegetables and Fruits Highest in Minerals (p. 49); Food Classes (p. 50); Pot Liquors and Fruit Juices (p. 51); Part III. Fruits (p. 52-78); Vegetables (p. 79-128).

A111. *The Work of Jack Dann: An Annotated Bibliography & Guide*, by Jeffrey M. Elliot, edited by Boden Clarke. BIBLIOGRAPHIES OF MODERN AUTHORS, Number 16. 128 p. LC 88-34679. OCLC #18908834. ISBN 0-8095-0506-1 cloth $19.95; ISBN 0-8095-1506-7 paper $9.95. Cover: standard series design by Highpoint Type & Graphics, cover photo by M. C. Valada, black ink on pale tangerine background. First Edition, April 1990.

A bibliography of and literary guide to the modern American writer, Jack Dann (1945-).

CONTENTS: Introduction: In Pity and Terror (p. 5-11); A Jack Dann Chronology (p. 12-16); A. Books (p. 17-37); B. Short Fiction (p. 38-56); C. Poetry (p. 57-60); D. Nonfiction (p. 61-69); E. Editorial Credits (p. 70-71); F. About the Author (p. 72-79); G. Honors and Awards (p. 80-81); H. Public Appearances (p. 82-92);

BP 300, by Robert Reginald & Mary Wickizer Burgess

I. Miscellanea (p. 93-94); Quoth the Critics (p. 95-103); Afterword: Advice to Aspiring Writers, by Jack Dann (p. 104-106); Postscript: Echoes of the Future: An Interview with Jack Dann, conducted by Gregory Feeley (p. 107-120); Title Index (p. 121-127); About Jeffrey M. Elliot (p. 128).

A112. *Across the Wide Missouri: The Diary of a Journey from Virginia to Missouri in 1819 and Back Again in 1822, with a Description of the City of Cincinnati*, by James Brown Campbell, edited by Mary Wickizer Burgess. STOKVIS STUDIES IN HISTORICAL CHRONOLOGY AND THOUGHT, Number 4. 139 p. LC 84-268. OCLC #10323054. ISBN 0-89370-169-6 cloth $19.95; ISBN 0-89370-269-2 paper $9.95. Illustrated with maps, tables, and photographs. Cover: standard series design by Judy Cloyd Graphic Design and Highpoint Type & Graphics, black ink on gold background. First Edition, May 1990.

The first publication of an historical diary written during the period 1819-1822.
   CONTENTS: Introduction: The Campbell Family, by Mary Wickizer Burgess (p. 5-10); Samuel Campbell of Gallia County, Ohio (p. 11-12); Alexander Campbell of Highland County, Virginia (p. 13-14); 1. Eighteen Nineteen (p. 15-35); 2. Eighteen Twenty (p. 36-61); 3. Eighteen Twenty-One (p. 62-100); 4. Eighteen Twenty-Two (p. 101-121); 5. A Description of the City of Cincinnati in 1822 (p. 122); Appendix: A James Brown Campbell Letter (p. 123); Name Index (p. 125-132); Place Index (p. 133-137).

A113. *What Are You Doing in My Universe?*, by Chuck Hillig, illustrated by Colleen McDougal Mills. [224] p., 8 x 5". LC 83-6426. OCLC #22776803. ISBN 0-89370-665-5 cloth $24.95; ISBN 0-89370-985-9 paper $14.95. Illustrated with drawings and diagrams. Cover design by Stephen D. Greenberg, adapted for the Borgo edition by Highpoint Type & Grapics; color: blue ink on a white background. First Borgo Edition, August 1990.

   b.   Second Printing, May 1991.

This reprint from the 1979 Newcastle edition features cover work adapted from the original. The book is a popular psychology guide that uses dots and figures to reveal truths about one's selves and what surrounds them.

A114. *The Work of George Zebrowski: An Annotated Bibliography & Guide, Second Edition, Revised and Expanded*, by Jeffrey M. Elliot and Robert Reginald, edited by Boden Clarke. BIBLIOGRAPHIES OF MODERN AUTHORS, Number 4. 118 p. LC 89-7093. OCLC #19518123. ISBN 0-8095-0514-2 cloth $19.95; ISBN 0-8095-1514-8 paper $9.95. Cover: standard series design by Highpoint Type & Graphics, photo of author by Jerry Bauer, black ink on gray background. Second Edition, September 1990.

A bibliography and literary guide to the works of the modern American writer, George Zebrowski (1945-).

CONTENTS: Introduction: Between Sensitivity and Concern (p. 5-8); A George Zebrowski Chronology (p. 9-16); A. Books (p. 17-33); B. Short Fiction (p. 34-47); C. Nonfiction (p. 48-65); D. Translations (p. 66); E. Editorial Credits (p. 67-69); F. Juvenilia (p. 70-73); G. Unpublished Works (p. 74); H. Other Media (p. 75); I. Honors and Awards (p. 76-77); J. Public Appearances (p. 78-82); K. About the Author (p. 83-88); L. Miscellanea (p. 89-91); Quoth the Critics (p. 92-108); Afterword: 6,250 Bits of Immortality, by George Zebrowski (p. 109-110); Index (p. 111-118); About the Authors (p. 118).

A revised and expanded version of **A72**; see also the Third Edition (**A249**).

A115. *To Kill or Not To Kill: Thoughts on Capital Punishment*, by Rep. William L. Clay Sr., edited by Michael and Mary Burgess. GREAT ISSUES OF THE DAY, Number 4. 208 p. LC 87-812. OCLC #15195192. ISBN 0-89370-331-1 cloth $24.95; ISBN 0-89370-431-8 paper $14.95. Illustrated with statistical charts and a two-page title-page photograph spread of the author. Cover: standard series design by Highpoint Type & Graphics, using photo of Congressman Clay, red and blue ink on white background. First Edition, October 1990.

A treatise on capital punishment by a leading African-American Democratic Congressman from Missouri.

CONTENTS: Introduction: The Question of Capital Punishment, by Gwen Giles (p. 7-8); Foreword: The Moral

Dilemma of State-Sponsored Murder, by Jeffrey M. Elliot (p. 9-12); Preface: A Few Words from Capitol Hill (p. 13-14); 1. The Position of America's Religious Leaders (p. 15-42); 2. Roman Justice (p. 43-56); 3. The Most Infamous Execution in History (p. 57-68); 4. The Death Penalty As a Deterrent (p. 69-94); 5. Why Not Public Executions? (p. 95-116); 6. Discrimination and Capital Punishment (p. 117-165); Notes (p. 166-171); Bibliography (p. 172-174); Appendix: Statistical Tables (p. 175-204); Index (p. 205-207); About the Author (p. 208).

A116. *The Work of Charles Beaumont: An Annotated Bibliography & Guide, Second Edition*, by William F. Nolan, edited by Boden Clarke. BIBLIOGRAPHIES OF MODERN AUTHORS, Number 6. 92 p. LC 90-15043. OCLC #22451636. ISBN 0-8095-0517-7 cloth $19.95; ISBN 0-8095-1517-2 paper $9.95. Cover: standard series design by Highpoint Type & Graphics using the same uncredited photo from the first edition, black ink on pale yellow background. Second Edition, November 1990.

A bibliography and literary guide to the works of the late American writer, Charles Beaumont (1929-1967).

CONTENTS: Preface to the Second Edition (p. 5-6); Introduction to the First Edition (p. 7-8); Chronology (p. 9-14); A. Books (p. 15-23); B. Short Fiction (p. 24-43); C. Nonfiction (p. 44-48); D. Screenplays (p. 49-51); E. Teleplays (p. 52-55); F. Comics (p. 56); G. Letters (p. 57); H. Unpublished Stories (p. 58-60); I. Verse (p. 61); J. Honors and Awards (p. 62); K. Artwork (p. 63); L. Editorial Credits (p. 64); M. About the Author (p. 65-72); N. Miscellanea (p. 73-74); Quoth the Critics (p. 75-76); Afterword: "My Grandmother's Japonicas," by Charles Beaumont (p. 77-84); Index (p. 85-91); About William F. Nolan (p. 92).

A revised and expanded version of **A71**.

A117. *The Work of Dean Ing: An Annotated Bibliography & Guide*, by Scott Alan Burgess, edited by Boden Clarke. BIBLIOGRAPHIES OF MODERN AUTHORS, Number 11. 82 p. LC 87-827. OCLC #15195579. ISBN 0-89370-395-8 cloth $19.95; ISBN 0-89370-495-4 paper $9.95. Cover: standard series design by Highpoint Type & Graphics, using photo of author, black ink on tan background. First Edition, December 1990.

BP 300, by Robert Reginald & Mary Wickizer Burgess

A bibliography and literary guide to the works of the modern American writer, Dean Ing (1931-).

CONTENTS: Introduction: "Delphi Must Be Near: Talking with Dean Ing" (p. 5-11); A Dean Ing Chronology (p. 12-15); A. Books (p. 17-32); B. Short Fiction (p. 33-38); C. Nonfiction (p. 39-56); D. Unpublished Works (p. 57); E. Editorial Credits (p. 58); F. Radio and Television Appearances (p. 59); G. Honors and Awards (p. 60); H. About the Author (p. 61-64); I. Miscellanea (p. 65); Quoth the Critics (p. 66-70); Afterword: "Excuse the Shouting...," by Dean Ing (p. 71-74); Index (p. 75-81); About Scott Alan Burgess (p. 82).

A118. *First Century Palestinian Judaism: A Bibliography of Works in English*, by David Ray Bourquin. STUDIES IN JUDAICA AND THE HOLOCAUST, Number 6. 104 p. LC 88-34665. OCLC #18908712. ISBN 0-89370-373-7 cloth $22.95; ISBN 0-89370-473-3 paper $12.95. Cover: standard series design by Highpoint Type & Graphics, black ink on tan background. First Edition, December 1990.

A bibliography of books and periodical articles dealing with first century Palestinian Judaism.

CONTENTS: Preface (p. 5-6); Introduction (p. 7-9); How to Use This Book (p. 10); A. Primary Sources (p. 11); B. Books (p. 13-47); C. Periodical and Serial Articles (p. 49-76); Index of Books (p. 77-89); Index of Periodical and Serial Article Titles (p. 91-100); Index of Periodicals and Serials (p. 101-103); About the Author (p. 104).

A119. *Victorian Criticism of American Writers: A Guide to British Criticism of American Writers in the Leading British Periodicals of the Victorian Period, 1824-1900*, by Arnella K. Turner. BORGO LITERARY GUIDES, Number 6. 456 p. LC 87-807. OCLC #15195171. ISBN 0-89370-816-X cloth $49.95; ISBN 0-89370-916-6 paper $39.95. Cover: standard series design by Highpoint Type & Graphics, blue ink on pale blue background. First Edition, April 1991.

A bibliography of criticism of American writers in British periodicals of the Victorian era.

BP 300, by Robert Reginald & Mary Wickizer Burgess

(Dublin) University Magazine, 1833-1880 (p. 301-321); 40. *The Foreign Review and Continental Miscellany*, 1828-1830 (p. 322); 41. *The London Quarterly Review*, 1853-1900 (p. 323-345); 42. *Longman's Magazine*, 1882-1900 (p. 346-350); 43. *Tait's Edinburgh Magazine*, 1832-1860 (p. 351-358).

Appendix. 44. *The Athenaeum*, 1828-1900 (p. 361-396); 45. *Chambers's Edinburgh Magazine*, 1844-1900 (p. 397-400); 46. *The Literary Chronicle and Weekly Review*, 1824, 1826 (p. 401); 47. *Ward's Miscellany*, 1837-1838 (p. 402-403).

Notes (p. 404-419); Bibliography (p. 420-435); About the Author (p. 436); Index (p. 437-456).

This was the longest Borgo Press book published to this date.

A120. ***The Beach Boys: Southern California Pastoral, Second Edition***, by Bruce Golden, updated by Paul David Seldis. THE WOODSTOCK SERIES: POPULAR MUSIC OF TODAY, Number 1. 104 p. LC 90-2538. OCLC #22242765. ISBN 0-89370-359-1 cloth $22.95; ISBN 0-89370-459-8 paper $12.95. Cover design by Highpoint Type & Graphics, black ink on gold background. Second Edition, April 1991.

b. Second Printing, with redesigned back cover copy featuring EAN Bookland bar codes, August 1994.

A popular guide to the music of the Beach Boys group.

CONTENTS: A Beach Boys Chronology (p. 5-8); Foreword to the Second Edition (p. 9-11); Introduction to the First Edition (p. 12-16); 1. "Surfin'" to *All Summer Long* (1962-1964) (p. 17-26); 2. *Beach Boys Today* to *Beach Boys Party* (1965) (p. 27-30); 3. *Pet Sounds* to *Holland* (1966-1973) (p. 31-42); 4. *Still Cruisin'* (1974-1990) (p. 43-47); 5. Afterword, by Dr. Bruce Golden (p. 49-50); An Overview of Beach Boys Releases (p. 51-54); Discography (p. 55-79); Bibliography (p. 80-83); Notes (p. 84-85); Index to Song and Album Titles (p. 87-93); Index to Individuals, Groups, and Subjects (p. 94-103); About the Authors (p. 104).

See also the First Edition (**A2**); the copyright page indicates the book is a "Second Edition," the cover and title page call it a "Revised Edition."

BP 300, by Robert Reginald & Mary Wickizer Burgess

A121. *At Wolfe's Door: The Nero Wolfe Novels of Rex Stout*, by J. Kenneth Van Dover. THE MILFORD SERIES: POPULAR WRITERS OF TODAY, Volume 52. 120 p. LC 88-34363. OCLC #18907358. ISBN 0-89370-189-0 cloth $22.95; ISBN 0-89370-289-7 paper $12.95. Cover: standard series design by Judy Cloyd Graphic Design and Highpoint Type & Graphics, black ink on gray background. First Edition, April 1991.

b. Second Printing, with updated back cover and altered spine copy, May 1993.

A critique of the late American writer, Rex Stout (1886-1975).
  CONTENTS: Preface (p. 5); Chronology (p. 6-8); Part One: Nero Wolfe. A. Introduction (p. 9-14); B. Synopses (p. 15-81); Part Two: Bonner, Fox, Cramer, Hicks, and Others. A. Introduction (p. 82-84); B. Synopses (p. 85-100); Part Three: Nero Wolfe and Perry Mason: From the Thirties to the Seventies (p. 101-109); Bibliography (p. 110-112); Index (p. 113-119); About J. Kenneth Van Dover (p. 120).

A122. *Jerzy Kosinski: The Literature of Violation*, by Welch D. Everman. THE MILFORD SERIES: POPULAR WRITERS OF TODAY, Volume 47. 160 p. LC 84-356. OCLC #10375583. ISBN 0-89370-176-9 cloth $29.95; ISBN 0-89370-276-5 paper $19.95. Cover: standard series design by Judy Cloyd Graphic Design and Highpoint Type & Graphics, black ink on tan background. First Edition, April 1991.

A critique of the late Polish-American writer, Jerzy Kosinski (1933-1991).
  CONTENTS: A Jerzy Kosinski Chronology (p. 5-6); 1. The Fiction of Jerzy Kosinski (p. 7-11); 2. The Literature of Violation/The Violation of Literature (p. 12-26); 3. *The Painted Bird* (p. 27-46); 4. *Steps* (p. 47-56); 5. *Being There* (p. 57-66); 6. *Being There*: The Film (p. 67-69); 7. *The Devil Tree* (p. 70-83); 8. *The Devil Tree*: The 1981 Edition (p. 84-89); 9. *Cockpit* (p. 90-102); 10. *Blind Date* (p. 103-117); 11. *Passion Play* (p. 118-133); 12. Violence/Philosophy/Literature (p. 134-136); 13. Epilogue: *Pinball* (p. 137-150); Primary Bibliography (p. 151-152); Secondary Bibliography (p. 153); Index (p. 155-158); About Welch D. Everman (p. 160).

A123. *The Second Marxian Invasion: The Fiction of the Strugatsky Brothers*, by Stephen W. Potts. THE MILFORD SERIES: POPULAR WRITERS OF TODAY, Volume 50. 104 p. LC 84-309. OCLC #10375504. ISBN 0-89370-179-3 cloth $22.95; ISBN 0-89370-279-X paper $12.95. Cover: standard series design by Judy Cloyd Graphic Design and Highpoint Type & Graphics, black ink on gray background. First Edition, April 1991.

A critique of the modern Russian writers, Arkady Strugatsky (1925-1991) and Boris Strugatsky (1933-).
  CONTENTS: A Strugatsky Chronology (p. 5-6); 1. The Strugatsky Brothers in Context (p. 7-17); 2. The Road to Utopia (p. 19-35); 3. Of History and Human Nature (p. 37-51); 4. Fantasy and Satire (p. 53-70); 5. Confronting the Alien (p. 71-89); 6. Conclusion (p. 91-95); Bibliographical Notes (p. 97-99); About Stephen W. Potts (p. 100); Index (p. 101-104).
  Winner of the 1993 J. Lloyd Eaton Award for Best Non-fiction Work of the Year.

A124. *Starclimber: The Literary Adventures and Autobiography of Raymond Z. Gallun*, by Raymond Z. Gallun with Jeffrey M. Elliot, edited by Paul David Seldis and Mary A. Burgess. BORGO BIOVIEWS, Number 1. 168 p. LC 89-82175. OCLC #22450791. ISBN 0-83970-348-6 cloth $24.95; ISBN 0-89370-448-2 paper $14.95. Illustrated with photographs of the author. Cover: standard series design by Highpoint Type & Graphics, using photo of author, black ink on gray background. First Edition, May 1991.

b. Second Printing, September 1993.

An autobiography of the late American writer, Raymond Z. Gallun (1911-1994).
  CONTENTS: Introduction, by Dr. Jeffrey M. Elliot (p. 5-7); 1. Back to Beaver Dam (p. 9-13); 2. Annie—And Others (p. 14-17); 3. An Eccentric Household (p. 18-23); 4. A New Beginning (p. 24-26); 5. Books—And More Books (p. 27-30); 6. Beginning Lines (p. 31-38); 7. Higher Education (p. 39-42); 8. A Milestone Story (p. 43-51); 9. A Poised Interval (p. 52-58); 10. Yarn Seeds (p. 59-72); 11. First Encounters (p. 73-81); 12. A Journey to

Myself (p. 82-87); 13. Paris, Refugees, and Catching Up (p. 88-98); 14. Drifting Away from Campbell (p. 99-107); 15. Back to the States (p. 108-113); 16. From the War to *Collier's* (p. 114-123); 17. Frieda (p. 124-129); 18. A Brush with Einstein (p. 130-141); 19. Finished Novels, Unfinished Thoughts (p. 142-160); Bibliography (p. 161-163); Index (p. 164-168).

A125. *David Lodge: How Far Can You Go?*, by Merritt Moseley, edited by Dale Salwak. THE MILFORD SERIES: POPULAR WRITERS OF TODAY, Volume 16. viii+112 p. LC 89-29632. OCLC #24360134. ISBN 0-8095-5204-3 cloth $22.95; ISBN 0-8095-5229-9 paper $12.95. Cover: standard series design by Judy Cloyd and Highpoint Type & Graphics, black ink on green background. First Edition, May 1991.

A critique of the modern British writer, David Lodge (1935-).
    CONTENTS: Preface and Acknowledgments (p. v-vi); Chronology (p. vii-viii); Chapter One: Introduction (p. 1-13); Chapter Two: Biography (p. 14-17); Chapter Three: Beginning: *The Picturegoers* (p. 18-26); Chapter Four: Scrupulous Realism: *Ginger, You're Barmy* (p. 27-34); Chapter Five: Life and Art: *The British Museum Is Falling Down* (p. 35-43); Chapter Six: Back into the Shelter: *Out of the Shelter* (p. 44-57); Chapter Seven: Maturity: *Changing Places* (p. 58-69); Chapter Eight: Catholics in the World: *How Far Can You Go?* (p. 70-79); Chapter Nine: Dons in Space: *Small World* (p. 80-91); Chapter Ten: The Condition of England: *Nice Work* (p. 92-100); Chapter Eleven: Lodge's Criticism (p. 101-106); Primary Bibliography (p. 107-108); Secondary Bibliography (p. 109-110); Index (p. 111-112).
    Originally intended to be published as STARMONT CONTEMPORARY WRITERS SERIES, Number 5, the insides of this book were already printed when Borgo Press assumed the contract; Borgo substituted a new title page and copyright page and a new cover; only two unbound copies exist of the original version.

A126. *The Italian Theater in San Francisco: Being a History of the Italian-Language Operatic, Dramatic, and Comedic Productions Presented in the San Francisco Bay Area Through the Depression Era, with Reminiscences of the Leading Players and Impresarios of the Times*, by Laurence Estavan, edited by Mary A. Burgess. CLIPPER STUDIES IN THE AMERICAN THEATRE,

BP 300, by Robert Reginald & Mary Wickizer Burgess

Number 3. 120 p. LC 87-869. OCLC #15196977. ISBN 0-89370-364-8 cloth $22.95; ISBN 0-89370-464-4 paper $12.95. Illustrated with photographs of some of the principal players. Cover: standard series design by Judy Cloyd Graphic Design as adapted by Highpoint Type & Graphics, black ink on yellow background. First Borgo Edition, May 1991.

This history of the Italian-language theatre in San Francisco prior to World War II was extensively reworked from its original 1939 appearance as a mimeographed WPA project.

BP 300, by Robert Reginald & Mary Wickizer Burgess

Part Two: Il Teatro Italiano. 1. The Italian Theatre (p. 77-78); 2. Mimi Aguglia (p. 79-80); 3. L'Aguglia and d'Annunzio (p. 81-82); 4. European Triumphs (p. 83); 5. L'Aguglia in America (p. 84-85); 6. Second Week at the Court (p. 86-87); 7. At Washington Square (p. 88); 8. Elenora Duse (p. 89-90); 9. The Return of Mimi Aguglia (p. 91-92); 10. The Aguglia Repertoire (p. 93-94); 11. Genesis of the Teatro Italiano (p. 95); 12. The Teatro Italiano at the Community Playhouse (p. 96-97); 13. Goldoni and Pirandello (p. 98); 14. The Teatro Italiano Carries On (p. 99-100); 15. At the Greenroom Playhouse (p. 101); 16. At the Golden Bough Playhouse (p. 102-103); 17. Seragnoli and the Popular Theatre (p. 104-105); 18. Conclusion (p. 106); Notes (p. 107); Bibliography (p. 108); Appendix I: Mimi Aguglia (p. 109-110); Appendix II: Repertoire of the Teatro Italiano (p. 111-112); Index (p. 113-119).

A127. *Mystery Voices: Interviews with British Crime Writers*, by Dale Salwak. BROWNSTONE MYSTERY GUIDES, Volume 8. A Brownstone Book. 112 p. LC 84-3115. OCLC #10404581. ISBN 0-89370-178-5 cloth $22.95; ISBN 0-89370-278-1 paper $12.95. Illustrated with photographs of the interviewees. Cover: standard series design by Highpoint Type & Graphics, black ink on cream background. First Edition, August 1991.

A collection of interviews with five modern British crime writers.
CONTENTS: Introduction: "On Being a Writer of Detective Fiction," by Catherine Aird (p. 5-10); A Catherine Aird Chronology (p. 11-12); I. An Interview with Catherine Aird (p. 15-33); Selected Secondary Bibliography (p. 34); A P. D. James Chronology (p. 35-36); II. An Interview with P. D. James (p. 39-56); Selected Secondary Bibliography (p. 57); An H. R. F. Keating Chronology (p. 59-61); III. An Interview with H. R. F. Keating (p. 63-79); Selected Secondary Bibliography (p. 79); A Ruth Rendell Chronology (p. 81-83); IV. An Interview with Ruth Rendell (p. 85-94); Selected Secondary Bibliography (p. 94); A Julian Symons Chronology (p. 95-97); V. An Interview with Julian Symons (p. 99-106); Selected Secondary Bibliography (p. 106-107); About Dale Salwak (p. 108); Index (p. 109-112).
The first of the "new" Brownstone Mystery Guides published by The Borgo Press. The spine erroneously gives the series number as "1."

74

BP 300, by Robert Reginald & Mary Wickizer Burgess

A128. *The Jewish Holocaust: An Annotated Guide to Books in English*, by Marty Bloomberg. STUDIES IN JUDAICA AND THE HOLOCAUST, Number 1. 248 p. LC 81-21605. OCLC #8034760. ISBN 0-89370-160-2 cloth $34.95; ISBN 0-89370-260-9 paper $24.95. Cover: standard series design by Highpoint Type & Graphics, adapting a manuscript page from Yitzhak Katzenelson's *The Song of the Murdered Jewish People*, blue ink on pale blue background. First Edition, August 1991.

b. Second Printing, August 1992.

An annotated bibliography of books in English relating to the Holocaust.
CONTENTS: Foreword: A Living Testimonial, by Dr. Jeffrey M. Elliot (p. 7-9); Introduction (p. 10); A. Reference Materials (p. 11-23); B. European Anti-Semitism (p. 24-31); C. Background Materials (p. 32-65); D. The Holocaust Years (p. 66-129); E. Jewish Resistance (p. 130-139); F. Concentration Camps and Death Camps (p. 140-153); G. Special Studies (p. 154-167); H. War Crimes Trials (p. 168-177); I. The Meaning of the Holocaust (p. 178-184); J. Art and Literature (p. 185-217); Core Title Recommendations (p. 218-225); About the Author (p. 226-227 [including portrait]); Index (p. 228-248).
See also the Second Edition (**A208**).

A129. *The Trilemma of World Oil Politics*, by Jeffrey M. Elliot and Sheikh R. Ali, edited by Michael Burgess and Paul David Seldis. GREAT ISSUES OF THE DAY, Number 2. 152 p. LC 84-275. OCLC #10323084. ISBN 0-89370-168-8 cloth $24.95; ISBN 0-89370-268-4 paper $14.95. Includes graphs and charts. Cover: standard series design by Highpoint Type & Graphics, black and red ink on gray background. First Edition, October 1991.

This treatise discusses the impending shortage of world petroleum products and the politics surrounding the supply and demand of this most vital of world resources.
CONTENTS: Introduction (p. 5-8); 1. The Politics of Oil (p. 9-25); 2. County-Company-Consumer Relationships (p. 26-36); 3. Arab Oil as a Volatire Weapon (p. 37-52); 4. American Peace Initiatives (p. 53-61); 5. The Impact of OPEC Petroleum (p. 62-71); 6. The Myth and Reality of Chinese Oil (p. 72-82); 7. Soviet

Oil Strategy in the World (p. 83-91); 8. Oil Hegemony and the International Crisis (p. 92-100); 9. After Oil, Then What? (p. 101-117); 10. Conclusions (p. 118-121); 11. Postscript (p. 122-126); Acronyms (p. 127); Appendix A: The Statute of the Organization of Petroleum Exporting Countries (p. 128-134); Appendix B: Resolution of Arab Oil Ministries (p. 135); Notes (p. 136-141); Bibliography (p. 142-145); Index (p. 146-151); About the Authors (p. 152).

A130. *The Work of Louis L'Amour: An Annotated Bibliography & Guide*, by Hal W. Hall, edited by Boden Clarke. BIBLIOGRAPHIES OF MODERN AUTHORS, Number 15. 192 p. LC 88-34678. OCLC #18908828. ISBN 0-8095-0510-X cloth $29.95; ISBN 0-8095-1510-5 paper $19.95. Cover: standard series design by Highpoint Type & Graphics, using photo of author, brown ink on tan background. First Edition, November 1991.

A bibliography of and literary guide to the works of the late American western writer, Louis L'Amour (1908-1988).

CONTENTS: Introduction: "The Several Literary Careers of Louis L'Amour," by Michael T. Marsden (p. 5-9); A Louis L'Amour Chronology (p. 10-14); A. Books (p. 15-89); B. Short Fiction (p. 90-114); C. Nonfiction (p. 115-117); D. Poetry (p. 118-125); E. Editorial Credits (p. 126); F. Audio Tapes and Records (p. 127-138); G. Motion Picture and Television Adaptations (p. 139-144); H. Secondary Sources (p. 145-160); I. Honors and Awards (p. 161); J. Miscellanea (p. 162); Quoth the Critics (p. 163-166); Afterword: "A Conversation with Louis L'Amour," by Michael T. Marsden and Kristine Fredriksson (p. 167-178); Presentation of an Honorary Ph.D. Degree (p. 179); Series Index (p. 181-182); Index (p. 183-191); About Hal W. Hall (p. 192).

A131. *The Little Kitchen Cookbook*, by Scottie Kimberlin. A Burgess & Wickizer Book. 160 p. LC 91-35071. OCLC #24468208. ISBN 0-89370-820-8 cloth $23; ISBN 0-89370-920-4 paper $12. Illustrated with photographs of the Little Kitchen and Scottie Kimberlin, including one of the LK on the back cover. Cover design by Highpoint Type & Graphics; color: white background with stylized Little Kitchen storefront overprinted in red; sign etched in green, LK stove logo in black, with blue backdrop. First Edition, November 1991.

b. Second Printing, December 1991.

A cookbook based around the popular San Bernardino restaurant, The Little Kitchen.
CONTENTS: About The Little Kitchen, by Jan Roddick (p. 9-10); Introduction (p. 11); Soups (p. 13-23); Salads (p. 24-46); Dressings for Green Salads (p. 47-48); Miscellaneous Relishes and Side Dishes (p. 49-56); Vegetables (p. 57-68); Main Dishes (p. 69-100); Breads (p. 101-109); Cookies (p. 110-120); Puddings (p. 120-122); Desserts (p. 123-128); Cakes (p. 129-141); Frostings and Icings (p. 142); Pies and Pie Crust (p. 143-154); Index (p. 155-160).
The first Burgess & Wickizer book published by The Borgo Press. See also the Second Edition (**A191**).

A132. *Reginald's Science Fiction and Fantasy Awards: A Comprehensive Guide to the Awards and Their Winners, Second Edition, Revised and Expanded*, by Daryl F. Mallett & Robert Reginald. BORGO LITERARY GUIDES, Number 1. 248 p. LC 90-15074. OCLC #22492499. ISBN 0-89370-826-7 cloth $29.95; ISBN 0-89370-926-3 paper $19.95. Cover: standard series design by Highpoint Type & Graphics, green ink on green background. Second Edition, November 1991.

A guide to the major and minor awards and honors presented in the science fiction, fantasy, and horror genres.
CONTENTS: Introduction (p. 7-8); How to Use This Book (p. 9); English-Language Awards (p. 13-145); Foreign-Language Awards (p. 147-170); Non-Genre Awards (p. 171-178); Appendices (p. 179-186); Author Index (p. 187-238); Statistical Tables (p. 239-245); Index to Award Names (p. 246-247); About the Authors (p. 248).
An expanded version of **A41**; see also the third edition (**A149**).

A133. *One Day with God: A Guide to Retreats and the Contemplative Life, Revised Edition*, by Karl Pruter. ST. WILLIBRORD STUDIES IN PHILOSOPHY AND RELIGION, Number 1. A St. Willibrord's Press Book. 56 p. LC 91-35733. OCLC #24543314. ISBN 0-912134-10-0 cloth $18; ISBN 0-912134-11-9 paper $8. Cover:

BP 300, by Robert Reginald & Mary Wickizer Burgess

standard series design by Highpoint Type & Graphics, black ink on beige background. First Edition, December 1991.

A guide to religious retreats and how to conduct them.

CONTENTS: Introduction (p. 9); 1. The Call to Retreat (p. 11-14); 2. Should You Go to a Silent Retreat? (p. 15-19); 3. The Mountain (p. 21-22); 4. A Postscript to the Mountain (p. 23); 5. Searching for God (p. 25-26); 6. Meditation on the Meaning of the Phrase, "Servant of God" (p. 27-28); 7. Silence (p. 29-32); 8. The God Who Speaks (p. 33-36); 9. What Does God Require of Thee? (p. 37-38); 10. Unceasing Prayer (p. 39-40); 11. For Whom Should We Pray? (p. 41-43); 12. Making This Day Count (p. 45-47); 13. The Greatest Thrill (p. 49-50); 14. The Loneliness of God (p. 51-52); Bibliography (p. 53); Index (p. 54-55); About the Author (p. 56).

The first of the "new" St. Willibrord's Press books published by The Borgo Press.

A134. *Science Fiction and Fantasy Research Index, Volume 9*, by Hal W. Hall. v+97 p. OCLC #24614822. ISBN 0-8095-6112-3 cloth $25. Photocopied from the original. First Edition, March 1992.

A continuing subject and author index to critical and bibliographical materials in the science fiction and fantasy genres.

A135. *Science Fiction and Fantasy Book Review Index, Volume 18, 1987*, by Hal W. Hall. v+70 p. ISBN 0-8095-6801-2 cloth $25. Photocopied from the original. First Edition, March 1992.

A continuing index to book reviews of science fiction, fantasy, and horror fiction and nonfiction.

A136. *Science Fiction and Fantasy Book Review Index, Volume 19, 1988*, by Hal W. Hall. 85 p. ISBN 0-8095-6802-0 cloth $25. Photocopied from the original. First Edition, March 1992.

A continuing index to book reviews of science fiction, fantasy, and horror fiction and nonfiction.

A137. *The Work of Robert Reginald: An Annotated Bibliography & Guide, Second Edition*, by Michael Burgess. BIBLIOGRAPHIES

BP 300, by Robert Reginald & Mary Wickizer Burgess

OF MODERN AUTHORS, Number 5. 176 p. LC 87-6306. OCLC #15318070. ISBN 0-8095-0505-3 cloth $27; ISBN 0-8095-1505-9 paper $17. Cover: standard series design by Highpoint Type & Graphics, photo by Paul Williams, black ink on light green. Second Edition, April 1992.

A bibliography of and literary guide to the works of the modern American author and publisher, Robert Reginald (1948-).

CONTENTS: Introduction: "Comets Don't Slow Down," by William F. Nolan (p. 5-7); Preface: "It Was Twenty Years Ago Today...," by Dr. Fran J. Polek (p. 8); A Robert Reginald Chronology (p. 9-16); A. Books (p. 17-65); B. Short Nonfiction (p. 66-81); C. Short Fiction (p. 82); D. Editorial Credits (p. 83-109); E. Documents (p. 110-112); F. Catalogs (p. 113-123); G. Book Production and Design (p. 124-126); H. Unpublished Works (p. 127-129); I. Juvenilia (p. 130-131); J. Public Appearances (p. 132-135); K. Secondary Sources (p. 136-141); L. Honors and Awards (p. 142-143); M. Miscellanea (p. 144-151); Quoth the Critics (p. 152-165); Afterthoughts: "Harvesting the Vineyards of Obscurity," by Robert Reginald (p. 166-167); Afterword: "Robert Reginald: Force Majeure," by Jack Dann (p. 168-170); Title Index (p. 171-176).

An expanded version of **A63**.

A138. *Inside Science Fiction: Essays on Fantastic Literature*, by James Gunn. I.O. EVANS STUDIES IN THE PHILOSOPHY AND CRITICISM OF LITERATURE, Number 11. 176 p. LC 91-32976. OCLC #24504894. ISBN 0-89370-312-5 cloth $27; ISBN 0-89370-412-1 paper $17. Cover: standard series design by Highpoint Type & Graphics, green ink on pale green background. First Edition, May 1992.

A collection of previously-published and original essays on fantastic literature.

CONTENTS: Introduction (p. 5-6); Part I: Getting Inside Science Fiction. 1. The Education of a Science Fiction Teacher (p. 9-15); 2. From the Pulps to the Classroom: The Strange Journey of Science Fiction (p. 16-29); 3. Science Fiction and the Mainstream (p. 30-51); 4. The Gatekeepers (p. 52-59); 5. Fifty Amazing, Astounding, Wonderful Years (p. 60-64).

Part II: Science Fiction and the Teacher. 6. Teaching Science Fiction Revisited (p. 67-72); 7. The Academic Viewpoint (p. 73-78); 8. Science Fiction As Literature (p. 79-91); 9. The City and the Critics (p. 92-98).

Part III: Science Fiction on Film and Television. 10. The Tinsel Screen (p. 101-112); 11. Television and "The Immortal" (p. 113-117); 12. The Great Science Fiction Radio Show (p. 118-120); 13. Looking Backward at *2001* (p. 121-123).

Part IV: Science Fiction and the Real World. 14. The Uses of Space (p. 127-133); 15. A Short History of the Space Program; or, A Funny Thing Happened on the Way to the Moon (p. 134-145); 16. Shapechangers and Fearmongers (p. 146-149); 17. Science Fiction and the Future (p. 150-153); 18. Science Fiction in the Nineties (p. 154-160); Acknowledgments (p. 161); About the Author (p. 162); A James Gunn Bibliography (p. 163); Index (p. 164-176).

A139. *Into the Flames: The Life Story of a Righteous Gentile*, by Irene Gut Opdyke with Jeffrey M. Elliot, edited by Mary A. Burgess. STUDIES IN JUDAICA AND THE HOLOCAUST, Number 8. 176 p. LC 91-41355. OCLC #24870548. ISBN 0-89370-375-3 cloth $27; ISBN 0-89370-475-X paper $17. Illustrated with photographs of the author and her family. Cover: standard series design by Highpoint Type & Graphics with large photo of Opdyke, black ink on cream background. First Edition, May 1992.

b. Second Printing, July 1992.
c. Third Printing, January 1993.
d. Fourth Printing, May 1993.
e. Fifth Printing, October 1993.
f. Sixth Printing, January 1994.
g. Seventh Printing, April 1994.
h. Eighth Printing, with redesigned back cover copy featuring EAN Bookland bar codes, July 1994.
i. Ninth Printing, February 1995.
j. Tenth Printing, April 1995.
k. Eleventh Printing, June 1995.
l. Twelfth Printing, September 1995.
m. Thirteenth Printing, December 1995.
n. Fourteenth Printing, March 1996.
o. Fifteenth Printing, June 1996.

BP 300, by Robert Reginald & Mary Wickizer Burgess

p. Sixteenth Printing, September 1996.

The memoir of a Righteous Gentile, Irene Gut Opdyke, describing how she saved a number of Polish Jews from death at the hands of the Nazis during World War II.
CONTENTS: Dedication and Acknowledgments (p. 4); Introduction, by Rabbi Harold Schulweis (p. 5); 1. Prologue (p. 6); 2. Radom (p. 7-11); 3. Tarnopol (p. 12-25); 4. Escape (p. 26-31); 5. Swietlana (p. 32-37); 6. A New Life (p. 38-41); 7. Christmases Past and Present (p. 42-47); 8. Return to Tarnopol (p. 48-61); 9. A Brief Reunion (p. 62-71); 10. Working for the Enemy (p. 72-82); 11. Janina (p. 83-94); 12. Into the Forest (p. 95-99); 13. A Miracle Takes Place (p. 100-109); 14. A New Way of Life (p. 110-122); 15. The Forester's Cottage (p. 123-132); 16. Dangerous Times (p. 133-138); 17. A Bargain Is Struck (p. 139-147); 18. Janek (p. 148-157); 19. End of the Line (p. 158-163); 20. A Stranger Among Strangers (p. 164-171); 21. Full Circle (p. 172); Citation of Distinguished Honor and Recognition (p. 173); Afterword, by Dr. Nathan Kravetz (p. 174); Index (p. 175-176).

A140. *The Work of Brian W. Aldiss: An Annotated Bibliography & Guide*, by Margaret Aldiss, edited by Boden Clarke. BIBLIOGRAPHIES OF MODERN AUTHORS, Number 9. 360 p. LC 87-746. OCLC #15163873. ISBN 0-89370-388-5 cloth $39; ISBN 0-89370-488-1 paper $29. Illustrated with photographs of the author. Cover: standard series design by Highpoint Type & Graphics, photo of author by Jerry Bauer, black ink on cream background. First Edition, July 1992.

A bibliography of and literary guide to the works of modern British writer, Brian W. Aldiss (1925-).
CONTENTS: Foreword (p. 5); Introduction: "Map and Territory," by David Wingrove (p. 6-8); A Brian W. Aldiss Chronology (p. 9-14); A. Books (with annotations by Brian W. Aldiss) (p. 15-126); B. Short Fiction (p. 127-228); C. Nonfiction (p. 229-260); D. Poetry (p. 261-265); E. Other Media (p. 266-270); F. Editorial Credits (p. 271-273); G. Secondary Sources (p. 274-286); H. Honors and Awards (p. 287-288); I. Miscellanea (p. 289-292); Quoth the Critics (p. 293-319); "A Walk in the Glass Forest: Autobiographical Reflections," by Brian W. Aldiss (p. 320-342); Afterword: "Slaves of the Megamachine?" by Brian W.

BP 300, by Robert Reginald & Mary Wickizer Burgess

Aldiss (p. 343-348); Title Index (p. 349-356); Index to Secondary Sources (p. 357-359); About Margaret Aldiss (p. 360).

A141. *Of Force and Violence and Other Imponderables: Essays on War, Politics, and Government*, by Reginald Bretnor, edited by Paul David Seldis. STOKVIS STUDIES IN HISTORICAL CHRONOLOGY AND THOUGHT, Number 6. 144 p. LC 84-306. OCLC #10375498. ISBN 0-89370-321-4 cloth $25; ISBN 0-89370-421-0 paper $15. Cover: standard series design by Highpoint Type & Graphics with old flintlock drawing, black ink on pale lemon background. First Edition, November 1992.

A collection of previously-published essays on war and politics.
CONTENTS: Foreword (p. 5); Acknowledgments (p. 6); 1. Of Force and Violence (p. 7-18); 2. The Noble Art of Murder (p. 19-24); 3. A Plea for Censorship (p. 25-34); 4. Conservatism and the Uncontrolled Experiment (p. 35-44); 5. California's Science Fiction Future (p. 45-50); 6. Disarmament: Deadend and Detour (p. 51-62); 7. The Children's Crusade (p. 63-79); 8. Where Is Our Intellectual Middle Class? (p. 81-84); 9. "Gun Control" and the Free Citizen (p. 85-91); 10. Cats, Rats, and the History of the West (p. 93-100); 11. The Prevention of War: About Unthinking the Thinkable (p. 101-106); 12. The Semantics of War: A Time for Revision? (p. 107-109); 13. The Words of War: Professionalism (p. 111-116); 14. Of Theory and Practice (p. 117-122); 15. Security: False Shield, False Promise (p. 123-136); Index (p. 137-143); About the Author (p. 144).

A142. *Vultures of the Void: A History of British Science Fiction Publishing, 1946-1956*, by Philip Harbottle and Stephen Holland, edited by Daryl F. Mallett. I.O. EVANS STUDIES IN THE PHILOSOPHY AND CRITICISM OF LITERATURE, Number 13. 128 p. LC 87-748. OCLC #15163889. ISBN 0-89370-315-X cloth $25; ISBN 0-89370-415-6 paper $15. Illustrated with reproductions of paperback cover art by Ron Turner. Cover design by Highpoint Type & Graphics incorporating cover drawing by Ron Turner, black ink on green background. First Edition, December 1992.

b. Second Printing, with redesigned back cover copy featuring EAN Bookland bar codes, August 1994.

BP 300, by Robert Reginald & Mary Wickizer Burgess

A history of British science fiction pulp paperback publishing during the postwar decade of 1946-56.

CONTENTS: Acknowledgments (p. 5); Introduction: Forgotten Fantasies (p. 7-8); Chronology (p. 9-11); 1. The Story Begins (p. 13-17); 2. The New Breed (p. 19-24); 3. Brave New (Trembling) World (p. 25-28); 4. The Crazy World (p. 29-35); 5. Invasion from Space (p. 37-41); 6. The Deluge Begins (p. 43-46); 7. *Authentic Science Fiction* (p. 47-56); 8. Prisoner in the Cellar (p. 57-65); 9. Blast-Off for Space Opera (p. 67-76); 10. Child of the Fifties (p. 77-85); 11. Burn Out for Space Opera (p. 87-94); 12. The End of an Era (p. 95-108); 13. "A Rose by Any Other Name..." (p. 109-113); Index (p. 115-126); About the Authors (p. 128).

A143. *The Cranberry Tea Room Cookbook*, by Richard Martinez, edited by Gloria Chavez. A Burgess & Wickizer Book. 144 p. LC 92-35047. OCLC #26809622. ISBN 0-8095-2950-5 cloth $23; ISBN 0-8095-3950-0 paper $12. Cover design by Highpoint Type & Graphics; colors: four-color stylized drawing on a silhouetted couple dining in the restaurant's, using cranberry red, gray, brown, black, and green. First Edition, December 1992.

A cookbook based around the San Bernardino restaurant, The Cranberry Tea Room.

CONTENTS: Introducing Richard Martinez: "A Touch of Class" (p. 7-8); Glossary (p. 9); Dedication (p. 10); Soups (p. 11-22); Salads and Sandwich Fillings (p. 23-37); Cranberry Tea Room Main Dishes (p. 39-58); From the Grill (p. 59-62); Richard's Mexican Specialties (p. 63-78); Casseroles and Side Dishes (p. 79-87); Sauces, Dips, and Spreads (p. 89-98); Breads (p. 99-107); Cakes (p. 109-118); Frostings, Icings, and Special Toppings (p. 98, 111, 115, 122, 130); Pies (p. 119-128); Puddings, Desserts, and Cookies (p. 129-140); Index (p. 141-144).

A144. *Shamrocks and Sea Silver, and Other Illuminations*, by Leonard Wibberley, edited by Christopher Wibberley and Paul David Seldis. I.O. EVANS STUDIES IN THE PHILOSOPHY AND CRITICISM OF LITERATURE, Number 8. 128 p. LC 84-345. OCLC #10375577. ISBN 0-89370-302-8 cloth $23; ISBN 0-89370-402-

BP 300, by Robert Reginald & Mary Wickizer Burgess

4 paper $13. Cover design by Highpoint Type & Graphics, with green shamrocks and type over tan background. First Edition, December 1992.

A collection of previously-published newspaper columns on life and literature by the late American writer, Leonard Wibberley (1915-1983).

CONTENTS: A Leonard Wibberley Chronology (p. 5-6); Introduction, by Robert Nathan (p. 7); Editors' Note (p. 8). 1979. 1. Child Finds Treasures (p. 11-12); 2. Whiskey a Better Buy Than a Novel (p. 13-14); 3. Toes Are an Anatomical Mystery (p. 15-16); 4. Never Associate Failure with Father (p. 17-18).

1980. 5. Death Common to All (p. 21-22); 6. Babies Have No Nerves (p. 23-24); 7. Turtles Near Extinction (p. 25-26); 8. Automobile Teaches Humility to Man (p. 27-28); 9. Mushrooms Are One Gift of the Rain (p. 29-30); 10. Newspapermen Are a Little Bit Crazy (p. 31-32); 11. Human Skull Is Superior to Computer (p. 33-34); 12. Portugal a Good Place for a Father (p. 35-36); 13. Kites Arouse Sense of Mild Adventure (p. 37-38); 14. Approach Impersonal (p. 39-40); 15. So Few Men Believe in Themselves (p. 41-42); 16. A Cup of Coffee Makes It All Worthwhile (p. 43-44); 17. Standardization Should Be the Rule (p. 45-46); 18. Cold Mile, Bread a Marvelous Meal (p. 47-48); 19. Life Consists of Sickness and Health (p. 49-50); 20. Objects Are Migratory (p. 51-52); 21. He's a Klutz When It's Modern Art (p. 53-54); 22. Dull Students Essential to Teachers (p. 55-56); 23. Parking Comes First, Faculty Second (p. 57-58); 24. Nozzles on Gas Hoses Test Character (p. 59-60); 25. Humor Is Absent Among Fanatics (p. 61-62).

1981. 26. Why Am I Still Alive? (p. 65-66); 27. A Day for Teachers (p. 67-68); 28. Today's Knives Are Dull (p. 69-70); 29. System Is Logical; Humans Are Not (p. 71-72); 30. Straightening a House Costs $7,000 (p. 73-74); 31. Punctuation a Favorite Wilderness (p. 75-76); 32. Soapdish Problem Remains Unsolved (p. 77-78); 33. Apes May Be Descended from Man (p. 79-80); 34. Let's Not Fight Chaos (p. 81-82); 35. Be Original with Nouns (p. 83-84); 36. Peculiar Heart Attack Cause of Fall (p. 85-86); 37. Cafe is Descendant of Coffee Houses (p. 87-88); 38. Slogans Do Not Represent Thinking (p. 89-90); 39. Child Wins Battle of Wits (p. 91-92); 40. Arising Late Can Be Dangerous to Health (p. 93-94); 41. Another Midlife Crisis (p. 95-96); 42. Censorship Works for School Libraries (p. 97-98); 43. Children Are All Different (p. 99-100); 44. Chablis an Effective Termite Pesticide (p. 101-102); 45. More Conveniences, But Fewer Services (0. 103-104).

1982. 46. Punishment Helps Students (p. 107-108); 47. A Visit to Treasure Island (p. 109-110); 48. Idleness Is Not Laziness (p. 111-112); 49. Reality Has Devoured Charm, Romance (p. 113-114); 50. Off to Gather Shamrocks (p. 115-116).

Undated. 51. Pay Heed to Foundation of Knowledge (p. 119-120); 52. Cats, Asthma, Vitamins (p. 121-122); 53. Interior at 47 (p. 123-124); 54. Fragrance of "Affair" Still Lingers (p. 125-126); Title Index (p. 127); About the Author (p. 128).

A145. *The Work of Katherine Kurtz: An Annotated Bibliography & Guide*, by Boden Clarke with Mary A. Burgess. BIBLIOGRAPHIES OF MODERN AUTHORS, Number 7. 128 p. LC 85-31401. OCLC #13063902. ISBN 0-89370-386-9 cloth $23; ISBN 0-89370-486-3 paper $13. Includes genealogical charts of the Haldane Kings. Cover: standard series design by Highpoint Type & Graphics, photo of the author by Beth Gwinn, black ink on peach background. First Edition, March 1993.

A bibliography of and literary guide to the works of the modern American author, Katherine Kurtz (1944-).

CONTENTS: Introduction: "Bridges: An Appreciation of Katherine Kurtz," by Andrew V. Phillips (p. 5-7); A Katherine Kurtz Chronology (p. 9-11); A. Books (p. 13-40); B. Short Fiction (p. 41-48); C. Short Nonfiction (p. 49-51); D. Songs (p. 52); E. Editorial Credits (p. 53); F. Scripts (p. 54); G. Other Media (p. 55); H. Unpublished Works (p. 56); I. Honors and Awards (p. 57); J. Secondary Sources (p. 58-63); K. Miscellanea (p. 64); Quoth the Critics (p. 65-82); Talking with Katherine Kurtz, by Jeffrey M. Elliot & Robert Reginald (p. 83-116); Afterword: "Imaginary History: A Genealogical Approach," by Katherine Kurtz (p. 117-124); Index (p. 125-127); About the Authors (p. 128).

A146. *A Directory of Autocephalous Bishops of the Churches of the Apostolic Succession, Sixth Edition*, by Karl Pruter. THE AUTOCEPHALOUS ORTHODOX CHURCHES, Number 1. A St. Willibrord's Press Book. 96 p. LC 92-24123. OCLC #26217486. ISBN 0-912134-12-7 cloth $23; ISBN 0-912134-13-5 paper $13. Cover design by Highpoint Type & Graphics showing an

BP 300, by Robert Reginald & Mary Wickizer Burgess

Orthodox archbishop, black ink on cream background. Sixth Edition, March 1993.

A directory of independent Orthodox and Old Catholic bishops, updated from earlier editions published by the independent St. Willibrord's Press.
CONTENTS: Preface (p. 5-6); Directory: United States and Canada (p. 7-87); Central and South America (p. 88); Index of Jurisdictions (p. 89-95); About the Author (p. 96).
Spine title reads: *Sixth Directory of Autocephalous Bishops*. See also the Seventh Edition (**A224**).

A147. *The Russian Orthodox Church Outside Russia: A History and Chronology*, by Rev. Fr. Alexey Young, edited by Bishop Karl Pruter and Paul David Seldis. THE AUTOCEPHALOUS ORTHODOX CHURCHES, Number 2. A St. Willibrord's Press Book. 136 p. LC 91-36884. OCLC #24669400. ISBN 0-8095-2300-0 cloth $25; ISBN 0-8095-3300-6 paper $15. Cover design by Highpoint Type & Graphics, showing the Metropolitan of the Church, black ink on gray background. First Edition, March 1993.

b.   Second Printing, with redesigned back cover copy featuring EAN Bookland bar codes, October 1994. Erroneously substitutes the drawing of the prelate from *The Directory of Autocephalous Bishops*.
c.   Third Printing, October 1995. Cover photo corrected.
d.   Fourth Printing, July 1996.
e.   Fifth Printing, July 1997.

A history of the Russian Orthodox Church Outside Russia, which split from the Russian Orthodox Church in 1921.
CONTENTS: Preface, by Bishop Karl Pruter (p. 5-7); A Chronology of Russian Orthodoxy (p. 9-11); Glossary (p. 13-15); Introduction (p. 17-20); 1. The Beginning (p. 21-26); 2. Confusion and Schism (p. 27-32); 3. The Church in America (p. 33-37); 4. The Russian Moses (p. 39-43); 5. Stress and Strain (p. 45-50); 6. The Transition (p. 51-56); 7. New Challenges (p. 57-63); 8. More New Challenges (p. 65-72); 9. A New Schism (p. 73-80); 10. Spiritual Life (p. 81-88); 11. The Future (p. 89-97); 12. Postscript (p. 99-104); Appendix I: Prelates (p. 105-106); Appendix II: Clergy and Parishes (p. 107-108); Appendix III: Monasteries and

Convents (p. 109); Appendix IV: Schools, Nursing Homes, Publications (p. 111); Appendix V: *Ukaz* No. 362 (p. 113-116); Appendix VI: *Protocol* #8 (p. 117-118); Appendix VII: An Appeal (p. 119-120); Appendix VIII: Primate Metropolitans (p. 121); Appendix IX: Patriarchs of Russia (p. 123); Footnotes (p. 125-130); Bibliography (p. 131-132); Index (p. 133-135); About the Author (p. 136).

A148. *The Transylvanian Library: A Consumer's Guide to Vampire Fiction*, by Greg Cox, edited by Daryl F. Mallett. BORGO LITERARY GUIDES, Number 8. 264 p. LC 88-36553. OCLC #18988294. ISBN 0-89370-335-4 cloth $30; ISBN 0-89370-435-0 paper $20. Cover: standard series design by Highpoint Type & Graphics, plus a bat, black and red ink on gray background. First Edition, March 1993.

   b.   Second Printing, February 1994.
   c.   Third Printing, with redesigned back cover copy featuring EAN Bookland bar codes, November 1994.

An annotated, humorous guide to the vampire in literature, from its earliest beginnings to modern times.
CONTENTS: Acknowledgments (p. 5); About the Author (p. 6); Introduction (p. 7-9); The Transylvanian Rating System (p. 10); The Transylvanian Library: 1. The History of the Vampire (p. 11-30); 2. In the Wake of Dracula (p. 31-72); 3. The Vampire Meets the Atomic Age (p. 73-87); 4. Return of the Heroic Vampire (p. 89-116); 5. The Heroic Vampire Triumps (p. 117-238); Afterword (p. 239-240); Appendix I: The Unread (p. 241-242); Appendix II: The Blood Countess on Film (p. 243); Selected Bibliography (p. 245-246); Author Index (p. 247-250); Character Index (p. 251-254); Miscellaneous and Publisher Index (p. 255-256); Title Index (p. 257-264).

A149. *Reginald's Science Fiction and Fantasy Awards: A Comprehensive Guide to the Awards and Their Winners, Third Edition, Revised and Expanded*, by Daryl F. Mallett & Robert Reginald. BORGO LITERARY GUIDES, Number 1. 248 p. LC 92-24445. OCLC #26362811. ISBN 0-8095-0200-3 cloth $30; ISBN 0-8095-1200-9 paper $20. Cover: standard series design by Highpoint Type & Graphics, red ink on pink background. Third Edition, March 1993.

b. Second Printing, October 1993.

A guide to the major and minor awards and honors presented in the science fiction, fantasy, and horror genres.
CONTENTS: Introduction (p. 9-10); How to Use This Book (p. 11); About the Authors (p. 12); Part One: Genre Awards (p. 13-140); Part Two: Non-Genre Awards (p. 141-162); Appendices (p. 163-174); Author Index (p. 175-244); Index to Award Names (p. 245-248).
An expanded version of **A132**.

A150. *The Catholic Priest: A Guide to Holy Orders*, by Karl Pruter, edited by Paul David Seldis. ST. WILLIBRORD STUDIES IN PHILOSOPHY AND RELIGION, Number 2. A St. Willibrord's Press Book. 88 p. LC 92-45059. OCLC #27186559. ISBN 0-912134-14-3 cloth $20; ISBN 0-912134-15-1 paper $10. Cover: standard series design by Highpoint Type & Graphics, black ink on rose background. First Edition, March 1993.

A guide to holy orders for the Catholic priest.
CONTENTS: Part One: Preparation. 1. The Call to Holy Orders (p. 7-11); 2. The Priesthood of Jesus (p. 13-16); 3. The Role of the Priest in Public Worship (p. 17-21); 4. The Priest As Confessor and Counselor (p. 23-31).
Part Two: Training. 5. The Priest As Preacher (p. 35-38); 6. The Role of the Priest at Weddings (p. 39-43); 7. The Priest As Missionary (p. 45-50); 8. The Priest As Healer (p. 51-56); 9. Preparation for the Holy and Priestly Life (p. 57-68).
Part Three: Practice. 10. The Priest As Teacher (p. 71-75); 11. Father to the Parish (p. 77-81); Notes and Bibliography (p. 82); Index (p. 83-87); About the Author (p. 88).

A151. *The Association Oath Rolls of the British Plantations [New York, Virginia, Etc.], A.D. 1696: Being a Contribution to Political History*, edited by William Gandy, introduction by Michael Burgess. STOKVIS STUDIES IN HISTORICAL CHRONOLOGY AND THOUGHT, Number 10. A Sidewinder Press Book. 86 p., illustrated. LC 93-3795. OCLC #27896339. ISBN 0-8095-

BP 300, by Robert Reginald & Mary Wickizer Burgess

0100-7 cloth $20; ISBN 0-8095-1100-2 paper $10. Includes one illustration of the original rolls. Cover: standard series design by Highpoint Type & Graphics, black ink on green background, with a backdrop of some of the signatures. First Borgo Edition, April 1993.

This facsimile reprint of the 1922 Gandy edition includes lists of loyalty oaths signed in the British colonies in the Americas in 1696.
    CONTENTS: Preface (p. 7); [New] Introduction, by Michael Burgess (p. 8); The Association Oath Rolls of the British Plantations, A.D. 1696 [Introductory Chapter] (p. 9-23); The Rolls (p. 25-74); Index of Surnames (p. 77-86).

A152. *More Monumental Inscriptions: Tombstones of the British West Indies*, by Vere Langford Oliver, introduction by Michael Burgess. STOKVIS STUDIES IN HISTORICAL CHRO-NOLOGY AND THOUGHT, Number 14. A Sidewinder Press Book. iv+267 p. LC 93-90. OCLC #27379807. ISBN 0-89370-322-2 cloth $33; ISBN 0-89370-422-9 paper $23. Cover: standard series design by Highpoint Type & Graphics, black ink on blue background. First Borgo Edition, April 1993.

This facsimile reprint of the 1927 Friary Press edition records tombstone inscriptions from the islands of the British West Indies except Barbados.
    CONTENTS: Preface (p. iii); [New] Introduction, by Michael Burgess (p. iv); Antigua (p. 1-4); Dominica (p. 5-38); Montserrat (p. 39-63); Nevis (p. 64-121); St. Kitts (p. 122-198); Grenada (p. 199-211); St. Lucia (p. 211); Tobago (p. 212-213); Trinidad (p. 214-222); Demerara (p. 223-239); Bahamas (p. 240-248); Naval and Military Burial Grounds (p. 249-260); Index Nominum (p. 261-267).

A153. *The State and Province Vital Records Guide*, by Michael Burgess, Mary A. Burgess, and Daryl F. Mallett. BORGO REFERENCE GUIDES, Number 5. 96 p. LC 87-6312. OCLC #15318074. ISBN 0-89370-815-1 cloth $20; ISBN 0-89370-915-8 paper $10. Cover: standard series design by Highpoint Type & Graphics, black ink on pale yellow background. First Edition, April 1993.

b. Second Printing, with redesigned back cover copy featuring EAN Bookland bar codes, May 1994, bright yellow covers.
c. Third Printing, November 1994.

A guide to the vital records available from the U.S. states and territories, and from the Canadian provinces and territories.
    CONTENTS: Introduction (p. 7-8); Part One: United States (p. 9-71); Part Two: U.S. Insular Areas and Territories (p. 73-81); Part Three: Canada (p. 83-95); About the Authors (p. 96).

A154. *An Annotated Narrative of Joe Blackburn's A Clown's Log*, as compiled by Charles H. Day, arranged and edited by William L. Slout. CLIPPER STUDIES IN THE THEATRE, Number 6. An Emeritus Enterprise Book. x+138 p. LC 92-44479. OCLC #27173336. ISBN 0-8095-6250-2 cloth $23; ISBN 0-8095-6251-0 paper $13. Illustrated with contemporary drawings. Nonstandard series design by the author, blue ink on pale blue background. First Edition, April 1993.

The first book publication of a history of an American clown's trip to England in the 1830s and '40s.
    CONTENTS: Preface (p. ix-x); Prologue (p. 3-11); Blackburn in America (p. 13-35); Blackburn in England (p. 37-103); Epilogue (p. 105-110); Notes (p. 111-119); Bibliography (p. 121-127); Index (p. 129-138).
    The first Emeritus Enterprise book.

A155. *The Mystery Fancier: An Index to Volumes I-XIII, November 1976-Fall 1992*, by William F. Deeck. BROWNSTONE MYSTERY GUIDES, Volume 9. A Brownstone Book. ix+170 p. LC 93-341. OCLC #27642983. ISBN 0-941028-11-9 cloth $27; ISBN 0-941028-12-7 paper $17. Cover: standard series design by Highpoint Type & Graphics, black ink on rose background. First Edition, April 1993.

A comprehensive index to the entire run of a semi-professional mystery fan magazine, *The Mystery Fancier*.
    CONTENTS: Reader's Guide (p. v-vi); Checklist of Issues Indexed (p. vii-ix); Cover Art (p. ix); The Index (p. 1-169); About the Author (p. [170]).

A156. *Adventures of a Freelancer: The Literary Exploits and Autobiography of Stanton A. Coblentz*, by Stanton A. Coblentz with Jeffrey M. Elliot, edited by Scott Alan Burgess. BORGO BIOVIEWS, Number 2. 160 p. LC 93-189506. OCLC #30548356. ISBN 0-89370-338-9 cloth $27; ISBN 0-89370-438-5 paper $17. Cover: standard series design by Highpoint Type & Graphics, using photo of author, black ink on tan background. First Edition, May 1993.

An autobiography of the late American poet and editor, Stanton A. Coblentz (1896-1982).

CONTENTS: Introduction, by Dr. Jeffrey M. Elliot (p. 5-9); About Jeffrey M. Elliot (p. 10); A Stanton A. Coblentz Chronology (p. 11-15); "Childhood Remembrance," by Stanton A. Coblentz (poem; p. 16); Preface (p. 17); 1. Earthquake, Fire, and Flood (p. 19-23); 2. Childhood Remembrances (p. 25-32); 3. New Pathways (p. 33-42); 4. A Mote in the Metropolis (p. 43-47); 5. Vicissitudes of a Book Reviewer (p. 49-51); 6. A Slippery Conquest (p. 53-54); 7. Path of Thorns and Daisies (p. 55-60); 8. The Publishing Doors Slide Open (p. 61-70); 9. A Rocky Road Opens Up (p. 71-76); 10. Shadows of the Depression (p. 77-80); 11. Fortune Still Twists and Turns (p. 81-89); 12. Editorial Flutterings (p. 91-97); 13. *Wings* Beings to Fly (p. 99-112); 14. Trials and Tribulations of an Editor (p. 113-120); 15. More of the Unexpected (p. 121-128); 16. A Novice on Publishers' Row (p. 129-134); 17. Challenging Giants (p. 135-144); 18. In Other Years (p. 145-153); Epilogue (p. 154); Bibliography (p. 155-156); Index (p. 157-160).

A157. *Still the Frame Holds: Essays on Women Poets and Writers*, edited by Sheila Roberts, additional editing by Yvonne Pacheco Tevis. I.O. EVANS STUDIES IN THE PHILOSOPHY AND CRITICISM OF LITERATURE, Number 10. 216 p. LC 87-823. OCLC #15195565. ISBN 0-89370-304-4 cloth $30; ISBN 0-89370-404-0 paper $20. Cover: modified series design by Highpoint Type & Graphics, black ink on pink background. First Edition, May 1993.

An anthology of previously-published and original essays on twentieth-century women writers.

BP 300, by Robert Reginald & Mary Wickizer Burgess

CONTENTS: Preface (p. 5); Introduction (p. 7-13); 1. Carolyn Forche: Poet of Witness, by Leonora Smith (p. 15-28); 2. Reforming the Body Politic: Radical Feminist Science Fiction, by Katherine Fishburn (p. 29-46); 3. Wakoski's Poems: Moving Past Confession, by Linda W. Wagner (p. 47-58); 4. Stevie Smith: An Appreciation, by Liz Holmes (p. 59-68); 5. H.D.: Gifts of Music, Gifts of Vision, by Lee Upton (p. 69-78); 6. Within the Bounds of Feminine Sensibility? The Poetry of Rosemary Dobson, Gwen Harwood, and Judith Wright, by Jennifer Strauss (p. 79-99); 7. Would Superwoman Fly? Some Notes, by Rose Moss (p. 101-108); 8. Two Utopias: Marge Piercy's *Woman on the Edge of Time* and Ursula Le Guin's *The Dispossessed*, by Barbara Drake (p. 109-127); 9. Words of Space: The Fiction of Sheila Watson and Sharon Riis, by Donna E. Smyth (p. 129-135); 10. An Archetype of Pain: From Plath to Atwood and Musgrave, by Catherine Ahearn (p. 137-156); 11. An Introduction to Violette Leduc, by Julie Whitby (p. 157-163); 12. *A Green Equinox*: The Nature of Love in the Fiction of Elizabeth Mavor, by Sheila Fugard (p. 165-171); 13. Film into Fiction: The Influence of Ruth Prawer Jhabvala's Cinema Work upon Her Fiction, by Yasmine Gooneratme (p. 173-189); 14. Barriers of Reticence and Reserve, by Rose Moss (p. 191-200); Notes (p. 201-209); About the Contributors (p. 210-211); Index (p. 212-216).

A158. *Science Fiction and Fantasy Book Review Index, Volume 20, 1989*, by Hal W. Hall. vi+90 p. ISBN 0-8095-6804-7 cloth $25. Photocopied from the original. First Borgo Edition, May 1993.

A continuing index to book reviews of science fiction, fantasy, and horror fiction and nonfiction.

A159. *The Magic That Works: John W. Campbell and the American Response to Technology*, by Albert I. Berger, edited by Mary A. Burgess. THE MILFORD SERIES: POPULAR WRITERS OF TODAY, Volume 46. 231 p. LC 84-373. OCLC #10404305. ISBN 0-89370-175-0 cloth $30; ISBN 0-89370-275-7 paper $20. Cover: standard series design by Highpoint Type & Graphics, with photo of Campbell by Jay Kay Klein, black ink on gray background. First Edition, June 1993.

BP 300, by Robert Reginald & Mary Wickizer Burgess

b. Second Printing, with redesigned back cover copy featuring EAN Bookland bar codes, November 1994. Includes new "About the Author" bio squib on new p. 232.

A critique of the late American writer and editor, John W. Campbell, Jr. (1910-1971).
CONTENTS: Acknowledgments (p. 5-6); A John Campbell Chronology (p. 7-8); 1. In the Beginning (p. 9-14); 2. The Pulp Writer As Philosopher (p. 15-32); 3. The Pulp Writer As Editor (p. 33-51); 4. The Editor As Celebrant, the Editor As Suspect (p. 53-72); 5. The Editor Validated (p. 73-86); 6. The Editor As Psychologist (p. 87-106); 7. The Editor in a Changing Market (p. 107-114); *ASF* Readers' Income v. U.S. Median Income (chart) (p. 115); 8. The Editor in the Age of Space, 1945-1958 (p. 117-130); 9. The Editor and the Problem of Unorthodox Science (p. 131-158); 10. The Editor As Elitist (p. 159-176); 11. The Editor As Authoritarian (p. 177-190); 12. Conclusions (p. 191-197); Notes (p. 199-224); Index (p. 225-231); About the Author (p. 232).
Winner of the 1995 J. Lloyd Eaton Award for Best Non-fiction Work of the Year. The "About the Author" page was accidentally omitted from the first printing of the book by the printer.

A160. *Mexico and the United States: Neighbors in Crisis: Proceedings from the Conference, Neighbors in Crisis, A Call for Joint Solutions*, edited by Daniel G. Aldrich, Jr. and Lorenzo Mayer, additional anonymous editing by Yvonne Pacheco Tevis. GREAT ISSUES OF THE DAY, Number 6. A UC MEXUS Book. x+390 p. LC 93-924. OCLC #27813016. ISBN 0-89370-345-1 cloth $40; ISBN 0-89370-445-8 paper $30. Illustrated with charts and graphs. Cover design by Highpoint Type & Graphics, blue and green ink on cream background. First Edition, June 1993.

The proceedings of a conference, Neighbors in Crisis: A Call of Joint Solutions, held at the University of California, Riverside in February of 1989.
CONTENTS: Foreword, by Arturo Gómez-Pompa (p. vii-ix); Introduction, by Lorenzo Meyer (p. 1-6); 1. Agriculture to the Rescue: A Solution to Binational Problems, by David Barkin and J. Edward Taylor (p. 7-34); Commentary, by Samuel Taylor (p.

35-36); Commentary, by Antonio Turrent Fernández (p. 37-39); 2. Mexico's Export Electronics Industry: International Competitiveness and Regional Impacts, by Luis Suárez-Villa, Bernardo González-Aréchiga, and José Carlos Ramírez Sánchez (p. 41-73); Commentary, by Eduardo G. Guajardo (p. 74-77); Commentary, by Chris Kraul (p. 78-81);

3. Mexican Migration to the United States and the Possibilities of Bilateral Cooperation: Four Conceptual Frameworks, by Manuel García y Griego and James W. Wilkie (p. 83-105); Commentary, by Edgardo Flores Rivas (p. 106-109); Commentary, by E. Michael Trominski (p. 110); 4. AIDS Control at the Frontier: A Binational Challenge to the United States and Mexico, by J. Dennis Mull and Vicente López Rocher (p. 111-128); Commentary, by Miguel Angel González Block (p. 129-133); 5. Human Rights and Indigenous Workers: The Mixtecs in Mexico and the United States, by Carole Nagengast, Rodolfo Stavenhagen (with the assistance of Joan Friedland), and Michael Kearney (p. 135-179); Commentary, by Evaristo López Herrera (p. 180-182); 6. Political Transition in Mexico: Its Impact Upon U.S.-Mexico Relations, by José Luis Reyna and Edgar W. Butler (p. 183-209); Commentary, by Marco Antonio Bernal Gutiérrez (p. 210-212); Commentary, by John Bailey (p. 213-215);

7A. The Debt Crisis: A View from Mexico, by Víctor L. Urquidi (p. 217-233); 7B. The Debt Crisis: A View from the United States, by Maxwell J. Fry (p. 235-246); 8A. The Possibilities for Better Mexican-U.S. Energy Cooperation: The United States As a Possible Market for Increased Mexican Crude and Refined Petroleum Exports, by Isidro Morales Moreno (p. 247-276); 8B. The Possibilities for Better Mexican-U.S. Energy Cooperation: Opportunities for Mexican Natural Gas and Electric Power Exports to the United States, by Walter J. Mead (p. 277-302); Commentary, by Richard Bilas (p. 303-306); Commentary, by Fausto Alzati (p. 307-310); 9. A Binational System of Agricultural Production: The Case of the Mexican Bajío and California, by Juan Vicente Palerm and José Ignacio Urquiola (p. 311-367); Commentary, by Gustavo Verduzco Igartua (p. 368-369); Index (p. 371-390).

A161. *The Trial of Dr. Jekyll: An Adaptation of Robert Louis Stevenson's "The Strange Case of Dr. Jekyll and Mr. Hyde": A Play in Two Acts*, by William L. Slout. CLIPPER STUDIES IN THE

BP 300, by Robert Reginald & Mary Wickizer Burgess

THEATRE, Number 7. An Emeritus Enterprise Book. x+75 p. LC 93-10112. OCLC #27814317. ISBN 0-8095-6252-9 cloth $20; ISBN 0-8095-6253-7 paper $10. Illustrated with stills from the first production of the play. Cover design by Highpoint Type & Graphics, using a photo still from the CSUSB production of the play, black ink on gray background. First Edition, July 1993.

The first publication of an original play adapted from Robert Louis Stevenson's well-known novella, "The Strange Case of Dr. Jekyll and Mr. Hyde," which was first produced on February 5, 1993, at California State University, San Bernardino.

CONTENTS: Author's Notes (p. v-vi); Cast of Characters (p. vii-viii); Designer Lee Lyons' Floor Plan for the Initial Production (p. ix); The Trial of Dr. Jekyll (p. 1-75).

A162. *Polemical Pulps: The Martin Beck Novels of Maj Sjöwall and Per Wahlöö*, by J. Kenneth Van Dover. BROWNSTONE MYSTERY GUIDES, Volume 11. A Brownstone Book. 96 p. LC 87-716. OCLC #15132395. ISBN 0-89370-184-X cloth $22; ISBN 0-89370-284-6 paper $12. Cover: standard series design by Highpoint Type & Graphics, black ink on sage green background. First Edition, July 1993.

A critique of the ten Martin Beck novels written by modern Swedish writers Maj Sjöwall (1935-) and Per Wahlöö (1926-1975).

CONTENTS: Note (p. 5); Acknowledgments (p. 6); Introduction: Polemical Pulps (p. 7-9); A Sjöwall and Wahlöö Chronology (p. 10-12); 1. *Roseanna* (p. 13-19); 2. *The Man Who Went Up in Smoke* (p. 21-24); 3. *The Man on the Balcony* (p. 25-30); 4. *The Laughing Policeman* (p. 31-35); 5. *The Fire Engine That Disappeared* (p. 37-41); 6. *Murder at the Savoy* (p. 43-50); 7. *The Abominable Man* (p. 51-55); 8. *The Locked Room* (p. 57-63); 9. *Cop Killer* (p. 65-69); 10. *The Terrorists* (p. 71-77); 11. The Significance of Sex (p. 79-83); 12. Reality and Truth (p. 85-87); 13. Martin Beck in 1993 (p. 89-92); Bibliography (p. 93); Index (p. 94-95); About J. Kenneth Van Dover (p. 96).

A163. *Geo. Alec Effinger: From Entropy to Budayeen*, by Ben P. Indick, edited by Daryl F. Mallett. ESSAYS ON FANTASTIC LITERATURE, Number 8. 96 p. LC 93-2880. OCLC #27430757.

BP 300, by Robert Reginald & Mary Wickizer Burgess

ISBN 0-89370-346-X cloth $22; ISBN 0-89370-446-6 paper
$12. Cover: standard series design by Highpoint Type &
Graphics, black ink on orange background. First Edition, July
1993.

A critical guide to the work of modern American writer, George
Alec Effinger (1947-2002).
    CONTENTS: Introduction: "Beginnings" (p. 5-77); A George
Alec Effinger Chronology (p. 9-10); 1. That Old Funny Stuff:
Gags and Games (p. 11-14); 2. *What Entropy Means to Me* (p. 15-
17); 3. *Relatives* (p. 19-22); 4. Early Short Stories (p. 23-26); 5.
Mixed Feelings (p. 27-30); 6. An Authorial Aside: *The Planet of
the Apes* Novels (p. 31-32); 7. Novels for the Mainstream and the
Jetstream (p. 33-36); 8. *Death in Florence* (p. 37-40); 9. Space
Exiles (p. 41-42); 10. Meanwhile, in the Short Story Department
(p. 43-45); 11. Comedy Tonight (p. 47-52); 12. A Caper (p. 53-
54); 13. A Slightly Alternate War Between the States (p. 55-57);
14. Computer Games and Books (p. 59-62); 15. "The Budayeen":
Effinger Gets It All Together (p. 63-79); Notes on the Text (p. 81-
83); A George Alec Effinger Bibliography (p. 85-86); A Note
About a Nickname (p. 87); Index (p. 89-95); About Ben P. Indick
(p. 96).

A164. *Defying the Holocaust: A Diplomat's Report*, by Aba Gefen,
    edited by Nathan Kravetz. STUDIES IN JUDAICA AND THE
    HOLOCAUST, Number 11. 248 p. LC 93-9283. OCLC
    #27432356. ISBN 0-89370-366-4 cloth $32. ISBN 0-89370-466-
    0 paper $22. Illustrated with photographs of the author. Cover:
    standard series design by Highpoint Type & Graphics with
    photo of author, black ink on gray background. First Edition,
    August 1993.

A memoir of the Holocaust survivor and Israeli diplomat, Aba
Gefen.
    CONTENTS: Dedication (p. 5); About the Author (p. 6);
Preface (p. 7); Foreword (p. 8); Part One: Inconceivable Savagery.
1. "Little America" (p. 11-19); 2. "God Be with You!" (p. 21-24);
3. Proud to Be a Jew (p. 25-29); 4. Drunk with Frightening
Regularity (p. 31-36); 5. In the Wheat Fields (p. 37-42); 6. The
Gun (p. 43-49); 7. Annoying Prediction (p. 51-54); 8. Intensified

Chase (p. 55-60); 9. The Continuing Search for Shelter (p. 61-64); 10. God Was with Us! (p. 65-67).

Part Two: Hour of Punishment. 11. O Lord, God of Vengeance! (p. 71-79); 12. Why Did the Jews Not Rebel? (p. 81-86); 13. Big Catch (p. 87-90); 14. Six Million Would-Be Accusers (p. 91-95).

Part Three: The Flight. 15. Tangible Goal (p. 99-107); 16. Glorious Week (p. 109-115); 17. A Pogrom and a Rabbi (p. 117-120); 18. God's Covenant with Abraham (p. 121-123); 19. Appeasement at Our Expense (p. 125-131); 20. Our Unfailing American Protector (p. 133-138); 21. A Woman of Valor and Piety (p. 139-142).

Part Four: Jewish Statehood Regained. 22. With Trust in Almighty God (p. 145-148); 23. No Second Masada! (p. 149-155); 24. Primary Responsibility (p. 157-161); 25. Sanctification of the Divine Name (p. 163-164); 26. To Hold Fast to the Bible (p. 165-170); 27. Critical Events (p. 171-177); 28. Missed Opportunities for Peace (p. 179-182); 29. As Recited in the Haggadah (p. 183-187); 30. Assignment in Argentina (p. 189-192); 31. On the Most Sacred Day (p. 193-198); 32. King, Emperor, or God? (p. 199-209); 33. Fighting a New Wave of Terrorism (p. 211-214); 34. Moscow's Excuses (p. 215-220); 35. Massive Return to Ancestral Homeland (p. 221-224); 36. Facing Another Hitler (p. 225-230); 37. Chances or Risks? (p. 231-236); 38. A Relationship Built to Endure (p. 237-242); Index (p. 243-248).

A165. *Stalin: An Annotated Guide to Books in English*, by Marty Bloomberg & Buckley Barry Barrett, edited by Michael Burgess and Paul David Seldis. BORGO REFERENCE GUIDES, Number 1. 128 p. LC 92-43368. OCLC #27172557. ISBN 0-8095-0701-3 cloth $25; ISBN 0-8095-1701-9 paper $15. Cover: standard series design by Highpoint Type & Graphics, illustration of Stalin by Boris Mukhametshin, black ink on peach background. First Edition, September 1993.

b. Second Printing, April 1995, featuring a redesigned back cover with EAN Bookland bar codes.

A bibliography of books by and about Soviet dictator, Joseph Stalin (1879-1953).

BP 300, by Robert Reginald & Mary Wickizer Burgess

CONTENTS: Introduction (p. 5-6); Chronology (p. 7-8); Abbreviations (p. 9); A. Bibliographies, Memoirs, and Related Works (p. 11-42); B. Stalinism (p. 43-80); C. Special Topics (p. 81-102); D. Fiction and Juvenile Nonfiction (p. 103-111); Author Index (p. 113-118); Title Index (p. 119-126); About the Authors (p. 128).

A166. *Phoenix Renewed: The Survival and Mutation of Utopian Thought in North American Science Fiction, 1965-1982, Revised Edition*, by Hoda M. Zaki. I.O. EVANS STUDIES IN THE PHILOSOPHY AND CRITICISM OF LITERATURE, Number 18. A Thaddeus Dikty Book. 112 p. LC 93-30397. OCLC #28721952. ISBN 1-55742-126-9 cloth $25; ISBN 1-55742-127-7 paper $15. Cover: standard series design by Highpoint Type & Graphics, black ink on beige background. Revised Edition, September 1993.

b. Second Printing, with redesigned back cover copy featuring EAN Bookland bar codes, October 1994.

A study of utopianism in modern American science fiction.
CONTENTS: Acknowledgments (p. 5); 1. Utopian Thought and Political Theory (p. 7-17); 2. Science Fiction (p. 19-28); 3. The Nebula Novels (p. 29-46); 4. Ursula K. Le Guin (p. 47-65); 5. Conclusion (p. 67-71); Appendix I: The Nebula Award-Winning Novels (p. 73); Appendix II: The Hugo Award-Winning Novels (p. 75-76); Notes (p. 77-93); Selected Bibliography (p. 95-106); Index (p. 107-112).
Revised and reset from the 1988 Starmont Edition (see **G67**).

A167. *J.R.R. Tolkien: The Art of the Myth-Maker, Revised Edition*, by David Stevens and Carol D. Stevens, edited by Roger C. Schlobin. THE MILFORD SERIES: POPULAR WRITERS OF TODAY, Volume 56. A Thaddeus Dikty Book. 1993. vi+178 p. LC 93-17850. OCLC #28112937. ISBN 1-55742-238-9 cloth $28; ISBN 1-55742-237-0 paper $18. Cover: standard series design by Highpoint Type & Graphics, black ink on light rose background. Revised Edition, October 1993.

b. Second Printing, with redesigned back cover copy featuring EAN Bookland bar codes, June 1994.

BP 300, by Robert Reginald & Mary Wickizer Burgess

A critique of the late British writer, J. R. R. Tolkien (1892-1973).

CONTENTS: Acknowledgments (p. iv); Preface (p. v); Chronology (p. 1-4); Chapter One: The Life and Works of J. R. R. Tolkien (p. 5-18); Chapter Two: Non-Fiction and Scholarly Works (p. 19-38); Chapter Three: The Evolution of *The Silmarillion* (p. 39-58); Chapter Four: *The Hobbit* (p. 59-67); Chapter Five: *The Lord of the Rings* (p. 68-136); Chapter Six: Tolkien's Minor Fiction (p. 137-148); A Selected Primary Bibliography (p. 149-156); A Selected Secondary Bibliography (p. 157-172); Index (p. 173-178).

Reproduced from the corrected plates of the Starmont Edition (see **G61**); the copies originally published by Starmont were scrapped due to incorrect page layout.

A168. *Mary Roberts Rinehart, Mistress of Mystery*, by Frances H. Bachelder, edited by Dale Salwak and Daryl F. Mallett. BROWNSTONE MYSTERY GUIDES, Volume 15. A Brownstone Book. 120 p. LC 93-342. OCLC #27429984. ISBN 0-8095-5150-0 cloth $24; ISBN 0-8095-5175-6 paper $14. Cover: standard series design by Highpoint Type & Graphics, black ink on lavender background. First Edition, October 1993.

   b. Second Printing, with redesigned back cover copy featuring EAN Bookland bar codes, July 1994.

A critique of the late American mystery writer, Mary Roberts Rinehart (1876-1958).

CONTENTS: Preface (p. 7); Chronology (p. 9-10); 1. *The Circular Staircase* (1908) (p. 11-18); 2. *The Case of Jennie Brice* (1913) (p. 19-28); 3. *The Red Lamp* (1925) (p. 29-37); 4. *Lost Ecstasy* (1927) (p. 39-47); 5. *The Door* (1930) (p. 49-57); 6. *The Great Mistake* (1940) (p. 59-67); 7. *The Haunted Lady* (1942) (p. 69-75); 8. *The Yellow Room* (1945) (p. 77-88); 9. *The Light in the Window* (1948) (p. 89-99); 10. *The Swimming Pool* (1952) (p. 101-109); 11. Conclusion (p. 111-112); Bibliography (p. 113-114); Index (p. 115-119); About the Author (p. 120).

A169. *William Eastlake: High Desert Interlocutor*, by W. C. Bamberger, edited by Mary A. Burgess and Paul David Seldis. THE MILFORD SERIES: POPULAR WRITERS OF TODAY, Volume 65. 136

BP 300, by Robert Reginald & Mary Wickizer Burgess

p. LC 92-24444. OCLC #26218245. ISBN 0-89370-196-3 cloth $26; ISBN 0-89370-296-X paper $16. Cover: standard series design by Highpoint Type & Graphics, black ink on gold background. First Edition, October 1993.

A critique of modern American writer, William Eastlake (1917-1997).
CONTENTS: A William Eastlake Chronology (p. 5-7); 1. Early Life and Work (p. 9-15); 2. *Go in Beauty* (p. 17-25); 3. *The Bronc People* (p. 27-36); 4. *Portrait of an Artist with Twenty-Six Horses* (p. 37-48); 5. *Castle Keep* (p. 49-61); 6. *Jack Armstrong in Tangier* (p. 63-72); 7. *The Bamboo Bed* (p. 73-87); 8. *A Child's Garden of Verses for the Revolution* (p. 89-98); 9. *Dancers in the Scalp House* (p. 99-109); 10. *The Long Naked Descent into Boston* (p. 111-120); 11. "Saying the End" (p. 121-122); Notes (p. 123-126); Bibliography (p. 127-129); About the Author (p. 130); Index (p. 131-136).

A170. *Wilderness Visions: The Western Theme in Science Fiction Literature, Second Edition, Revised and Expanded*, by David Mogen, edited by Daryl F. Mallett. I.O. EVANS STUDIES IN THE PHILOSOPHY & CRITICISM OF LITERATURE, Number 1. 128 p. LC 92-46389. OCLC #27226104. ISBN 0-89370-300-1 cloth $26; ISBN 0-89370-400-8 paper $16. Cover: standard series design by Highpoint Type & Graphics, black ink on tan background. Second Edition, October 1993.

b.   Second Printing, with redesigned back cover copy featuring EAN Bookland bar codes, May 1994.

A critique focusing on the western theme in modern science fiction.
CONTENTS: Preface to the Second Edition (p. 5); Introduction (p. 7-8); Part I: The Frontier Heritage Enters the Space Age. 1. Science Fiction "Westerns" and American Literature (p. 11-21); 2. The Frontier Metaphor in American Culture (p. 23-32); 3. The Frontier Metaphor as Prophecy (p. 33-38); 4. Blazing Trails to Outer Space: Heinlein, Asimov, and *The Space Merchants* (p. 39-66).
Part II: New Frontiers, Old Horizons. 5. Regenerative Frontiers: New Worlds in Outer Space (p. 69-91); 6. Regressive

Frontiers: Pastoralism and Other Survivors (p. 93-107); 7. Aesthetics and the Science Fiction Frontier (p. 109-118); Bibliography and Works Cited (p. 119-121); Index (p. 123-127); About the Author (p. 128).

See also the First Edition (**A48**).

A171. ***Libido into Literature: The "Primera Época" of Benito Pérez Galdós***, by Clark M. Zlotchew, edited by Daryl F. Mallett. THE MILFORD SERIES: POPULAR WRITERS OF TODAY, Volume 60. 136 p. LC 93-338. OCLC #27429957. ISBN 0-89370-198-X cloth $26; ISBN 0-89370-298-6 paper $16. Cover: standard series design by Highpoint Type & Graphics with inset photo of Pérez Galdós, black ink on pale green background. First Edition, November 1993.

A critique on the late Spanish writer, Benito Pérez Galdós (1843-1920).

CONTENTS: Acknowledgments (p. 4); Introduction, by Douglass M. Rogers (p. 5-7); Preface (p. 8-10); Foreword: The State of Galdosian Criticism (p. 11-13); Chronology (p. 14-16); 1. The Individual and the Group-Organism: *La Fontana de Oro* (p. 17-29); 2. Social Evolution: *El audaz* (p. 31-39); 3. Capture the Bride: *Doña Perfecta* (p. 41-49); 4. Mythic Narrative and Hierogamy: *Gloria* (p. 51-62); 5. The Turning Point: *Marianela* (p. 63-72); 6. Modus Vivendi: *La sombra* Through *La familia de León Roch* (p. 73-83); 7. Conclusion (p. 85-89); Appendix A: Galdós and the Collective Unconscious (p. 91-98); Appendix B: Galdós's Hebrew and Sephardic Origins (p. 99-104); Notes on the Text (p. 105-120); Select Bibliography (p. 121-128); Index (p. 129-135); About the Author (p. 136).

A172. ***The Price of Paradise: The Magazine Career of F. Scott Fitzgerald***, by Stephen W. Potts, edited by Paul David Seldis & John Hansen Gurley. THE MILFORD SERIES: POPULAR WRITERS OF TODAY, Volume 58. 136 p. LC 93-344. OCLC #27429996. ISBN 0-89370-187-4 cloth $26; ISBN 0-89370-287-0 paper $16. Cover: standard series design by Highpoint Type & Graphics, black ink on pale yellow background. First Edition, November 1993.

BP 300, by Robert Reginald & Mary Wickizer Burgess

b. Second Printing, with redesigned back cover copy featuring EAN Bookland bar codes, October 1994.
c. Third Printing, February 1995.
d. Fourth Printing, June 1995.

A critique on the late American writer, F. Scott Fitzgerald (1896-1940).
CONTENTS: An F. Scott Fitzgerald Chronology (p. 5-7); Introduction (p. 9-11); 1. The Gates of Paradise (p. 13-33); 2. Spokesman for the Jazz Generation (p. 35-53); 3. Hitched to the Past (p. 55-75); 4. False Starts and False Endings (p. 77-96); 5. Pasting It Together (p. 97-114); 6. The End of a Life, the Beginning of a Legend (p. 115-119); About the Author (p. 120); Bibliography (p. 121-124); Index (p. 125-136).

A173. *Dragons & Martinis: The Skewed Realism of John Cheever*, by Michael D. Byrne, edited by Paul David Seldis & John Hansen Gurley. THE MILFORD SERIES: POPULAR WRITERS OF TODAY, Volume 55. 136 p. LC 93-337. OCLC #27429950. ISBN 0-8095-2000-1 cloth $26; ISBN 0-8095-3000-7 paper $16. Cover: standard series design by Highpoint Type & Graphics, black ink on sky blue background. First Edition, November 1993.

b. Second Printing, with redesigned back cover copy featuring EAN Bookland bar codes, November 1994.

A critique of the late American writer, John Cheever (1912-1982).
CONTENTS: A John Cheever Chronology (p. 5-6); Introduction (p. 7-21); Part I: Early Cheever: The Critic and the Dreamer. 1. City Life (p. 25-39); 2. Yankee Virtues (p. 41-54). Part II: Maturity: The Imperiled Humanist. 3. The Sanctity of Suburbia (p. 57-66); 4. Forceful Absurdities (p. 67-76); 5. The End of the Spool (p. 77-88). Part III: Late Cheever: The Optimistic Imagination. 6. The Triumph of Nostalgia (p. 91-99); 7. The Triumph Over Chaos (p. 101-114); Notes (p. 115-123); Selected Secondary Bibliography (p. 125-128); Index (p. 129-135); About the Author (p. 136).

A174. *Generous Rafaela: A Novel*, by Juan Valera, translated from the Spanish by Robert G. Trimble (from the novel *Genio y Figura...*). An Emeritus Enterprise Book. iv+187 p. LC 93-

30398. OCLC #28799009. ISBN 0-913960-30-6 cloth $28; ISBN 0-913960-31-4 paper $18. Cover drawing of Rafaela by Barbara Trimble, cover design by Highpoint Type & Graphic; black type on a cream background. First Edition, November 1993.

b.   Second Printing, with redesigned back cover copy featuring EAN Bookland bar codes, September 1994.

A new English-language translation of a classic nineteenth-century novel by Spanish writer, Juan Valera (1824-1905).

A175. ***Doors into the Play: A Few Practical Keys for Theatricians***, by Sydney H. Spayde with Douglas A. Mackey. CLIPPER STUDIES IN THE THEATRE, Number 10. 159 p. LC 93-9431. OCLC #27432916. ISBN 0-89370-316-8 cloth $26; ISBN 0-89370-416-4 paper $16. Cover design of four doors by Highpoint Type & Graphics, black ink on tan background. First Edition, December 1993.

b.   Second Printing, March 1994.

A treatise on acting, developed from a series of interviews with Sydney H. Spayde.
CONTENTS: Preface (p. 5-9); Introduction (p. 10-13); I. Training (p. 15-37); II. Auditioning (p. 39-64); III. Rehearsing (p. 65-108); IV. Playing (p. 109-149); Suggested Reading (p. 151-153); Index (p. 155-159).

A176. ***Displaced German Scholars: A Guide to Academics in Peril in Nazi Germany During the 1930s***, introduction by Dr. Nathan Kravetz. STUDIES IN JUDAICA AND THE HOLOCAUST, Number 7. ii+126 p. LC 93-2897. OCLC #27430803. ISBN 0-89370-374-5 cloth $24; ISBN 0-89370-474-1 paper $14. Cover: standard series design by Highpoint Type & Graphics, black ink on rose background. First Borgo Edition, December 1993.

b.   Second Printing, with redesigned back cover copy featuring EAN Bookland bar codes, November 1994.

BP 300, by Robert Reginald & Mary Wickizer Burgess

This facsimile reprint of the 1936 edition is a list of mostly Jewish German scholars who at that time were seeking to flee the Reich for positions in the West.

CONTENTS: [New] Preface, by Dr. Nathan Kravetz (p. 1-2); Introduction (p. 3-4); Example of How the Text Should Be Read (p. 6); List of Displaced German Scholars (p. 7-108); Index to Subjects (p. 109); Register of Names (p. 111-125); Note (p. 126).

A177. *A Wayfarer in a World in Upheaval*, by Bernard L. Ginsburg, edited by Dr. Nathan Kravetz and Daryl F. Mallett. STUDIES IN JUDAICA AND THE HOLOCAUST, Number 12. 128 p. LC 93-12024. OCLC #27339468. ISBN 0-8095-0400-6 cloth $24; ISBN 0-8095-1400-1 paper $14. Illustrated with photographs and maps of the author and the region. Cover: standard series design by Highpoint Type & Graphics with photo of author, black ink on yellow background. First Edition, December 1993.

b.   Second Printing, April 1994.

A memoir of Holocaust survivor, Bernard L. Ginsburg.

CONTENTS: Acknowledgments (p. 5-6); Editor's Preface (p. 7); Foreword (p. 9-10); Introduction (p. 11-12); 1. A Thunderous Awakening (p. 13-19); 2. Under Soviet Rule (p. 21-28); 3. Dnepropetrovsk (p. 29-35); 4. Tashkent (p. 37-45); 5. "Druzhba Narodov" (p. 47-51); 6. Split-Second Turn: From Endangered to "Spasitiel" (p. 53-64); 7. Not an Hour Without a Crisis (p. 65-74); 8. Jubilation: The Defeat of Germany (p. 75-83); 9. Kiev (p. 85-92); 10. Berlin! (p. 93-103); 11. Events in the Tragic Drama (p. 105-119); 12. Toward the New World (p. 121-123); Index (p. 125-128).

A178. *Science Fiction and Fantasy Research Index, Volume 10*, by Hal W. Hall. iv+153 p. OCLC #24614822. ISBN 0-8095-6803-9 cloth $30. Photocopied from the original. First Edition, March 1994.

A continuing subject and author index to critical and bibliographical materials in the science fiction and fantasy genres.

A179. *Black Paradise: The Rastafarian Movement, Revised Edition*, by Peter B. Clarke, with a New Bibliography on the Rastafarians by

BP 300, by Robert Reginald & Mary Wickizer Burgess

Bonnie L. Petry. BLACK POLITICAL STUDIES, Number 5. 126 p. LC 93-32884. OCLC #28798194. ISBN 0-8095-8008-X cloth $25; ISBN 0-8095-8005-5 paper $15. Illustrated with photographs. Cover: standard series design by Highpoint Type & Graphics, using photo of the Emperor Haile Selassie, brown ink on yellow background. Revised Edition, March 1994.

b. Second Printing, with redesigned back cover copy featuring EAN Bookland bar codes, August 1994.
c. Third Printing, June 1995. This printing, which was produced for distribution by Quality Books, only features one EAN Bookland bar code on the back cover (for the paper edition).
d. Fourth Printing, July 1995.
e. Fifth Printing, October 1995.
f. Sixth Printing, June 1997.
g. Seventh Printing, November 1997.

This facsimile reprint of the 1986 Aquarian Press (Thorsons Publishers) edition is a popular history of the Rastafarian movement.

CONTENTS: Acknowledgements (p. 10); Introduction: The Rastafarian Movement and New Religions in Britain (p. 11-16); 1. The African Diaspora (p. 17-26); 2. The Back-to-Africa Movement and the Rise of Ethiopianism (p. 27-35); 3. Marcus Garvey: Black Moses and Prophet of God in Ethiopia (p. 36-44); 4. Babylon: The Rise and Development of the Rastafarian Movement in Jamaica and Britain (p. 45-62); 5. Beliefs (p. 63-78); 6. Rastafarian Lifestyle and Rituals (p. 79-94); 7. From Self-Awareness to the Brotherhood of Man (p. 95-100); Notes (p. 101-107); A Bibliography on the Rastafarians (p. 109-121); Index (p. 122-126).

See also the original edition (**A93**).

A180. *Starvation Camp*, by Bill Pronzini. A MYSTERY SCENE READER'S EDITION. 192 p. LC 93-8123. OCLC #28064897. ISBN 0-913960-24-1 cloth $23; ISBN 0-913960-25-X paper $8.95. Cover drawing of a stylized Mountie by Beatty; cover design by Highpoint Type & Graphics; color: brown ink on cream background. First Borgo Edition, March 1994.

BP 300, by Robert Reginald & Mary Wickizer Burgess

This facsimile reprint of the 1984 Doubleday edition of this historical mystery set in the Yukon Territory was published in conjunction with *Mystery Scene* magazine.

CONTENTS: [New] Introduction: The Challenge of the Yukon, by Bill Pronzini (p. iii-vii); Starvation Camp (p. 1-180).

A181. *A Triumph of the Spirit: Ten Stories of Holocaust Survivors*, edited by Jacob Biber, additional editing by Mary A. Burgess and Nathan Kravetz. STUDIES IN JUDAICA AND THE HOLOCAUST, Number 9. 128 p. LC 93-9208. OCLC #27339399. ISBN 0-89370-339-7 cloth $24; ISBN 0-89370-439-3 paper $14. Illustrated with a photograph of "Triumph," a sculpture in wood by Chaim Goldberg (p. 4). Cover: standard series design by Highpoint Type & Graphics with photo of Biber on the back cover, black ink on beige background. First Edition, April 1994.

b. Second Printing, June 1995, featuring EAN Bookland bar code for the paperback edition only. Cover: black ink on white background.

An anthology of ten Holocaust survivors' accounts.

CONTENTS: Foreword (p. 5-6); 1. Introduction, by Jacob Biber (p. 7-22); 2. Itzchok Gochman (p. 23-29); 3. Halina Laster (p. 31-38); 4. Yechiel M. Strohly (p. 39-49); 5. Harry Parzen (p. 51-56); 6. Ruth Joseovitz Rosenblum (p. 57-63); 7. Rose Milder (p. 65-70); 8. Leon Faigenbam (p. 71-82); 9. Abraham Mahler (p. 83-90); 10. Selig Schwitzer (p. 91-96); 11. Eva Cherniak Biber (p. 97-122): Index (p. 123-128).

A182. *The Work of Jack Vance: An Annotated Bibliography & Guide*, by Jerry Hewett & Daryl F. Mallett, edited by Boden Clarke. BIBLIOGRAPHIES OF MODERN AUTHORS, Number 29. A Borgo Press/Underwood-Miller Book. xxii+293 p., 6 x 9". LC 92-28056. OCLC #26309718. ISBN 0-8095-0509-6 library cloth $35; ISBN 0-8095-1509-1 paper $25; ISBN 0-88733-165-3 trade cloth $35; ISBN 0-88733-166-1 signed, slipcased edition $50. Cover: standard series design by Highpoint Type & Graphics, using photo of author, brown ink on tan background. First Edition, May 1994.

BP 300, by Robert Reginald & Mary Wickizer Burgess

A bibliography of and literary guide to the works of modern American writer, Jack Vance (1916-), jointly published with Underwood-Miller.

CONTENTS: Foreword: "Two Years and Two Hundred Hours" (p. ix-x); "Introduction: The World of Jack Vance," by Robert Silverberg (p. xi-xiii); A Jack Vance Chronology (p. xv-xxii); A. Books (p. 1-163); B. Short Fiction (p. 164-209); C. Verse and Poetry (p. 210); D. Nonfiction (p. 211-213); E. Other Media (p. 214-215); F. Interviews (p. 216); G. Maps and Drawings (p. 217-218); H. Phantom Editions and Works (p. 219-220); I. Unpublished Manuscripts (p. 221); J. Honors and Awards (p. 222-223); K. Guest of Honor Appearances (p. 224); L. Interviews with Jack Vance (p. 225-226); M. Secondary Sources (p. 227-247); N. Miscellanea (p. 248-249); "The Genesee Slough Murders: Outline for a Novel," by Jack Vance (p. 250-266); Afterword: "Jack Vance: The Man and the Myth," by Tim Underwood (p. 267-268); Index (p. 269-293).

A183. *Hard-Boiled Heretic: The Lew Archer Novels of Ross Macdonald*, by Mary S. Weinkauf, edited by Mary Wickizer Burgess. BROWNSTONE MYSTERY GUIDES, Volume 12. A Brownstone Book. 128 p. LC 84-282. OCLC #10349868. ISBN 0-89370-172-6 cloth $24; ISBN 0-89370-272-2 paper $14. Cover: standard series design by Highpoint Type & Graphics, black ink on sky blue background. First Edition, July 1994.

A critique of the late American author, Ross Macdonald (Kenneth Millar, 1915-1983).

CONTENTS: About the Author (p. 4); Chronology (p. 5-9); A Critic's View (p. 10); 1. The "Hard-Boiled" Heretic (p. 11-16); 2. A Humanist Priest in a Secular World (p. 17-20); 3. What Makes Lew Tick (p. 21-29); 4. The Calling (p. 31-40); 5. Sleeping with the Enemy (p. 41-44); 6. Tools of the Trade (p. 45-54); 7. Judgment Day (p. 55-61); 8. Through a Mirror Darkly (p. 63-71); 9. The Lonely Streets (p. 73-82); 10. Sermons on the Mount (p. 83-96); 11. The Tie That Binds (p. 97-108); Conclusion: Father Confession (p. 109-115); Notes (p. 116-121); A Ross Macdonald Bibliography (p. 122-123); Selected Secondary Bibliography (p. 124-125); Index (p. 126-128).

A184. *The House of the Burgesses: Being a Genealogical History of William Burgess of Richmond (Later King George) County, Virginia, His Son, Edward Burgess of Stafford (Later King George) County, Virginia, with the Descendants in the Male Line of Edward's Sons: Garner Burgess of Fauquier County, Virginia, William Burgess of Stafford County, Virginia, Edward Burgess, Jr. of Fauquier County, Virginia, Moses Burgess of Orange County, Virginia, Reuben Burgess of Rowan (Later Davie) County, North Carolina, Second Edition, Revised and Expanded*, by Michael Burgess with Mary A. Burgess. BORGO FAMILY HISTORIES, Number 1. A Burgess & Wickizer Book. xx+708 p., 8.5 x 11". LC 87-6316. OCLC #15283912. ISBN 0-89370-379-6 cloth $60; ISBN 0-89370-479-2 paper $50. Illustrated with photographs, maps, and charts. Cover design by Highpoint Type & Graphics, utilizing an 1879 illustration depicting the farm of Greenberry Fields Burgess in Shelby County, Indiana, with an inset photo of the author at age two with his grandfather, Roy P. Burgess; color: beige background with brown ink. Second Edition, July 1994.

A genealogical history of the Burgess family of King George County, Virginia.

CONTENTS: Introduction (p. vii-xvii); A Word of Appreciation (p. xviii); Abbreviations (p. xix); The First Generations (p. 3-14); Garner Burgess—The First Branch (p. 15-66); William Burgess—The Second Branch (p. 69-202); Edward Burgess, Jr.—The Third Branch (p. 203-362); Moses Bur-gess—The Fourth Branch (p. 363-442); Reuben Burgess—The Fifth Branch (p. 443-637); Index (p. 638-708).

This was the largest book published by The Borgo Press to date. See also the First Edition (**A52**).

A185. *W.E.B. Du Bois: His Contributions to Pan-Africanism*, by Kwadwo O. Pobi-Asamani, edited by Daryl F. Mallett. BLACK POLITICAL STUDIES, Number 4. 136 p. LC 93-4385. OCLC #28111942. ISBN 0-89370-351-6 cloth $26; ISBN 0-89370-451-2 paper $16. Cover: standard series design by Highpoint Type & Graphics, using photo of Du Bois, black ink on beige background. First Edition, August 1994.

b. Second Printing, December 1994.

BP 300, by Robert Reginald & Mary Wickizer Burgess

c. Third Printing (Corrected), June 1995. This printing, which was produced for distribution by Quality Books, only features one EAN Bookland bar (for the paperback edition) on its back cover.

d. Fourth Printing (Corrected), July 1998.

An analysis of the contributions to Pan-Africanism of the late African-American writer, W. E. B. Du Bois (1868-1963).

CONTENTS: Acknowledgments (p. 4); Acronyms (p. 4); Foreword, by Henry Ponder (p. 5-6); Introduction, by Sterling Stuckey (p. 7-8); Preface (p. 9); As I Face Africa..., by W. E. B. Du Bois (p. 10); A W. E. B. Du Bois Chronology (p. 11-15); 1. W. E. B. Du Bois: His Contributions to Pan-Africanism (p. 17-28); 2. The Origins and Development of Pan-Africanism (p. 29-39); 3. The First Pan-African Congress (p. 41-44); 4. The Second and Third Pan-African Congresses (p. 45-48); 5. The Fourth Pan-African Congress (p. 49-56); 6. The Fifth Pan-African Congress (p. 57-60); 7. Pan-Africanism, Independence, and Unity (p. 61-68); 8. Pan-Africanism or Socialism (p. 69-74); 9. African Unity: Pan-Africanism Then and Now (p. 75-80); Conclusion (p. 81-83).

Appendix A: Address to the Nations of the World by the Races Congress in London, 1900 (p. 84-85); Appendix B: Memorandum to M. Blaise Diagne and Others on a Pan-African Congress to Be Held in Paris in February, 1919 (p. 86-87); Appendix C: Resolution of the Fifth Pan-African Congress, Manchester, 1945 (p. 88-93); Appendix D: The Charter of the Organization of African Unity (p. 94-99); Appendix E: First Conference of Independent African States (p. 100-107); Appendix F: Organization of African Unity (p. 108-110); Appendix G: The Hottentot Massacres, Bondelschwartz Region, South Africa (p. 111); Appendix H: Resolutions of the Pan-African Congress, Paris, February, 1919 (p. 112-114); Appendix I: An African-American Historical Chronology (p. 115-118); Appendix J: Letters Honoring W. E. B. Du Bois (p. 119-120); Appendix K: Resolution of the National Congress of British West Africa, Accra, March 1920 (p. 121-124); Appendix L: Summary of Arusha Resolution, Jan. 26-29, 1967 (p. 125); Notes (p. 126-128); Bibliography (p. 129-132); Index (p. 133-135); About the Author (p. 136).

A186. *The Egyptian Gods: A Handbook, Revised Edition*, by Alan W. Shorter, with a new bibliography by Bonnie L. Petry. STOKVIS STUDIES IN HISTORICAL CHRONOLOGY AND THOUGHT, Number 12. xii+148 p. LC 94-14146. OCLC #30109222. ISBN 0-89370-557-8 cloth $26; ISBN 0-89370-535-7 paper $16. Illustrated with photographs of monumental representations of the Egyptian gods. Cover: standard series design by Highpoint Type & Graphics with reproduction of an Egyptian stone engraving, black ink on lavender background. Revised (First Borgo) Edition, August 1994.

    b.   Second Printing, April 1995. Background color is lighter on this printing.
    c.   Third Printing, July 1995.

This facsimile reprint of the 1937 Kegan Paul, Trench, Trübner, and Company edition provides a comprehensive survey of Egyptian mythology.
Preface (p. vii-viii); Table of Egyptian History (p. ix-x); Introduction (p. 1-3); 1. The Sun-God—The Creation—The Great Gods—Åmen, God of Thebes (p. 4-18); ; 2. An Egyptian Temple—The Temple of Thebes—The Gods of the Common People (19-36); 3. Osiris—Judgement After Death—Immortality (p. 37-60); 4. The Book of the Dead—The Book of Åm Tuat—The Book of Gates (p. 61-94); 5. The Nature of the Gods—The Gods and Magic—The Monotheism of King Akhenåten (p. 95-123); Descriptive List of the Principal Egyptian Gods (p. 125-143); [New] Bibliography, by Bonnie L. Petry (p. 144-148).

A187. *Roald Dahl: From The Gremlins to The Chocolate Factory, Second Edition, Revised and Expanded*, by Alan Warren, edited by Daryl F. Mallett. THE MILFORD SERIES: POPULAR WRITERS OF TODAY, Volume 57. 128 p. LC 93-12020. OCLC #27339466. ISBN 0-8095-2001-X cloth $24; ISBN 0-8095-3001-5 paper $14. Cover: standard series design by Highpoint Type & Graphics, black ink on cream background. Second Edition, August 1994.

    b.   Second Printing, March 1995.

A critique of the late British writer, Roald Dahl (1916-1990).

BP 300, by Robert Reginald & Mary Wickizer Burgess

CONTENTS: Dedication and About the Author (p. 4); A Roald Dahl Chronology (p. 5-7); Introduction: "I Found About 35 Plots" (p. 9-16); 1. Biography: "Did You Know You Were a Writer?" (p. 17-23); 2. The Short Stories: "What's Horrible Is Basically Funny" (p. 25-63); 3. The Children's Fiction: "A Crock of Gold" (p. 65-81); 4. Novels and Nonfiction Books: *My Uncle Oswald* (p. 83-91); 5. Media Adaptations: *Tales of the Unexpected* (p. 93-95); 6. The Marriage Group (p. 97-104); 7. The Ogre (p. 105-110); 8. Conclusion (p. 111-114); Notes (p. 115); Bibliography of Primary Sources (p. 116-119); Bibliography of Secondary Sources (p. 120-122); Index (p. 123-128).

See also the original Starmont edition (**D1**).

A188. *The Dance of Consciousness: Enlightenment in Modern Literature*, by Douglas A. Mackey. I.O. EVANS STUDIES IN THE PHILOSOPHY AND CRITICISM OF LITERATURE, Number 16. 156 p. LC 94-27641. OCLC #30700737. ISBN 0-89370-305-2 cloth $26; ISBN 0-89370-405-9 paper $16. Cover: standard series design by Highpoint Type & Graphics, black ink on light blue background. First Edition, August 1994.

A treatise on Maharishi Mahesh Yogi's "seven states of consciousness" as evidenced in specific examples of modern literature.

CONTENTS: Preface (p. 5-6); I. Invitation to the Dance (p. 7-14); II. Absurdity: Beckett, Pirandello, Strindberg (p. 15-36); III. Transcendence: Bergman, Jung, Pynchon (p. 37-61); IV. Enlightenment: Jiménez, Scriabin, Lawrence (p. 62-84); V. Celebration: Crane, Rilke (p. 85-108); VI. Unity: Pirsig, Joyce, Powys (p. 109-135); VII. The Enlightened Artist (p. 136-139); Notes (p. 140-146); Bibliography (p. 147-150); Index (p. 151-156); About the Author (p. 157).

A189. *An Irony of Fate: The Fiction of William March*, by Abigail Ann Martin, edited by Mary A. Burgess. THE MILFORD SERIES: POPULAR WRITERS OF TODAY, Volume 53. 136 p. LC 93-6559. OCLC #27380806. ISBN 0-83970-182-3 cloth $26; ISBN 0-89370-282-X paper $16. Cover: standard series design by Highpoint Type & Graphics, black ink on cream background. First Edition, August 1994.

BP 300, by Robert Reginald & Mary Wickizer Burgess

A critique of the late American writer, William March (1893-1954).

CONTENTS: Foreword (p. 4); Chronology (p. 5-6); 1. A Brief Biography (p. 7-14); 2. The War Fiction: *Company K* (p. 15-28); 3. The Pearl County Novels and Stories (p. 29-31), The Inevitability of Fate: *Come in at the Door* (p. 32-41), More About Fate: *The Tallons* (p. 42-53), A Plot of Suffering: *The Looking Glass* (p. 54-61), Short Stories of Pearl County (p. 62-64); 4. Religion as a Factor (p. 65-69), Slaying the Sacred Cow: *October Island* (p. 70-75); 5. The Abnormal as a Factor (p. 77-79), Something Too Dreadful to Endure: *The Bad Seed* (p. 80-87), Maxwell Anderson's Play (p. 88-91); 6. *99 Fables* (p. 93-98); 7. March in His Work (p. 99-113); Primary Bibliography (p. 115); Secondary Bibliography (p. 116); Notes (p. 117-129); Index (p. 130-136).

A190. *Rex Stout: A Biography*, by John J. McAleer. BROWNSTONE MYSTERY GUIDES, Volume 6. A Brownstone Book. x+622 p. LC 93-335. OCLC #27429945. ISBN 0-941028-09-7 cloth $56; ISBN 0-941028-10-0 paper $46. Illustrated with photographs of the author's life. Cover: standard series design by Highpoint Type & Graphics, black ink on gray background. First Brownstone Edition, September 1994.

b. Second Printing, August 1996.

This facsimile reprint of the 1977 Little, Brown edition is the standard biography of the late American writer, Rex Stout (1886-1975).

CONTENTS: Foreword, by P. G. Wodehouse (p. ix-x); Family Chart (p. 2); Introduction (p. 3-13); In the Beginning (p. 14-15).

Book I: Heritage. 1. Rootstock and Genes—The Stouts (p. 19-24); 2. Rootstock and Genes—The Todhunters (p. 25-31).

Book II: A Prairie Boyhood. 3. Cabbages and Kings (p. 35-41); 4. John and Lucetta (p. 42-46); 5. Stout Traits—Todhuntery Ways (p. 47-53); 6. Everything Alive (p. 54-62); 7. Hackberry Hall (p. 63-69); 8. Mr. Brilliance (p. 70-80); 9. Know-It-All in Knee Pants (p. 81-87); 10. Dramatic Interlude (p. 88-93).

Book III: The Nomadic Years. 11. The *Mayflower* Years (p. 97-109); 12. Logic and Life (p. 110-113); 13. A Brownstone in

BP 300, by Robert Reginald & Mary Wickizer Burgess

New York (p. 114-118); 14. Literary Apprenticeship (p. 119-130); 15. Underground Novelist (p. 131-138); 16. The Heart Has Reasons (p. 139-143); 17. Crime Fiction (p. 144-155).

Book IV: A Liberal Awakening. 18. Melons and Millions (p. 159-166); 19. Pied Piper of Thrist (p. 167-184); 20. Civil Libertarian (p. 185-195); 21. His Own Man (p. 196-203); 22. Expatriate Novelist (p. 204-216).

Book V: The Years of Choice. 23. Squire of High Meadows (p. 219-226); 24. A Literary Farmer (p. 227-233); 25. Stout Fellow (p. 234-241); 26. Lazy Bloodhound (p. 242-253); 27. Mystery Monger (p. 254-261); 28. Commander Over the Earth (p. 262-271).

Book VI: Minister of Propaganda. 29. King's Gambit (p. 275-284); 30. Nero Wolfe Gets Smaller (p. 285-292); 31. Crusader by Inner Compulsion (p. 293-302); 32. The Lie Detective (p. 303-310); 33. Chairman Rex (p. 311-320); 34. Hunting with the Hounds (p. 321-328); 35. Ideological Racketeer (p. 329-336); 36. A Man of Sovereign Parts (p. 337-349).

Book VI: Citizen of the World. 37. Under Viking Sail (p. 353-369); 38. A Superman Who Talks Like a Superman (p. 370-378); 39. Beyond High Meadow (p. 379-384); 40. King Rex (p. 385-392); 41. Watch Out for Rex Stout (p. 393-408); 42. The King in Action (p. 409-414); 43. More Than a Duke (p. 415-420); 44. Master of Mystery (p. 421-431); 45. The Best We Have (p. 432-437); 46. A Majesty's Life (p. 438-449).

Book VIII: A King's Ransom. 47. A Fish at Wolfe's Door (p. 453-464); 48. Champion of Justice (p. 465-478); 49. The One and True Paradigm (p. 479-485); 50. A Man Who Gloriously Acts and Decides (p. 486-500); 51. Nero Equals Archie (p. 501-508); 52. Sage of High Meadow (p. 509-517); 53. Hip Hooroy, You Bearded Boy (p. 518-532).

Notes (p. 535-578); A Rex Stout Checklist (p. 581-591); Acknowledgments (p. 595-599); Index (p. 601-621); About the Author (p. 622).

A191. *The Little Kitchen Cookbook, Second Edition, Revised and Expanded*, by Scottie Kimberlin, ed. by Mary Wickizer Burgess. A Burgess & Wickizer Book. 167 p. LC 94-16908. OCLC #30360986. ISBN 1-877880-08-6 cloth $26; ISBN 1-877880-09-4 paper $16. Illustrated with photographs of the Little Kitchen and Scottie Kimberlin. Cover design by Highpoint Type &

BP 300, by Robert Reginald & Mary Wickizer Burgess

Graphics (same design as first edition); color: white background with gray, red, and black overprinting; backcover photo of Little Kitchen has been replaced with EAN Bookland bar codes. Second Edition, September 1994.

A cookbook based around the popular San Bernardino restaurant, The Little Kitchen.
CONTENTS: Introduction to the Second Edition, by Mary Wickizer Burgess (p. 9); About The Little Kitchen, by Jan Roddick (p. 10-11); Introduction (p. 12); Soups (p. 13-24); Salads (p. 25-48); Dressings for Green Salads (p. 49-50); Miscellaneous Relishes and Side Dishes (p. 51-58); Vegetables (p. 59-71); Main Dishes (p. 72-105); Breads (p. 106-115); Cookies (p. 116-127); Puddings (p. 128-129); Desserts (p. 130-136); Cakes (p. 137-149); Frostings and Icings and Fudge! (p. 150-151); Pies and Pie Crust (p. 152-164); Index (p. 165-167).
See also the First Edition (**A131**).

A192. *British Science Fiction Paperbacks and Magazines, 1949-1956: An Annotated Bibliography and Guide*, by Philip Harbottle and Stephen Holland, edited by Daryl F. Mallett and Michael Burgess. BORGO LITERARY GUIDES, Number 7. 232 p. LC 87-752. OCLC #15163899. ISBN 0-89370-821-6 cloth $30; ISBN 0-89370-921-2 paper $20. Cover: standard series design by Highpoint Type & Graphics, black ink on lime green background. First Edition, September 1994.

An annotated guide to the pulp SF paperbacks published by fly-by-night houses in Great Britain in the post-World War II period.
CONTENTS: Dedication (p. 4); Acknowledgments (p. 5); How to Use This Book (p. 6); Introduction (p. 7-8); A. Original Science Fiction Paperbacks, 1946-1956 (p. 9-129); B. Paperback Books from Established Houses, 1949-1956 (p. 130-147); C. A Checklist of British Science Fiction Magazines, 1949-1956 (p. 148-155); D. A Complete Author Index to the Stories in the British Science Fiction Magazines, 1949-1956 (p. 156-216); Book Title Index (p. 217-221); Short Story Title Index (p. 222-231); About the Authors (p. 232).
See also the Revised Edition (**A231**).

A193. *The Work of Elizabeth Chater: An Annotated Bibliography & Guide*, by Daryl F. Mallett and Annette Y. Mallett, edited by Boden Clarke. BIBLIOGRAPHIES OF MODERN AUTHORS, Number 27. 80 p. LC 93-333. OCLC #27429937. ISBN 0-89370-390-7 cloth $20; ISBN 0-89370-490-3 paper $10. Cover: standard series design by Highpoint Type & Graphics, using photo of author, black ink on lavender background. First Edition, September 1994.

   b.   Second Printing (Corrected), April 1995.

A bibliography of and literary guide to the works of American romance writer, Elizabeth Chater (1910-2004).

CONTENTS: Dedication (p. 4); Acknowledgments (p. 5); Foreword: "Milady Elizabeth" (p. 7-9); Introduction: "Bette," by Greg Bear (p. 11-14); An Elizabeth Chater Chronology (p. 15-17); About the Format (p. 18); A. Books (p. 19-33); B. Short Fiction (p. 35-37); C. Poetry (p. 39); D. Nonfiction (p. 41-42); E. Secondary Sources (p. 43-44); F. Honors and Awards (p. 45); G. Miscellanea (p. 47).

Five Works by Elizabeth Chater: "Just Another Wooden House..." (p. 51-52); "The Week the Traveling Salesman Came to Town" (p. 53-58); "Optomendacity" (p. 59-66); Epilogue: "You Want to Talk About Endings...?" (p. 67-70); "All the World's a Screen..." (p. 71); Index (p. 73-79); About the Authors (p. 80).

A194. *Amphitheatres and Circuses: A History from Their Earliest Date to 1861, with Sketches of Some of the Principal Performers*, by Col. T. Allston Brown, edited by William L. Slout. CLIPPER STUDIES IN THE THEATRE, Number 9. An Emeritus Enterprise Book. xiv+87 p. LC 94-22302. OCLC #30701142. ISBN 0-913960-32-2 cloth $24; ISBN 0-913960-33-0 paper $14. Illustrated with reproductions of contemporary woodcuts. Cover design by Highpoint Type & Graphics, black ink on green background. First Edition, September 1994.

The first book publication of a circus history first serialized in the *New York Clipper* in 1860-61.

CONTENTS: Introduction, by William L. Slout (p. ix-xiv); I. Roman Games and Amphitheatres (p. 3-9); II. James Hall, Rope Dancer (p. 9-15); III. Ambroise & Co. (p. 15-23); IV. Sandford

Erects Mount Pitt Circus (p. 23-30); V. Ricketts in Boston (p. 30-38); VI. Robinson & Eldred (p. 39-44); VII. About Rufus Welch (p. 44-50); VIII. Circuses in Albany (p. 50-60); IX. Astley's Amphitheatre (p. 60-70); X. John May (p. 70-76); Index (p. 79-87).

A195. *Christopher Hampton: An Introduction to His Plays*, by William J. Free, edited by Dale Salwak. THE MILFORD SERIES: POPULAR WRITERS OF TODAY, Volume 49. 136 p. LC 93-345. OCLC #27430002. ISBN 0-8095-5206-X cloth $26; ISBN 0-8095-5231-0 paper $16. Cover: standard series design by Highpoint Type & Graphics, with inset photo of Hampton, black ink on light blue background. First Edition, September 1994.

A critique of the works of the modern British playwright, Christopher Hampton (1929-).
    CONTENTS: Acknowledgments (p. 5); A Christopher Hampton Chronology (p. 7-9); 1. Christopher Hampton: An Introduction (p. 11-17); 2. *When Did You Last See My Mother?* (p. 19-30); 3. *Total Eclipse* (p. 31-41); 4. *The Philanthropist* (p. 43-60); 5. *Savages* (p. 61-76); 6. *Treats* (p. 77-86); 7. *Tales from Hollywood* (p. 87-102); 8. *Les Liaisons Dangereuses* (p. 103-119); 9. Conclusion (p. 121-125); Notes (p. 127-128); Bibliography (p. 129-130); Index (p. 131-134); Character Index (p. 135); About William J. Free (p. 136).

A196. *The Work of William Eastlake: An Annotated Bibliography & Guide*, by W. C. Bamberger, edited by Boden Clarke and Daryl F. Mallett. BIBLIOGRAPHIES OF MODERN AUTHORS, Number 21. 104 p. LC 93-340. OCLC #27429977. ISBN 0-89370-398-2 cloth $24; ISBN 0-89370-498-9 paper $14. Cover: standard series design by Highpoint Type & Graphics, photo of author by Larry Ketchum, black ink on tan background. First Edition, September 1994.

b.   Second Printing, February 1995.

A bibliography of and literary guide to the works of American writer, William Eastlake (1917-1997).
    CONTENTS: Foreword (p. 5-8); Introduction, by Ron Querry (p. 9-11); About the Format (p. 12); A William Eastlake

BP 300, by Robert Reginald & Mary Wickizer Burgess

Chronology (p. 13-15); A. Books (p. 17-31); B. Short Fiction (p. 32-44); C. Short Nonfiction (p. 45-53); D. Poetry (p. 54); E. Other Media (p. 55); F. Unpublished Works (p. 56-57); G. Honors and Awards (p. 58); H. Interviews with the Author (p. 59); I. Secondary Sources (p. 60-69); J. Miscellanea (p. 70); Quoth the Critics (p. 71-72); "Ishimoto's Land: An Excerpt," by William Eastlake (p. 73-81); "The Failure of Western Writing," by William Eastlake (p. 83-90); Index (p. 91-103); About W. C. Bamberger (p. 104).

A197. *Speaking of Horror: Interviews with Writers of the Supernatural*, by Darrell Schweitzer, edited by Daryl F. Mallett. THE MILFORD SERIES: POPULAR WRITERS OF TODAY, Volume 48. 136 p., illustrated. LC 84-357. OCLC #10404287. ISBN 0-89370-177-7 cloth $26; ISBN 0-89370-277-3 paper $16. Illustrated with photographs of the interviewees. Cover: standard series design by Highpoint Type & Graphics, black ink on cream background. First Edition, September 1994.

b.   Second Printing, December 1994.
c.   Third Printing, April 1995.

A collection of previously-published interviews with eleven modern American and British writers of horror fiction.
CONTENTS: Introduction (p. 5); List of Illustrations (p. 6); 1. Robert Bloch (p. 9-22); 2. Ramsey Campbell (p. 23-36); 3. Dennis Etchison (p. 37-46); 4. Charles L. Grant (p. 47-57); 5. Tanith Lee (p. 59-66); 6. Thomas Ligotti (p. 67-74); 7. Brian Lumley (p. 75-79); 8. William F. Nolan (p. 81-92); 9. Manly Wade Wellman (p. 93-101); 10. Chet Williamson (p. 103-112); 11. F. Paul Wilson (p. 113-125); Index (p. 127-135); About Darrell Schweitzer (p. 136).

A198. *George Orwell's Guide Through Hell: A Psychological Study of 1984, Revised Edition*, by Robert Plank, edited by Robert Reginald. THE MILFORD SERIES: POPULAR WRITERS OF TODAY, Volume 41. 136 p. LC 94-30950. OCLC #30972341. ISBN 0-89370-313-3 cloth $26; ISBN 0-89370-413-X paper $16. Cover: standard series design by Highpoint Type & Graphics, black ink on lemon background. Revised Edition, September 1994.

BP 300, by Robert Reginald & Mary Wickizer Burgess

b.   Second Printing, March 1995.

A critique of the late British writer, George Orwell (1903-1950), and his seminal work, *Nineteen Eighty-Four*.
    CONTENTS: Dedication (p. 4); Chronology (p. 5-6); Introduction (p. 7-10); I. Preparing to Descend into Hell (p. 11-15); II. Who Is Winston Smith? (p. 17-21); III. The Ghostly Bells of London (p. 23-31); IV. The Chestnut Tree Cafe (p. 33-39); V. The World in a Globe of Glass (p. 41-55); VI. The Inquisitor (p. 57-71); VII. Trust and Betrayal (p. 73-81); VIII. The Sanctity of the Word (p. 83-97); IX. Julia and the Rats (p. 99-105); X. Power and Paranoia (p. 107-119); The End of the Voyage Through Hell (p. 121-125); Notes (p. 126-131); Bibliography (p. 132-133); Index (p. 134-136).
    See also the First Edition (**A77**).

A199. ***Broadway Below the Sidewalk: Concert Saloons of Old New York***, edited by William L. Slout. CLIPPER STUDIES IN THE THEATRE, Number 4. xvi+115 p. LC 94-26402. OCLC #30738786. ISBN 0-8095-0301-8 cloth $26; ISBN 0-8095-1301-3 paper $16. Cover: standard series design by Judy Cloyd Graphic Design as adapted by Highpoint Type & Graphics, black ink on pink background. First Edition, October 1994.

A series of nineteenth-century articles on concert saloons reprinted from the pages of the *New York Clipper*.
    CONTENTS: Preface, by William L. Slout (p. vii-xv).
    Part One: Broadway Below the Sidewalk. Frank Burns' "Oriental" (p. 3-7); Kate Stanton's "Champion Music Hall (p. 8-12); St. Nicholas "Casino" (p. 12-20); George Heydon's "Melodeon" (p. 20-24); The "Bon Ton" (p. 24-27); Ballard's "What Is It" (p. 27-31); William E. Allen's "Occidental" (p. 32-37); Shafer's "Eureka" (p. 37-42); Collins & Williamson's "Opera Saloon" (p. 42-49); Lee and Hatstatt's "Eureka" (p. 49-52); Prescott Hall (p. 53-56); The "Reveille" (p. 56-61); The "Boulevard" (p. 61-65); The "New Oriental" (p. 65-70); Notes (p. 70-74).
    Part Two: The Rest of the Story. Recollections of Hours Passed in the "Shades" (p. 77-80); Canterbury Hall (p. 81-84); Concert Saloons, by Edward Winslow Martin [McCabe] (p. 85-89); Variety Dives and Concert Saloons, by John J. Jennings (p.

89-99); Harry Hill's Dance House, by Matthew Hale Smith [Burleigh] (p. 99-104); John Allen's Dance House, by Matthew Hale Smith [Burleigh] (p. 104-107); Notes (p. 107-110); Index (p. 111-115).

A200. *The Work of William F. Temple: An Annotated Bibliography & Guide*, by Mike Ashley, edited by Boden Clarke. BIBLIOGRAPHIES OF MODERN AUTHORS, Number 28. 112 p. LC 93-334. OCLC #27642974. ISBN 0-8095-0507-X cloth $24; ISBN 0-8095-1507-5 paper $14. Cover: standard series design by Highpoint Type & Graphics, photo of author by Joan Temple, black ink on tan background. First Edition, October 1994.

b. Second Printing, February 1995.

A bibliography of and literary guide to the works of the late British writer, William F. Temple (1914-1989).
CONTENTS: Preface (p. 5); About Mike Ashley (p. 6); "Reminiscences," by Arthur C. Clarke (p. 7-8); William F. Temple: A Short Biography (p. 9-19); A William F. Temple Chronology (p. 21-24); William F. Temple: An Introduction to His Works (p. 25-29); About the Format (p. 30); A. Books (p. 31-38); B. Short Fiction (p. 39-60); C. Short Nonfiction (p. 61-64); D. Editorial Credits (p. 65); E. Fan Writings (p. 66-70); F. Unpublished Works (p. 71-76); G. Other Media (p. 77-78); H. Honors and Awards (p. 79); I. Public Appearances (p. 80); J. Secondary Sources (p. 81-85); K. Miscellanea (p. 86); Quoth the Critics (p. 87-92); "I Loved You, Bill: An Afterword," by Forrest J Ackerman (p. 93-94).
Appendices: Selected Early Writings of William F. Temple. "The Hunting of the Flat" (p. 96-98); "Chingford Chiar-oscuro (A Layman's First Experimental Meeting" (p. 99-101); "The British Fan, No. 7: William F. Temple," by Arthur C. Clarke (p. 102-103); "The Final Word," by Joan Temple (p. 104); Index (p. 105-112).

A201. *Firefly: A Novel of the Far Future*, by Brian Stableford. CLASSICS OF FANTASTIC LITERATURE, Number 1. A Unicorn & Son Book. 136 p. LC 93-339. OCLC #27429968. ISBN 0-89370-376-1 cloth $26; ISBN 0-89370-476-8 paper $16. Cover:

BP 300, by Robert Reginald & Mary Wickizer Burgess

standard series design by Highpoint Type & Graphics, black and red ink on yellow background. First Edition, October 1994.

An early, previously unpublished science fiction novel by British writer, Brian Stableford. In the far future of Earth, the planet is dying. The cities have decayed, time is running down. Society has reverted to a more primitive way of life, much like that of the Middle Ages. Two men, Matthew and his brother John, the man who calls himself "Firefly," set out on a quest to find the time traveller, the one person who can give purpose to their existence, the one individual who can access past technology.

A202. *Eastern Europe: A Resource Guide: A Selected Bibliography on Social Studies and Humanities*, by Suzanne D. Gyeszly. BORGO REFERENCE GUIDES, Number 6. vi+242 p. LC 93-3166. OCLC #27679075. ISBN 0-8095-0702-1 cloth $30; ISBN 0-8095-1702-7 paper $20. Cover: standard series design by Highpoint Type & Graphics, black ink on sage background. First Edition, October 1994.

A comprehensive guide to the monographs and journals published in and about the social sciences and the humanities on the countries of Poland, Hungary, and Czechoslovakia.
  CONTENTS: Introduction (p. v); Acknowledgments (p. vi).
  Part One: The Region as a Whole. General Works (p. 1-5); Arts (p. 6); Economics and Foreign Trade (p. 7-9); Geography (p. 10); Government, Law, and Politics (p. 11-12); History (p. 13-14); Literature (p. 15); Sociology (p. 16-17).
  Part Two: Czech Republic and Slovakia (formerly Czechoslovakia). General Works (p. 18-21); Arts (p. 22); Economics and Foreign Trade (p. 23-28); Geography (p. 29); Government, Law, and Politics (p. 30-33); History (p. 34-41); Languages and Linguistics (p. 42-44); Literature (p. 45-52); Sociology (p. 53-55); Newspapers and Periodicals (p. 56-57).
  Part Three: Hungary. General Works (p. 58-66); Arts (p. 67-73); Economics and Foreign Trade (p. 74-80); Geography (p. 81-82); Government, Law, and Politics (p. 83-86); History (p. 87-109); Languages and Linguistics (p. 110-112); Literature (p. 113-128); Sociology (p. 129-131); Newspapers and Periodicals (p. 132-133).

BP 300, by Robert Reginald & Mary Wickizer Burgess

A203. *Christopher Isherwood: A World in Evening*, by Kay Ferres, edited by Dale Salwak. THE MILFORD SERIES: POPULAR WRITERS OF TODAY, Volume 43. 152 p. LC 93-343. OCLC #27429989. ISBN 0-8095-5202-7 cloth $26; ISBN 0-8095-5227-2 paper $16. Cover: standard series design by Highpoint Type & Graphics, black ink on gray background. First Edition, November 1994.

A critique on the late British and American writer, Christopher Isherwood (1904-1986).

CONTENTS: About Kay Ferres (p. 4); A Christopher Isherwood Chronology (p. 5-10); 1. Autobiography and Fiction (p. 11-21); 2. My Generation—Right or Wrong (p. 23-42); 3. Many a Civil Monster: Politics and the Narrator in the Berlin Fiction (p. 43-63); 4. Exile and Attachment: *Prater Violet* and *The World in the Evening* (p. 65-85); 5. The Coriolanus Myth: *Down There on a Visit* (p. 87-101); 6. Out in the Open: *A Single Man* and *A Meeting by the River* (p. 103-124); 7. Coda: On His Queerness (p. 125-129); Notes (p. 131-137); Primary Bibliography (p. 138); Secondary Bibliography (p. 139-147); Index (p. 149-152).

A204. *"We, the People!": Bay Area Activism in the 1960s: Three Case Studies*, by Richard DeLuca. GREAT ISSUES OF THE DAY, Number 7. 144 p. LC 93-16623. OCLC #27684153. ISBN 0-89370-154-8 cloth $26; ISBN 0-89370-254-4 paper $16. Illustrated with maps and photographs. Cover: standard series design by Highpoint Type & Graphics, using photograph by Vincent Maggiore of occupation of Alcatraz Island by the Indians, red and blue ink on white background. First Edition, November 1994.

The history of three separate confrontations which occurred in the San Francisco Bay Area during the 1960s: the "Black Friday" demonstration in May of 1960 by students against the House of Representatives Committee on Un-American Activities; San Francisco's freeway revolt; and the Indian occupation of Alcatraz Island in November of 1969.

CONTENTS: Acknowledgments (p. 4); Foreword (p. 5); 1. "We Shall Not Be Moved": San Francico's Black Friday and the Origins of the Berkeley Free Speech Movement (p. 7-45); 2. "Save Us from the Freeway!": San Francisco's Freeway Revolt and the Rise of Environmentalism in the Bay Area After World War II (p. 49-92); 3. "We Hold the Rock!": The Indian Attempt to Reclaim Alcatraz Island (p. 95-113); 4. "We, the People!": The Significance of Social Activism in the 1960s (p. 115-121); Notes (p. 122-139); Index (p. 140-143); About the Author (p. 144).

A205. *Science Fiction and Fantasy Book Review Index, Volume 21, 1990*, by Hal W. Hall. 105 p. ISBN 0-8095-6805-5 cloth $25. Photocopied from the original. First Edition, November 1994.

A continuing index to book reviews of science fiction, fantasy, and horror fiction and nonfiction.

A206. *Sermons in Science Fiction: The Novels of S. Fowler Wright*, by Mary S. Weinkauf, edited by Michael Burgess. THE MILFORD SERIES: POPULAR WRITERS OF TODAY, Volume 51. LC 94-36012. OCLC #31206681. 128 p. ISBN 0-89370-180-7 cloth $24; ISBN 0-89370-280-3 paper $14. Cover: standard series design by Highpoint Type & Graphics, black ink on red-orange background. First Edition, December 1994.

b. Second Printing, March 1995.

A critical guide to the writings of the late British writer, S. Fowler Wright (1874-1965).

CONTENTS: Acknowledgments (p. 4); An S. Fowler Wright Chronology (p. 5-8); 1. Who Is S. Fowler Wright? (p. 9-14); 2. The Short Stories (p. 15-26); 3. The Mysteries (p. 27-38); 4. Past and Future Warfare (p. 39-53); 5. The Survivors (p. 55-80); 6. Disaster: *Deluge* and *Dawn* (p. 81-94); 7. Societies Far and Near (p. 95-113); 8. Conclusion (p. 115-117); Notes (p. 118-121); Primary Bibliography (p. 122); Secondary Bibliography (p. 123-124); Index (p. 125-128).

A207. *Algebraic Fantasies and Realistic Romances: More Masters of Science Fiction*, by Brian Stableford. THE MILFORD SERIES: POPULAR WRITERS OF TODAY, Volume 54. 128 p. LC 94-31347. OCLC #31044966. ISBN 0-89370-183-1 cloth $25; ISBN 0-89370-283-8 paper $15. Cover: standard series design by Highpoint Type & Graphics, black ink on tan background. First Edition, February 1995.

   b.   Second Printing, October 1995.

A collection of previously published literary essays by British critic and novelist, Brian Stableford (1948-).
   CONTENTS: About Brian Stableford (p. 4); Introduction (p. 5); 1. The Future Between the Wars: The Speculative Fiction of John Gloag (p. 7-24); 2. Algebraic Fantasies: The Science Fiction of Bob Shaw (p. 25-44); 3. Realistic Romances: The Fantastic Fiction of Edgar Fawcett (p. 45-72); 4. The Politics of Evolution: Philosophical Themes in the Speculative Fiction of M. P. Shiel (p. 73-98); 5. Galactic Hitch-Hiker: The Sudden Rise of Douglas Adams (p. 99-104); 6. The Chronicles of Stephen R. Donaldson: The Fantasist (p. 105-111); 7. Animal Spirits: The Erotic and the Supernatural in Michael Jackson's "Thriller" Video (p. 113-119); Notes (p. 120-121); Bibliography (p. 122-123); Index (p. 124-128).

A208. *The Jewish Holocaust: An Annotated Guide to Books in English, Second Edition, Revised and Expanded*, by Marty Bloomberg and Buckley Barry Barrett. STUDIES IN JUDAICA AND THE HOLOCAUST, Number 1. 312 p. LC 94-29741. OCLC #30913248. ISBN 0-8095-0406-5 cloth $37; ISBN 0-8095-1406-0 paper $27. Cover: standard series design by Highpoint Type & Graphics, adapting a manuscript page from Yitzhak Katzenelson's *The Song of the Murdered Jewish People*, black ink on gray background. Second Edition, February 1995.

   b.   Second Printing, January 1996.

An annotated bibliography of books in English relating to the Holocaust.

BP 300, by Robert Reginald & Mary Wickizer Burgess

CONTENTS: Dedication (p. 6); Foreword: Lest We Forget, by Dr. Jeffrey M. Elliot (p. 7-9); Introduction to the Second Edition (p. 11); Abbreviations (p. 12); A. Reference Materials (p. 13-21); B. European Anti-Semitism (p. 23-30); C. Background Materials (p. 31-65); D. The Holocaust Years (p. 67-165); E. Jewish Resistance (p. 167-177); F. Concentration Camps and Death Camps (p. 179-198); G. Special Studies (p. 199-216); H. War Crimes Trials (p. 217-226); I. The Meaning and the Impact of the Holocaust (p. 227-240); J. Art and Literature (p. 241-281); About the Authors (p. 282); Core Title Recommendations (p. 283-290); Index (p. 291-312).
See also the First Edition (**A128**).

A209. *Monumental Inscriptions: Tombstones of the Island of Barbados*, by Vere Langford Oliver, introduction by Michael Burgess. STOKVIS STUDIES IN HISTORICAL CHRONOLOGY AND THOUGHT, Number 13. A Sidewinder Book. viii+224 p. LC 94-36625. OCLC #31207184. ISBN 0-89370-811-9 cloth $33; ISBN 0-89370-911-5 paper $23. Cover: standard series design by Highpoint Type & Graphics, black ink on red background. New Borgo Edition, February 1995.

This facsimile reprint of the 1915 Mitchell Hughes and Clarke edition is a compilation of headstone readings from the British colony of Barbados copied in 1913-14 by the author. This version is retitled to correspond with *More Monumental Inscriptions*, and includes new coverwork to match its companion volume.
CONTENTS: Preface (p. v-vii); [New] Introduction: A Monumental Work, by Michael Burgess (p. viii); Monumental Inscriptions in Barbados (p. 1-208); Index Nominum (p. 209-223); Abbreviations (p. [224]).
See also the previous Borgo edition (**A98**).

A210. *Popular Amusements in Horse & Buggy America: An Anthology of Contemporaneous Essays*, edited by William L. Slout. CLIPPER STUDIES IN THE THEATRE, Number 2. 208 p., illustrated. LC 84-12310. OCLC #10913762. ISBN 0-89370-361-3 cloth $30; ISBN 0-89370-461-X paper $20. Illustrated with contemporaneous photographs and drawings. Cover: standard series design by Judy Cloyd Graphic Design as adapted by

BP 300, by Robert Reginald & Mary Wickizer Burgess

Highpoint Type & Graphics, black ink on lavender background. First Edition, February 1995.

b.   Second Printing, October 1995.

An anthology of twenty-nine vivid contemporaneous essays on popular amusements taken from nineteenth-century newspapers and popular periodicals.

CONTENTS: Preface, by William L. Slout (p. 5); Dedication (p. 6).

Part One: Thoughts About Amusements. 1. First Impressions of America (p. 10-15); 2. Amusements for the Poor (p. 16-20); 3. Americans at Play, by Edward Eggleston (p. 21-23); 4. Christianity and Popular Amusements, by Washington Gladden (p. 24-31).

Part Two: Summer Resorts and Watering Places. 5. Domestic Tourism (p. 34-38); 6. Watering-Place Worries (p. 39-48); 7. Life at Long Branch, by Olive Logan (p. 49-60); 8. The New Narragansett Pier, by Brander Matthews (p. 61-66).

Part Three: The Agricultural Fair. 9. Cattle-Fair Day in New England (p. 68-75); 10. The Alabama State Fair (p. 76-77); 11. The County Fair, by Nelson Lloyd (p. 78-88); 12. The Spectator (*at the Fair*) (p. 89-91).

Part Four: World's Expositions. 13. The Great Exhibition and Its Visitors (p. 94-98); 14. A Sennight of the Centennial, by W. D. Howells (p. 99-105); 15. In and Out of the New Orleans Exposition, by Eugene V. Smalley (p. 106-111); 16. At the Fair, by M. G. Van Rensselaer (p. 112-116).

Part Five: Amusement Parks. 17. Niblo's Seen by a Child (p. 118-122); 18. Sunday in Jones's Wood (p. 123-125); 19. The Trolley-Park, by Day Allen Willey (p. 126-128); 20. New York's New Summer Playground, by Theodore Waters (p. 129-132); 21. The Amusement Park, by Rollin Lynde Hartt (p. 133-143).

Part Six: The Traveling Circus. 22. Circus (p. 146-154); 23. Living in the Country (p. 155-156); 24. Circus Day, by Eugene Wood (p. 157-170); 25. On the Road with the "Big Show," by Charles Theodore Murray (p. 171-176).

Part Seven: Vaudeville. 26. Sketches of the People Who Oppose Our Sunday Laws (p. 178-184); 27. The Roof-Gardens of New York, by Vance Thompson (p. 185-190); 28. The Vaudeville

Theatre, by Edwin Milton Royle (p. 191-196); 29. The Life of a Vaudeville Artiste, by Norman Hapgood (p. 197-200).
Index (p. 201-206); About William L. Slout (p. 208).

A211. *Ink from a Circus Press Agent: An Anthology of Circus History from the Pen of Charles H. Day*, by Charles H. Day, edited and with a Circus Personnel Reference Roster by William L. Slout. CLIPPER STUDIES IN THE THEATRE, Number 5. xxi+201 p. LC 94-28522. OCLC #30701140. ISBN 0-8095-0302-6 cloth $31; ISBN 0-8095-1302-1 paper $21. Illustrated with reproductions of contemporaneous drawings and woodcuts. Cover: standard series design by Judy Cloyd Graphic Design as adapted by Highpoint Type & Graphics, black ink on orange background. First Edition, February 1995.

b.   Second Printing, October 1995. The background color stock used on the cover of this printing is lighter than on the first edition.

The first book publication of a collection of newspaper articles by nineteenth-century circus historian, Charles H. Day (1842-1907).
CONTENTS: Acknowledgments (p. vi); Introduction, by William L. Slout (p. vii-xv); The Day Chronology (p. xvii-xxi).
Part One: Ballyhoo: The Charles H. Day Anthology. The Press Agent's Antiquity (p. 3-4); The Press Agents of Way Back (p. 5-8); The Intelligence of the Old-Time Circus Manager (p. 9-12); Prominent Circus Managers (p. 13-16); Taking One's Own Medicine (p. 17-19); With Tights and Spangles (p. 20-23); Happy Days at the St. Charles (p. 24-31); On the Road (p. 32-34); Considering and Concerning the Children (p. 35-40); Shop Talk (p. 41-44); Recollections and Reflections of a Retired Gymnast (p. 45-49); Barnum on the Tented Field (p. 50-52); Charles Stow, Circus Writer (p. 53-55); The Invented Advertisement (p. 56-60); Making Much of Music (p. 61-65); The Elephant as an Advertisement (p. 66-69); The Eventful Career of Levi J. North (p. 70-85); Circus Managers (p. 86-91); Notes for Part One (p. 92-100).
Part Two: Sawdust: From the Townsend Walsh Scrapbook. 1884 (p. 103-116); 1885 (p. 117-158); 1886 (p. 159-165); 1887 (p. 166-170); Notes for Part Two (p. 171-174).
Circus Personnel Reference Roster, by William L. Slout (p. 176-188); Index (p. 189-201).

A212. *Kansas and Me: Memories of a Jewish Childhood*, by Annette Peltz McComas, edited by Nathan Kravetz. STUDIES IN JUDAICA AND THE HOLOCAUST, Number 10. 152 p. LC 94-40787. OCLC #31434559. ISBN 0-8095-0408-1 cloth $27; ISBN 0-8095-1408-7 paper $17. Illustrated with photographs from the author's life. Cover: standard series design by Highpoint Type & Graphics with a cover photo of the author, black ink on light rose background. First Edition, February 1995.

b.   Second Printing, October 1995.

The autobiography of the late Jewish teacher, writer, and theatrical director, Annette Peltz McComas (1911-1994), particularly focusing on her early days in Hutchinson, Kansas.

CONTENTS: Foreword (p. 5-6).

Part One: The Arrival. 1. Kansas and Me (p. 9-10); 2. Settling In (p. 10-13); 3. Keeping Warm in Kansas (p. 13-14); 4. The House Next Door (p. 14-18); 5. The Upstairs Ladies (p. 18-20); 6. The Beginning of a Lifelong Passion: Theatre (p. 20-22).

Part Two: Growing Up. 7. I Learn About the Amish (p. 23-27); 8. I Face the Judgment Day (p. 27-28); 9. God and I (p. 28-30); 10. He Was a Nice Jew Like Us (p. 30-33); 11. Freedom's Return, November 11, 1918 (p. 33-34); 12. That Perfect Child (p. 35-37); 13. A Scandal Too (p. 37-40); 14. I Adopt a Protégée (p. 40-47); 15. Hooray for the Red, White, and Blue (p. 47-49); 16. The Winds of Change (p. 49-54); 17. A Small Bite of the Big Apple (p. 54-63).

Part Three: Community Concerns. 18. The Isaacs: A Community Dilemma (p. 65-70); 19. Katja's Sorrow: A Community Outrage (p. 71-76); 20. Naomi's Plight: A Community Concerned (p. 76-80); 21. Salvation's Army: A Community Fights Back! (p. 80-83).

Part Four: Like in the Movies. 22. Sometimes I Am Tarzan of the Apes (p. 85-87); 23. Spanish Influenza (p. 87-90); 24. My Captive Audience (p. 90-93); 25. Like in the Movies (p. 94-96); 26. Adieu to Fantasy (p. 97-99); 27. A Quart Full of Theatre (p. 99-103); 28. On the Wings of Song (p. 103-105).

Part Five: Goodbye, Childhood. 29. The Birds, the Bees, and S-E-X! (p. 107-113); 30. Friday's Child—That's Me! (p. 113-118); 31. The Perils of Summer (p. 118-120); 32. Onward

BP 300, by Robert Reginald & Mary Wickizer Burgess

(Christian) Soldiers (p. 121-125); 33. All That Jazz (p. 125-127); 34. Love and Marriage (p. 128-129); 35. Grown-Up Clothes, Boyfriend Woes, and the Junior/Senior Fling (p. 130-133); 36. I Return to the Promised Land (p. 133-136).

Afterword. 37. A Brief History of My Family (p. 137-146); Index (p. 147-151); About the Author (p. 152).

A213. *Imaginative Futures: Proceedings of the 1993 Science Fiction Research Association Conference: June 17-19, 1993, Reno, Nevada*, edited by Milton T. Wolf and Daryl F. Mallett. SFRA STUDIES IN SCIENCE FICTION, FANTASY, AND HORROR, Number 2. An SFRA Press Book Published by Jacob's Ladder Books. 364 p. LC 94-46643. OCLC #31738604. ISBN 0-913960-34-9 cloth $41; ISBN 0-913960-35-7 paper $31. Illustrated by Jim Clark; includes charts. Cover art by Jim Clark, cover concept by Daryl F. Mallett, cover design by Highpoint Type & Graphics, black ink on gray background. First Edition, March 1995.

A collection of papers and essays presented at the 1993 SFRA Conference, distributed by Borgo Press.

CONTENTS: Dedication (p. 5); Introduction (p. 7-8); "Monolude: The Imaginative Future," by Frederik Pohl (p. 9-12).

Part One: Infosurfing and Virtual Reality: The Imaginative Future of Database Storage and Retrieval. "Virtual Reality and Other Electronic Intimacies," by Howard L. Davidson (p. 15-29); "Database Visualization and Future Innovations in Information Retrieval," by Martin Halbert (p. 31-51); "The Electronic Book in Future Information Access," by E. Susan Baugh (p. 53-59); "Claims-Making in Artificial Intelligence Research," by B. Diane Miller (p. 61-74); "Bilude: The Imaginative Future," by Lisa Goldstein (p. 75-79).

Part Two: Cybercerebralism and Hyperlearning: The Imaginative Future of Education, Research, Bibliography, and Criticism. "In Research of Wonder: The Future of Science Fiction Criticism," by Gary Westfahl (p. 83-93); "Surprises in the Heinlein Bibliography," by Marie Guthrie Ormes (p. 95-113); "New Light on the Work of John Taine," by Constance Reid (p. 115-124); "Trilude: Imagining the Future," by James Gunn (p. 125-134).

Part Three: "A Klingon, a Ferengi, and a Monk Walk into a Bar...": The Imaginative Future of Interpersonal and Technohumanoid Relationships: Gender, Cyborgism, Science/Humanity, and Sexualism. "Social Adjustments to a Robotic Future," by Joanne E. Pransky (p. 137-146); "Postmodern Images of Sexuality in Vampire Literature," by Martha Kearns (p. 147-159); "Bells and Time: A Review of *Doomsday Book* by Connie Willis," by Joan Slonczewski (p. 161-166); "Feminist Nurturers and Psychic Healers," by Susan Stone-Blackburn (p. 167-178); "Mary Shelley's Machines in the Garden: Victor Frankenstein and His Monster," by Mark L. Waldo (p. 179-190); "Youth, Culture, and Cybernetic Technologies," by Rob Latham (p. 191-201); "Science, Fiction, and Artificial Paradise: Villiers de L'Isle-Adam's *Future Eve*," by Miriella Melara (p. 203-216); "Signal to Noise: On the Meaning of Cyberpunk Subculture," by Anne Balsamo (p. 217-227); "*Homo Electronicus*: The Future of Human-Enhancement," by Mel Seesholtz (p. 229-244); "Putting the Abortion Controversy into the Deep Freeze," by Anna Livia (p. 245-247); "Quatrolude: Epistle to the SFRAns," by Poul Anderson (p. 249-260).

Part Four: Imaginative Miscellany: The Imaginative Future of Literature, Censorship, Humor, Imagery, Characterization. "Humor in Science Fiction," by Fiona Kelleghan (p. 263-277); "Wildmen, Witches, and Wanderlust: No Basque Science Fiction?" by Linda White (p. 279-292); "Maggots, Tropes, and Metafictional Challenge: John Fowles' *A Maggot*," by Peter Brigg (p. 293-305); "Perry Mason in Space: A Call for More Inventive Lawyers in Television Science Fiction Series," by Paul Joseph and Sharon Carton (p. 307-318); "Machen, Williams, and Autobiography: Fantasy and Decadence," by Donald M. Hassler (p. 319-327); "Kim Stanley Robinson: Premodernist," by Bud Foote (p. 329-340); "A Golem of Her Own: The Fantastic Art and Literature of Leilah Wendell," by Jane P. Davidson (p. 341-352); "Pentalude: Science Fiction as Fantasy," by Kim Stanley Robinson (p. 353-357); About the Contributors (p. 359-364).

A214. *Calendar of Coroners Rolls of the City of London, A.D. 1300-1378*, edited by Reginald R. Sharpe. STOKVIS STUDIES IN HISTORICAL CHRONOLOGY AND THOUGHT, Number 9. A Sidewinder Book. xxviii+324 p. LC 95-1542. OCLC #31937136. ISBN 0-913330-04-3 cloth $39; ISBN 0-913330-05-1 paper $29. Cover: standard series design by Highpoint Type &

BP 300, by Robert Reginald & Mary Wickizer Burgess

Graphics, black ink on red-orange background, with a backdrop of some of the signatures. First Borgo Edition, March 1995.

This facsimile reprint of the 1913 Richard Clay and Sons edition is a unique transcript of part of the *Liber Horn*, which includes the only surviving inquests into each "death other than his rightful death" that occurred in the City of London between the years 1300 and 1378, with some gaps. The nine rolls, labeled A through I, were evidently part of a longer series of such records, the rest of which have now been lost. Most of the cases include a complete list of the jurors examining the circumstances of the deaths. The comprehensive index includes some 4500 names of medieval Londoners.

CONTENTS: *Liber Horn* (p. vi); Introduction (p. vii-xxviii); Roll A (p. 1-32); Roll B (p. 33-69); Roll C. (p. 70-93); Roll D (p. 94-131); Roll E (p. 132-171); Roll F (p. 172-200); Roll G (p. 201-234); Roll H (p. 235-271); Roll I (p. 272-276); Appendix: Appraisement of Deodands (p. 277-278); Index (p. 279-324).

A215. *Voices of the River Plate: Interviews with Writers of Argentina and Uruguay*, by Clark M. Zlotchew, edited by Paul David Seldis. I.O. EVANS STUDIES IN THE PHILOSOPHY AND CRITICISM OF LITERATURE, Number 6. 200 p. LC 93-6560. OCLC #27380811. ISBN 0-89370-317-6 cloth $31; ISBN 0-89370-417-2 paper $21. Illustrated with photographs of the interviewees. Cover: modified series design by Highpoint Type & Graphics with stylized lizard design, black ink on sage background. First Edition, April 1995.

b. Second Printing (Corrected), October 1995.

A selection of mostly previously-published interviews with eleven writers of South America.

CONTENTS: About Clark M. Zlotchew (p. 4); Preface, by Edna Aizenberg (p. 5); Acknowledgments (p. 6).

Part One: Voices of the River Plate: Interviews with Writers of Argentina and Uruguay. Introduction to Part One (p. 9-15); 1. Jorge Luis Borges (p. 17-39); 2. Marco Denevi (p. 41-50); 3. Antonio Elio Brailovsky (p. 51-66); 4. Fernando Sorrentino (p. 67-76); 5. Julio Ricci (p. 77-92); 6. Enrique Cadícamo (p. 93-

105); 7. José Gobello (p. 107-120); 8. William Shand (p. 123-135).

Part Two: From the River Plate to the River Jordan: Interviews with South American Writers Living and Working in Israel. Introduction to Part Two (p. 139-140); 9. Leonardo Senkman (p. 141-154); 10. Samuel Pecar (p. 155-165); 11. José Luis Najenson (p. 167-182); Notes (p. 183-194); Index (p. 195-200).

A216. *Chaos Burning on My Brow: Don Juan Valera in His Novels*, by Robert G. Trimble. THE MILFORD SERIES: POPULAR WRITERS OF TODAY, Volume 61. 160 p. LC 95-2050. OCLC #31937533. ISBN 0-89370-987-5 cloth $29; ISBN 0-89370-989-1 paper $19. Cover: standard series design by Highpoint Type & Graphics with drawing of Valera by Barbara Trimble, black ink on cream background. First Edition, April 1995.

 b. Second Printing, October 1995.

A critique on the late Spanish writer, Juan Valera (1824-1905). CONTENTS: Preface (p. 4); 1. Andalucía—Córdoba— Doña Mencía (p. 5-7); 2. Don Juan Valera—A Brief Biography (p. 8-10); 3. Valera—The Nature of His Art (p. 11-18); 4. Categories of Authorial Presence in Valera's Novels (p. 19-24); 5. *Pepita Jiménez* (1874) (p. 25-36); 6. *Las Ilusiones del Doctor Faustino* (1875) (p. 37-50); 7. *El Comendador Mendoza* (1876) (p. 51-58); 8. *Pasarse de Listo* (1878) (p. 59-68); 9. *Doña Luz* (1879) (p. 69-82); 10. *Juanita la Larga* (1895) (p. 83-94); 11. *Genio y Figura...* (1897) (p. 95-111); 12. *Morsamor* (1899) (p. 112-125); 13. Conclusion (p. 126-129); Appendix I: The Katherine Bayard Affair (p. 130-143); Appendix II: The Exchange with Enrique Gómez Carrillo (p. 144-149); Notes (p. 150-153); Bibliography (p. 154-155); Index (p. 156-159); About the Author (p. 160).

A217. *It's Down the Slippery Cellar Stairs: Essays and Speeches on Fantastic Literature, Second Edition, Revised and Expanded*, by R. A. Lafferty. I.O. EVANS STUDIES IN THE PHILOSOPHY AND CRITICISM OF LITERATURE, Number 17. 104 p. LC 95-5201. OCLC #31970488. ISBN 0-8095-0901-6 cloth $25; ISBN 0-8095-1901-1 paper $15. Cover: standard series design by

BP 300, by Robert Reginald & Mary Wickizer Burgess

Highpoint Type & Graphics, black ink on gold background. Second Edition, April 1995.

b.   Second Printing, October 1995.

A collection of previously published literary essays and speeches by American author, R. A. Lafferty (1914-2002).

CONTENTS: Acknowledgments (p. 4); Introduction, by Robert Reginald (p. 5-6); An R. A. Lafferty Chronology (p. 7-8); 1. The World's Narration (p. 9-13); 2. The Ten Thousand Masks of the World (p. 15-18); 3. Great Awkward Gold (p. 19-23); 4. Something New Under the Black Suns (p. 25-30); 5. More Worlds Than One? (p. 31-35); 6. For a Little Bit of Gold (p. 37-40); 7. Riddle-Writers of the Isthmus (p. 41-45); 8. Through the Red Fire (p. 47-51); 9. Tell It Funny, Og (p. 53-57); 10. Rare Earths and Pig-Weeds (p. 59-63); 11. The Gathering of the Tribes (p. 65-71); 12. The Day After the World Ended: Notes for a Speech for DeepSouthCon '79, New Orleans, July 21, 1979 (p. 73-82); 13. Rogue Raft (p. 83-87); 14. The Roots of Folklore (p. 89-93); 15. It's Down the Slippery Cellar Stairs (p. 95-98); Index (p. 99-103); About the Author (p. 104).

See also the original edition (**A76**).

A218. ***The Jack Vance Lexicon: The Coined Words of Jack Vance, from Ahulph to Zipangote***, by Jack Vance, edited and with an introduction by Dan Temianka. BORGO LITERARY GUIDES, Number 2. 136 p. LC 95-5330. OCLC #31970910. ISBN 0-8095-0203-8 cloth $27; ISBN 0-8095-1203-3 paper $17. Cover: standard series design by Highpoint Type & Graphics, black ink on bright pink background. First Borgo Edition, April 1995.

b.   Second Printing, October 1995.

This facsimile reprint of the 1992 Underwood-Miller edition includes an A-Z listing of Jack Vance's created words, with illustrative quotations from Vance's works.

CONTENTS: Introduction (p. ix-xvi); References (p. xvii); Abbreviations (p. xix-xxi); The Coined Words of Jack Vance (p. 25-136).

A219. *Opening Minds: Essays on Fantastic Literature*, by Brian Stableford. I.O. EVANS STUDIES IN THE PHILOSOPHY AND CRITICISM OF LITERATURE, Number 14. 144 p. LC 95-5020. OCLC #31934203. ISBN 0-89370-303-6 cloth $27; ISBN 0-89370-403-2 paper $17. Cover: standard series design by Highpoint Type & Graphics, black ink on yellow background. First Edition, April 1995.

b. Second Printing, October 1995.

A collection of previously-published essays by the British critic and novelist, Brian Stableford.
CONTENTS: About Brian Stableford (p. 4); Introduction (p. 5-7); 1. SF: The Nature of the Medium (p. 9-14); 2. William Wilson's Prospectus for Science-Fiction, 1851 (p. 15-22); 3. Opening Minds (p. 23-28); 4. Science Fiction and the Mythology of Progress (p. 29-35); 5. The Concept of Mind in Science Fiction (p. 37-51); 6. The Mythology of Man-Made Catastrophe (p. 53-90); 7. The Plausibility of the Impossible (p. 91-98); 8. Marxism, Science Fiction, and the Poverty of Prophecy: Some Comparisons and Contrasts (p. 99-110); 9. Future Wars, 1890-1950 (p. 111-134); Notes (p. 135-137); Selected Bibliography (p. 138); Index (p. 139-144).

A220. *Self-Portrait: Ceaselessly into the Past*, by Ross Macdonald, edited by Ralph B. Sipper. BROWNSTONE MYSTERY GUIDES, Volume 13. A Brownstone Book. x+134 p. LC 95-1610. OCLC #32130291. ISBN 0-941028-25-9 cloth $27; ISBN 0-941028-26-7 paper $17. Cover: standard series design by Highpoint Type & Graphics, black ink on orange background. First Brownstone Edition, April 1995.

b. Second Printing, October 1995.

This facsimile reprint from the 1981 Capra Press edition includes a selection of autobiographical and critical pieces by the late American writer, Ross Macdonald [Kenneth Millar] (1915-1983), with a new index added.
CONTENTS: Foreword, by Eudora Welty (p. i-iv); 1. Down These Streets a Mean Man Must Go (p. 3-9); 2. A Collection of Reviews (p. 11-14); 3. Archer in Jeopardy (p. 15-16); 4. Lew

BP 300, by Robert Reginald & Mary Wickizer Burgess

Archer, Private Investigator (p. 17-21); 5. Kenneth Millar/Ross Macdonald—A Checklist (p. 23-28); 6. Archer at Large (p. 29-32); 7. Find the Woman (p. 33-34); 8. Archer in Hollywood (p. 35-37); 9. In the First Person (From the Davidson Films Shooting Script) (p. 39-46); 10. Writing *The Galton Case* (p. 47-59); 11. From *South Dakota Review* (p. 61-62); 12. A Death Road for the Condor (p. 63-67); 13. Life with The Blob (p. 69-79); 14. Black Tide (Adapted from Foreword to Book by Robert Easton) (p. 81-85); 15. An Interview with Ross Macdonald, by Ralph B. Sipper (p. 87-93); 16. *Great Stories of Suspense* (p. 95-104); 17. The Death of the Detective (World Crime Writers Conference, 1978) (p. 105-107); 18. Homage to Dashiell Hammett (p. 109-112); 19. The Writer as Detective Hero (p. 113-122); 20. F. Scott Fitzgerald (From Kenneth Millar's Notebooks) (p. 123-124); 21. Eudora Welty (Santa Barbara Writers Conference, 1977) (p. 125-126); Afterword: A Personal Appreciation, by Ralph B. Sipper (p. 127-129); Books by Ross Macdonald (p. 130); [New] Index (p. 131-134).

A221. *The State and Local Government Political Dictionary*, by Jeffrey M. Elliot and Sheikh R. Ali. BORGO REFERENCE GUIDES, Number 7. x+325 p. LC 95-11397. OCLC #32167223. ISBN 0-8095-0703-X cloth $39; ISBN 0-8095-1703-5 paper $29. Cover: standard series design by Highpoint Type & Graphics, black ink on cream background. First Borgo Edition, June 1995.

b.　Second Printing, April 1996.

This facsimile reprint of the 1988 ABC-CLIO edition is a guide to the major terms used in state and local government.
　　　　CONTENTS: Dedication (p. vi); Preface (p. vii-viii); How to Use This Book (p. ix); 1. Federal and State Constitutions (p. 3-26); 2. Intergovernmental Relations (p. 27-53); 3. Parties and Elections (p. 55-91); 4. The Legislative Branch (p. 93-119); 5. The Executive Branch (p. 121-142); 6. The Judicial Branch (p. 143-171); 7. Bureaucracy and Civil Service (p. 173-199); 8. Counties, Districts, and Towns and Townships (p. 201-225); 9. Cities and Metropolitan Areas (p. 227-250); 10. Financing State and Local Government (p. 251-282); 11. Citizen Needs and Government Policy (p. 283-304); Notes (p. 305-310); Index (p. 311-325).

A222. *Old Gotham Theatricals: Selections from a Series, "Reminiscences of a Man about Town,"* by Col. Tom Picton, edited by William L. Slout. CLIPPER STUDIES IN THE THEATRE, Number 12. x+170 p. LC 95-2057. OCLC #31937551. ISBN 0-89370-362-1 cloth $29; ISBN 0-89370-462-8 paper $19. Illustrated with reproductions of contemporaneous drawings and woodcuts. Cover: standard series design by Judy Cloyd Graphic Design as adapted by Highpoint Type & Graphics, black ink on blue background. First Edition, June 1995.

These recollections of nineteenth-century New York theatre life from the 1830s through the 1850s were originally published in the newspaper, the *New York Clipper*, between 1868-1869 by critic and historian Thomas Picton (1822-1891).

CONTENTS: Introduction, by William L. Slout (p. vii-ix); Broadway a Quarter of a Century Since (p. 3-5); Our Drama's Semi-Centennial (p. 6-12); Niblo's Garden (p. 13-20); Niblo's and Its Surroundings (p. 22-31); Niblo's and the Dancing Days of Yore (p. 32-40); "Old Drury" (p. 41-49); Memories of the Park Theatre (p. 50-57); "London Assurance" and Who Played in It (p. 58-65); Palmo's Opera House (p. 67-76); Richmond Hill and the Tivoli (p. 77-85); Mitchell's Olympic (p. 86-93); The Olympian Gods and Goddesses (p. 95-102); The Olympic's Patrons (p. 103-110); About Some Defunct Theatres (p. 111-120); Other Defunct Theatres (p. 121-130); Private Theatricals (p. 131-140); Notes (p. 141-160); Index (p. 161-170).

A223. *Bibi Mkuba: My Experiences During Wartime in German East Africa*, by Ada Schnee, translated and edited by Sam E. Edelstein from *Meine Erlebnisse Während der Kriegszeit in Deutsch-Ostafrika*, additional editing by Barbara Ann Quarton. BORGO BIOVIEWS, Number 8. 112 p. LC 93-32761. OCLC #29025421. ISBN 0-89370-319-2 cloth $25; ISBN 0-89370-419-9 paper $15. Illustrated with reproductions of contemporaneous photographs and maps. Cover: standard series design by Highpoint Type & Graphics, using photo of a native soldier and a British officer, black ink on lime green background. First Edition, June 1995.

The first English-language translation of an account by the English wife of the last German Governor of German East Africa of the war in Africa between Britain and Germany during World War I.

CONTENTS: Preface, by Sam E. Edelstein (p. 5); Prologue, by Sam E. Edelstein (p. 7); Foreword (p. 9); Chronology (p. 10-11); Acknowledgments, by Sam E. Edelstein (p. 12); 1. Our First News of War (p. 13-22); 2. Bombardment of Dar-es-Salaam (p. 23-30); 3. Our Achievements (p. 31-40); 4. Raiding the Uganda Railroad (p. 41-46); 5. The Great Offensive (p. 47-53); 6. Occupation of Tabora (p. 55-65); 7. My Particular Fate (p. 67-78); 8. My Journey Homeward (p. 79-86); 9. My Cousin's Hardships (p. 87-92); 10. My Emancipation (p. 93-95); Epilogue, by Sam E. Edelstein (p. 97); Notes (p. 99-104); Bibliography (p. 105); Index (p. 107-111); About the Translator (p. 112).

A224. *A Directory of Autocephalous Bishops of the Churches of the Apostolic Succession, Seventh Edition, Revised and Expanded,* by Bishop Karl Pruter. THE AUTOCEPHALOUS ORTHODOX CHURCHES, Number 1. A St. Willibrord's Press Book. 96 p. LC 95-5114. OCLC #31899978. ISBN 0-912134-24-0 cloth $23; ISBN 0-912134-25-9 paper $13. Cover design by Highpoint Type & Graphics showing an Orthodox archbishop, black ink on light green background. Seventh Edition, June 1995.

A directory of independent Orthodox and Old Catholic bishops.

CONTENTS: Rest in Peace (p. 5); Preface (p. 7-8); Directory: United States and Canada (p. 9-85); Central and South America (p. 86); Index of Jurisdictions (p. 87-93); Geographic Index (p. 94-95); About the Author (p. 96).

Spine title reads: *The Seventh Directory of Autocephalous Bishops*. See also the Sixth Edition (**A146**).

A225. *Sextet: Six Essays: On Turning Eighty, Reflections on the Death of Mishima, First Impressions of Greece, The Waters Reglitterized, Reflections on the Maurizius Case, Mother, China, and the World Beyond,* by Henry Miller. I.O. EVANS STUDIES IN THE PHILOSOPHY AND CRITICISM OF LITERATURE, Number 29. 192 p. LC 95-9979. OCLC #32132584. ISBN 0-8095-0903-2 cloth $29; ISBN 0-8095-1903-8 paper $19. Cover: standard series design by Highpoint Type & Graphics with inset photo of Henry Miller, black ink on cream background. First Borgo Edition, June 1995.

b. Second Printing, October 1995.

This facsimile reprint of the 1977 Capra Press edition includes six previously-published essays by the late American author, Henry Miller (1891-1980), plus new index.
CONTENTS: Editor's Note (p. 6); On Turning Eighty: Journey to an Antique Land: Foreword to *The Angel Is My Watermark* (p. 7-22); Reflections on the Death of Mishima (p. 23-55); First Impressions of Greece (p. 56-89); The Waters Reglitterized: The Subject of Water Color in Some of Its More Liquid Phases (p. 90-125); Reflections on the Maurizius Case (A Humble Appraisal of a Great Book) (p. 127-170); Mother, China, and the World Beyond (p. 171-188); [New] Index (p. 189-192).

A226. *World War I: A Cataloging Reference Guide*, by Buckley Barry Barrett. BORGO CATALOGING GUIDES, Number 4. iv+380 p. LC 93-19745. OCLC #28067012. ISBN 0-89370-824-0 cloth $41; ISBN 0-89370-924-7 paper $31. Cover: standard series design by Highpoint Type & Graphics, black ink on green background. First Edition, July 1995.

A guide to Library of Congress and Dewey Decimal cataloging practice in regard to World War I and related topics.
CONTENTS: Acknowledgments (p. iv); Introduction (p. 1-2); 1. Library of Congress Classification System (LC) (p. 3-115); 2. Dewey Decimal Classification System (DDC) (p. 116-157); 3. Index to Library of Congress & Dewey Classification (p. 158-290); 4. Library of Congress Subject & Other Headings (p. 291-379); About the Author (p. 380).

A227. *Black Women at the United Nations: The Politics, a Theoretical Model, and the Documents*, by Hanes Walton, Jr., edited by Paul David Seldis and Mary A. Burgess. BLACK POLITICAL STUDIES, Number 1. 144 p. LC 87-805. OCLC #15195167. ISBN 0-89370-323-0 cloth $27; ISBN 0-89370-423-7 paper $17. Includes tables. Cover: standard series design by Highpoint Type & Graphics, photo of Mary McLeod Bethune, black ink on tan background. First Edition, July 1995.

b. Second Printing, October 1995.

A history of the participation of Black women in the official U.S. delegations to the United Nations.

CONTENTS: Dedication (p. 4); Poems, by Ja. A. Jahannes (p. 4 and 7); Preface (p. 5-7); Foreword, by Bettye Collier-Thomas (p. 8-10).

Part One: Historical Background. 1. A State Department Perspective, by Ronald D. Branch (p. 13-15); 2. Black Women at the Founding Conference, by Shelby Lewis (p. 16-23); 3. The Ralph Bunche Connection, by Lois Banks Hollis (p. 25-28).

Part Two: An Analytical Framework. 4. A Systemic Overview (p. 31-39); 5. The Role of Black Women in Shaping International Politics (p. 40-44).

Part Three: The Delegates and the Documents. 6. Mary McLeod Bethune (p. 46-53); 7. Edith Sampson (p. 54-66); 8. Marian Anderson (p. 67-72); 9. Patricia Roberts Harris (p. 73-77); 10. Helen G. Edmonds (p. 78-88); 11. Jewel Lafontant (p. 89-99); 12. Margaret B. Young (p. 100-102); 13. Pearl Bailey (p. 103-106); 14. Ersa Hines Poston (p. 107-108); 15. Hannah Diggs Atkins (p. 109-123); 16. Other Delegates: Zelma Watson George, Elizabeth Duncan Koontz, Coretta Scott King, Joan Wallace Dawkins (p. 124-127).

Notes (p. 128-134); Bibliography (p. 135-138); List of Contributors (p. 139-140); Index (p. 141-144).

A228. *The New Hard-Boiled Dicks: Heroes for a New Urban Mythology, Second Edition, Revised and Expanded*, by Robert E. Skinner. BROWNSTONE MYSTERY GUIDES, Volume 2. A Brownstone Book. 192 p. LC 93-16090. OCLC #27336206. ISBN 0-941028-13-5 cloth $29; ISBN 0-941028-14-3 paper $19. Cover: standard series design by Highpoint Type & Graphics with a stylized drawing of a private detective's head on cover, black ink on red background. Second Edition, July 1995.

b.   Second Printing, October 1995.

A personal guide to the major hard-boiled detectives of the modern era, much expanded from the earlier 1987 Brownstone Books edition (see **C5**).

CONTENTS: Dedication (p. 4); Preface to the Second Edition (p. 5-6); 1. The Hard-Boiled Hero: Evolution of an Urban

Myth (p. 7-28); 2. Kosher Krime: Andrew Bergman (p. 29-36); 3. Alcohol, Guilt, and Crime: James Lee Burke (p. 37-48); 4. Man of a Thousand Voices: Robert Campbell (p. 49-57); 5. Crime and Class Struggle: James Colbert (p. 58-64); 6. One-Armed Tough Guy: Michael Collins (p. 65-71); 7. New Wild West: James Crumley (p. 72-80); 8. "K" Is for Kinsey: Sue Grafton (p. 81-87); 9. The Professional: Donald Hamilton (p. 88-99); 10. To Go Where No Man Has Gone Before: Joseph Hansen (p. 100-109); 11. The Black Knights: Chester Himes (p. 110-117); 12. Overnight Success: Elmore Leonard (p. 118-124); 13. Pistol Packin' Mama: Sara Paretsky (p. 125-135); 14. Marlowe's Heir: Robert B. Parker (p. 136-144); 15. Hard-Boiled Plunderer: Richard Stark (p. 145-157); 16. The Meanest Streets: Andrew Vachss (p. 158-165); 17. Man from the Big Easy: Chris Wiltz (p. 166-171); About the Author (p. 172); Notes (p. 173-179); Series Index (p. 180-187); Index (p. 188-192).

A229. *The Work of Gary Brandner: An Annotated Bibliography & Guide*, by Martine Wood, edited by Boden Clarke and Daryl F. Mallett. BIBLIOGRAPHIES OF MODERN AUTHORS, Number 23. 112 p. LC 93-2881. OCLC #27430764. ISBN 0-8095-0519-3 cloth $25; ISBN 0-8095-1519-9 paper $15. Cover: standard series design by Highpoint Type & Graphics, using photo of author, black ink on light blue background. First Edition, July 1995.

A bibliography of and literary guide to the modern American writer, Gary Brandner (1933-).

CONTENTS: Dedication (p. 4); Preface: "The Hemingway of Horror" (p. 5-10); Foreword: Gary Brandner: "Oh, Yeah?" by Richard Laymon (p. 11-12); Introduction: My Introduction to Gary Brandner, by Kim Greenblatt (p. 13); A Gary Brandner Chronology (p. 14-18); A. Books (p. 19-51); B. Short Fiction (p. 52-61); C. Short Nonfiction (p. 62-65); D. Other Media (p. 66-70); E. Interviews (p. 71-73); F. Secondary Sources (p. 74-75); G. Speeches and Public Appearances (p. 76-78); H. Miscellanea (p. 79-83); Quoth the Critics (p. 84-87); Martine Wood Interviews Gary Brandner (p. 88-97); "Sweet Lusting Heart," by Lurana Duchamp as Told to Gary Brandner (p. 98-99); Afterword: "How It Feels," by Gary Brandner (p. 100-101); About Martine Wood

(p. 101); A Gary Brandner Cyclopedia (p. 102-109); Index (p. 110-112).

A230. *From Here to Absurdity: The Moral Battlefields of Joseph Heller, Second Edition, Revised and Expanded*, by Stephen W. Potts. THE MILFORD SERIES: POPULAR WRITERS OF TODAY, Volume 36. 176 p. LC 95-5019. OCLC #31934197. ISBN 0-89370-318-4 cloth $29; ISBN 0-89370-418-0 paper $19. Cover: standard series design by Highpoint Type & Graphics, black and mustard ink on khaki background, with military star and flag design. Second Edition, August 1995.

   b.   Second Printing, October 1995.

A critique on the modern American writer, Joseph Heller (1923-1999).
    CONTENTS: About Stephen W. Potts (p. 4); A Joseph Heller Chronology (p. 5-6); Introduction (p. 7-10); 1. *Catch-22*: From Here to Absurdity (p. 11-25); 2. *Catch-22*: The Moral Battlefield (p. 26-40); 3. Dramas and Dramatizations (p. 41-61); 4. *Something Happened* (p. 62-79); 5. *Good as Gold* (p. 80-96); 6. *God Knows* (p. 97-110); 7. *No Laughing Matter* (p. 111-125); 8. *Picture This* (p. 126-137); 9. *Closing Time* (p. 138-153); 10. Conclusion (p. 154-158); Notes (p. 159-168); Primary Bibliography (p. 169); Secondary Bibliography (p. 170); Index (p. 171-176).
    See also the First Edition (**A51**).

A231. *British Science Fiction Paperbacks and Magazines, 1949-1956: An Annotated Bibliography and Guide, Revised Edition*, by Philip Harbottle and Stephen Holland, edited by Daryl F. Mallett and Michael Burgess. BORGO LITERARY GUIDES, Number 7. 232 p. LC 95-19142. OCLC #32509236. ISBN 0-8095-0204-6 cloth $31; ISBN 0-8095-1204-1 paper $21. Cover: standard series design by Highpoint Type & Graphics, black ink on lime green background. Revised Edition, July 1995.

An annotated guide to the pulp SF paperbacks published by fly-by-night houses in Great Britain in the post-World War II period. This version has roughly thirty-two pages with corrections and updates.

BP 300, by Robert Reginald & Mary Wickizer Burgess

CONTENTS: Dedication (p. 4); Acknowledgments (p. 5); How to Use This Book (p. 6); Introduction (p. 7-8); A. Original Science Fiction Paperbacks, 1946-1956 (p. 9-129); B. Paperback Books from Established Houses, 1949-1956 (p. 130-147); C. A Checklist of British Science Fiction Magazines, 1949-1956 (p. 148-155); D. A Complete Author Index to the Stories in the British Science Fiction Magazines, 1949-1956 (p. 156-216); Book Title Index (p. 217-221); Short Story Title Index (p. 222-231); About the Authors (p. 232).

See also the First Edition (**A192**).

A232. *Lords Temporal and Lords Spiritual: A Chronological Checklist of the Popes, Patriarchs, Katholikoi, and Independent Archbishops and Metropolitans of the Autocephalous and Autonomous Monarchical Churches of the Christian East and West, Second Edition, Revised and Expanded*, by Michael Burgess. STOKVIS STUDIES IN HISTORICAL CHRONOLOGY AND THOUGHT, Number 1. 336 p. LC 87-6319. OCLC #15318082. ISBN 0-89370-326-5 cloth $39; ISBN 0-89370-426-1 paper $29. Cover: standard series design by Highpoint Type & Graphics with drawing of two bishops by Michael Pastucha adapted from the first edition, black ink on light green background. Second Edition, September 1995.

Histories of each of the Eastern Orthodox Churches, with checklists of their patriarchs.

CONTENTS: Introduction: *Primus Inter Pares* (p. 5-8); Glossary (p. 9); Dedication (p. 10); 1. Aght'amar (p. 11-13); 2. Aghunie (Caucasian Albania) (p. 14-16); 3. Albania (p. 17-18); 4. Alexandria (Coptic) (p. 19-23); 5. Alexandria (Coptic Catholic) (p. 24-25); 6. Alexandria (Greek) (p. 26-29); 7. Alexandria (Latin) (p. 30-31); 8. America (p. 32-35); 9. Antioch (Greek) (p. 36-41); 10. Antioch (Greek Melkite) (p. 42-47); 11. Antioch (Latin) (p. 48-50); 12. Antioch (Maronite) (p. 51-54): 13. Antioch (Syrian Catholic) (p. 55-59); 14. Antioch (Syrian Orthodox) (p. 60-64); 15. Armenia (p. 65-70); 16. Assyria (Church of the East) (p. 71-76); 17. Austria and Hungary (p. 77-82); 18. Babylon (Chaldean Catholic Church) (p. 83-87); 19. Belarus (p. 88-89); 20. Bulgaria (p. 90-94); 21. Cilicia (Armenian Apostolic Church) (p. 95-97); 22. Cilicia (Armenian Catholic) (p. 98-99); 23. Constantinople (Armenian) (p. 100-103); 24. Constantinople (Greek) (p. 104-

BP 300, by Robert Reginald & Mary Wickizer Burgess

See also the First Edition (**A66**).

A233. ***Outside the Human Aquarium: Masters of Science Fiction, Second Edition, Revised and Expanded***, by Brian Stableford. THE MILFORD SERIES: POPULAR WRITERS OF TODAY, Volume 32. 152 p. LC 95-9971. OCLC #32132568. ISBN 0-89370-357-5 cloth $27; ISBN 0-89370-457-1 paper $17. Cover: standard series design by Highpoint Type & Graphics, black ink on blue background. Second Edition, September 1995.

A collection of previously-published essays on science fiction authors by British critic and novelist, Brian Stableford.

CONTENTS: About Brian Stableford (p. 4); Introduction (p. 5-6); 1. Edmond Hamilton and Leigh Brackett: An Appreciation (p. 7-17); 2. Locked in the Slaughterhouse: The Novels of Kurt Vonnegut (p. 18-27); 3. Insoluble Problems: Barry Malzberg's Career in Science Fiction (p. 28-36); 4. The Metamorphosis of Robert Silverberg (p. 37-48); 5. Utopia—And Afterwards: Socioeconomic Speculation in the SF of Mack Reynolds (p. 49-75); 6. Outside the Human Aquarium: The Fantastic Imagination of Clark Ashton Smith (p. 76-98); 7. Little Victories: The Heartfelt Fiction of Philip K. Dick (p. 99-107); 8. Gernsback's Pessimist: The Futuristic Fantasies of David H. Keller (p. 108-116); 9. Schemes of Salvation: The Literary Explorations of Theodore Sturgeon (p. 117-125); 10. The Lost Pioneer: The Science Fiction of Stanley G. Weinbaum (p. 126-134); Notes (p. 135-136); Selected Bibliography (p. 137-138); Index (p. 139-152).

BP 300, by Robert Reginald & Mary Wickizer Burgess

See also the First Edition, *Masters of Science Fiction* (**A44**).

A234. *The Chinese Economy: A Bibliography of Works in English*, by Robert Goehlert and Anthony C. Stamatoplos, edited by Daryl F. Mallett, Mary A. Burgess, and Xiwen Zhang. BORGO REFERENCE GUIDES, Number 4. 240 p. LC 93-329. OCLC #27429932. ISBN 0-8095-0700-5 cloth $33; ISBN 0-8095-1700-0 paper $23. Cover: standard series design by Highpoint Type & Graphics, black ink on red-orange background. First Edition, September 1995.

b.   Second Printing, January 1996.

A bibliographical guide to books and periodical articles on the economy of the People's Republic of China.
CONTENTS: About the Authors (p. 6); Preface: "The Tallest Tree in the Forest," by Richard D. Reynnells (p. 7-8); Introduction (p. 9-10); Research Sources (p. 11-20); A. General Works (p. 21-46); B. Economic Development (p. 47-57); C. Politics and Economics (p. 58-63); D. Economic System (p. 64-70); E. Fiscal Planning (p. 71-73); F. Monetary and Financial System (p. 74-86); G. Industry (p. 87-98); H. Agriculture (p. 99-121); I. Transportation (p. 122-124); J. Natural Resources (p. 125-132); K. Human Resources (p. 133-139); L. Special Topics (p. 140-166); Author Index (p. 167-182); Title Index: Books (p. 183-192); Title Index: Articles (p. 193-224); Subject Index (p. 225-240).

A235. *Street Kids and Other Plays*, by Brio Burgess, edited by Daryl F. Mallett. An Angel Enterprises Book. 168 p. LC 94-47230. OCLC #31739257. ISBN 0-913960-26-8 cloth $29; ISBN 0-913960-27-6 paper $19. Illustrated by Lawrence Ferlinghetti and James C. Burgess. Cover drawings by Lawrence Ferlinghetti and James C. Burgess, cover design by Highpoint Type & Graphics, black ink on gray background. First Edition, September 1995.

b.   Second Printing, February 1996.

A collection of original plays and verse by American poet and playwright, Brio Burgess (1943-).
CONTENTS: Dedication (p. 4); Preface (p. 5-6); *Lost City Nights* (p. 7-56); *Street Kids; or, Les Enfants sans Maisons* (p. 57-

97); *Rooftops* (p. 99-128); *Space Visions; or, Chanson à Dieu* (p. 129-162); Poems (p. 163-164); About the Author (p. 165); Quoth the Critics (p. 167-168).

A236. *Politics Quaker Style: A History of the Quakers from 1624 to 1718*, by John H. Ferguson, anonymously edited by Douglas A. Mackey. STOKVIS STUDIES IN HISTORICAL CHRONOLOGY AND THOUGHT, Number 15. viii+208 p. LC 95-1515. OCLC #31971819. ISBN 0-8095-0101-5 cloth $31; ISBN 0-8095-1101-0 paper $21. Cover: standard series design by Highpoint Type & Graphics, black ink on gray background. First Edition, October 1995.

A history of the first century of the Quakers in America.
   CONTENTS: About the Author (p. iv); Foreword (p. v-viii); 1. Quaker Beginnings (p. 1-21); 2. The Ideological Setting (p. 22-50); 3. Steps Toward Institutionalized Quakerism (p. 51-71); 4. Beleaguered Monarchs and Protectors (p. 72-109); 5. Ideological Conflicts and Persecution Within England (p. 110-144); 6. William Penn's Maturation and Colonial Governance (p. 145-172); Notes (p. 173-188); Bibliography (p. 189-197); Index (p. 198-208).

A237. *Merry Wheels and Spokes of Steel: A Social History of the Bicycle*, by Robert A. Smith. STOKVIS STUDIES IN HISTORICAL CHRONOLOGY AND THOUGHT, Number 16. xii+269 p. LC 95-9980. OCLC #32166581. ISBN 0-8095-0104-X cloth $35; ISBN 0-8095-1104-5 paper $25. Illustrated with drawings. Cover: standard series design by Highpoint Type & Graphics with drawing of early bicyclist, brown ink on cream background. First Borgo Edition, October 1995.

A reprint of *The Social History of the Bicycle*, published by American Heritage Press in 1972. The illustrations in the original edition were resized for this version.
   CONTENTS: Preface (p. ix-x); Acknowledgments (p. xi-xii); 1. "Hurrah, Hurrah, for the Merry Wheel": The Early Development of the Bicycle (p. 1-15); 2. "The Sundries Cost More Than the Wheel": The Bicycle Industry and the Bicycle Craze (p. 17-40); Illustrations (p. 41-46); 3. "From 'Farmer's Rest' to 'Bicycler's Retreat'": The Economic Effects of the Bicycle (p. 47-

61); 4. "A Scientific Angel": The Debate Over Health, Religion, Morals, and Manners (p. 63-82); Illustrations (p. 83-91); 5. "Sing a Song of Bloomers Out for a Ride": The Clothing Revolution (p. 93-109): 6. "It Has Put the Human Race on Wheels": The Bicycle as an Instrument for Social Change (p. 111-119); Illustrations (p. 121-126); 7. "Let Him Ride to Death": The Crazy Fringe (p. 127-141); 8. "Diamonds Flash from His Tie": Cycle Racing: The Amateurs (p. 143-155); 9. "Clear Out If You Value Your Life": Cycle Racing: The Professionals (p. 157-171); Illustrations (p. 173-181); 10. "I Am the Scorcher Full of Zeal": The Clash Between Cyclers and Non-Cyclers (p. 183-203); 11. "Scarcely Jackassable": The Drive for Better Roads (p. 205-225); 12. "The Elusive Bicycle Corps": The Military Role of the Bicycle (p. 227-234); Illustrations (p. 235-240); 13. "Goodbye and Hello": The Eclipse and Restoration of the Bicycle (p. 241-251); Notes (p. 253-255); Bibliography (p. 257-259); Index (p. 261-269).

A238. *Numbery: Poems*, by Richard Mathews. BORGO LAUREATE SERIES, Number 1. xii+59 p. LC 95-19143. OCLC #32509244. ISBN 0-913960-13-6 cloth $20; ISBN 0-919360-14-4 paper $10. Book design by Ana Montalvo. Cover format by Highpoint Type & Graphics, illustration, "Don't Walk," by Robert Cottingham, black and red ink on cream background. Printed on cream-colored paper. First Edition, October 1995.

Selected poems by American writer, Richard Mathews (1944-).

CONTENTS: Section 1. The Reception (p. 3); Imaginary Numbers (p. 4); A Distant Reach (p. 5); Partly Skies (p. 6); Poem for You (p. 7); Pot Holders (p. 8); Who Else (p. 9); Detail: His Memories (p. 10); Late Encounter with the Muse (p. 11); Barbara's Marriage (p. 12); The Skier (p. 13); The War Has Departed (p. 14-15).

Section 2. My Attic Is High and Unfinished (p. 19); Sixty-Four Words (p. 20); The Visits (p. 21); The Relative Dark (p. 22); The Kingdom of Words (p. 23); Childhood Forest (p. 24); Naomi (p. 25); Tranxene 3.75 (p. 26); Come Closer (p. 27); The Antique Supermarket (p. 28-29); This Sickness Will (p. 30-31); The Man Across (p. 32-35).

Section 3. Mornings (p. 39); A Political Poem for Michael Horovitz (p. 40); Fast Deals (p. 41); SWAT Team Poets Cautiously Approach the Slum (p. 42); Myth for Fred White (p. 43);

Hanging the Lamp (p. 44); Planned Redevelopment (p. 45); The Sunken Mine (p. 46); Notes on the Thirtieth (p. 47-48); Dear Patty, Dear Tania (p. 49-50); For John Berryman (p. 51-52); The Neon Waltz for Robert Cottingham (p. 53-55); Acknowledgments (p. 57); About the Author and Illustrator (p. 59).

A239. *Justyna's Diary: Jewish Resistance to the Nazis in Wartime Poland*, by Justyna (Gusta Dawidsohn Draenger), translated by Majka Shephard, edited and with an introduction by Nathan Kravetz. STUDIES IN JUDAICA AND THE HOLOCAUST, Number 14. 120 p. LC 95-5199. OCLC #31934526. ISBN 0-8095-0402-2 cloth $25; ISBN 0-8095-1402-8 cloth $15. Cover: standard series design by Highpoint Type & Graphics with photo of Justyna, black ink on bright yellow background. First Edition, November 1995.

This first English-language translation of *Pamietnik Justyny*, published by the Jewish Historical Commission, Krakow (1946), is a first-person account of a Jewish resistance fighter in Poland during World War II.
    CONTENTS: About the Translator (p. 4); Foreword, by Dr. Nathan Kravetz (p. 5-7); Preface, by the Jewish Historical Commission, Krakow (p. 8); Introduction, by Jozef Wulf (p. 9-16); Gusta/Justyna, by Bernard Johannes (p. 17-18); Justyna's Diary (p. 19-112); Notes (p. 113-115); Index (p. 116-120).

A240. *The Coachella Valley Preserve: The Struggle for a Desert Wetlands*, by Yvonne Pacheco Tevis, with a bibliography by M. Louise Reynnells. GREAT ISSUES OF THE DAY, Number 5. 136 p. LC 87-866. OCLC #15196970. ISBN 0-89370-332-X cloth $27; ISBN 0-89370-432-6 paper $17. Illustrated with photographs and maps. Cover: new standard series design by Highpoint Type & Graphics, using photo of fringe-toed lizard courtesy of Jim Cornett, black ink on beige background. First Edition, November 1995.

The story of the struggle between developers and environmentalists in the Coachella Valley of California, over the vanishing habitat of the fringe-toed lizard.
    CONTENTS: Preface (p. 5); List of Characters (p. 7-9); Glossary (p. 11-16); 1. A Hankering for Open Space (p. 17-21); 2.

BP 300, by Robert Reginald & Mary Wickizer Burgess

The Bulldozed Desert (p. 23-29); 3. The Coachella Valley Fringe-Toed Lizard (p. 31-36); 4. Listing the Lizard (p. 37-60); 5. The Lizard Club and the Balance of Terror (p. 61-75); 6. A Desert Wetlands (p. 77-88); 7. A Conservation Plan Emerges (p. 89-99); 8. A Wilderness Preserved (p. 101-106); 9. Epilogue: A Model for the Future (p. 107-110); Notes (p. 112-116); Bibliography, by M. Louise Reynnells (p. 117-129); Index (p. 131-135); About Yvonne P. Tevis (p. 136).

A241. *Centurions, Knights, and Other Cops: The Police Novels of Joseph Wambaugh*, by J. K. Van Dover. Brownstone Mystery Guides, Volume 19. A Brownstone Book. 128 p. LC 95-5344. OCLC #31971065. ISBN 0-89370-195-5 cloth $25; ISBN 0-89370-295-1 paper $15. Cover: standard series design by Highpoint Type & Graphics, black ink on blue background. First Edition, November 1995.

A critique of the works of the modern American writer, Joseph Wambaugh (1937-).

CONTENTS: Dedication (p. 4); Preface (p. 5-6); A Joseph Wambaugh Chronology (p. 7-8); Introduction (p. 9-10); 1. *The New Centurions* (1970) (p. 11-24); 2. *The Blue Knight* (1972) (p. 25-35); 3. *The Onion Field* (1973) (p. 37-45); 4. *The Choirboys* (1975) (p. 47-57); 5. *The Black Marble* (1978) (p. 59-65); 6. *The Glitter Dome* (1981) (p. 67-75); 7. *The Delta Star* (1983) (p. 77-83); 8. *Lines and Shadows* (1984) (p. 85-90); 9. *The Secrets of Harry Bright* (1985) (p. 91-94); 10. *Echoes in Darkness* (1987), *The Blooding* (1989) (p. 95-98); 11. *The Golden Orange* (1990) (p. 99-103); 12. *Fugitive Nights* (1992) (p. 105-108); 13. *Finnegan's Week* (1993) (p. 109-112); 14. Conclusion (p. 113-114); Notes (p. 115-119); Primary Bibliography (p. 120); Secondary Sources (p. 121); Index (p. 123-127); About J. K. Van Dover (p. 128).

A242. *A Voyage to America Ninety Years Ago: The Diary of a Bohemian Jew on His Voyage from Hamburg to New York in 1847*, by S. E. Rosenbaum, edited by Guido Kisch, newly translated and with an introduction by Nathan Kravetz. Studies in Judaica and the Holocaust, Number 3. 120 p. LC 93-2898. OCLC #27430811. ISBN 0-89370-371-0 cloth $25; ISBN 0-89370-471-7 paper $15. Cover: standard series design by

147

BP 300, by Robert Reginald & Mary Wickizer Burgess

Highpoint Type & Graphics, dark blue ink on blue background. First Edition, November 1995.

The first English-language translation of a diary of a Jewish immigrant who came to American in the year 1847, packaged with the German original.
CONTENTS: Foreword, by Dr. Nathan Kravetz (p. 5-6); Introduction, by Guido Kisch (p. 7-19); Preface, by Mary A. Burgess (p. 20-22); The Diary in Translation (p. 23-66); The Diary: The Original Text (p. 69-114); Notes (p. 115-116); Index (p. 117-120).

A243. *Welcome to the Revolution: The Literary Legacy of Mack Reynolds*, by Curtis C. Smith, edited by Roger C. Schlobin. THE MILFORD SERIES: POPULAR WRITERS OF TODAY, Volume 64. A Thaddeus Dikty Book. 136 p. LC 95-5022. OCLC #31934209. ISBN 1-55742-235-4 cloth $27; ISBN 1-55742-236-2 paper $17. Cover: standard series design by Highpoint Type & Graphics with large photo of Reynolds, black ink on rose background. First Edition, December 1995.

A biography of the late American writer, Mack Reynolds (1917-1983), together with a critique of his works.
CONTENTS: Dedication (p. 4); A Mack Reynolds Chronology (p. 5-7); Abbreviations (p. 8); 1. Introduction: A Red Diaper Baby (p. 9-26); 2. The Short Stories (p. 27-40); 3. The Year 2000 (p. 41-63); 4. Primitive and Advanced Societies (p. 65-72); 5. The Joe Mauser Series (p. 73-79); 6. Interplanetary Fiction (p. 81-88); 7. Lagrangia (p. 89-95); 8. Other Works (p. 97-101); 9. The Legacy of Mack Reynolds (p. 103-107); Notes (p. 109-114); Primary Bibliography (p. 115-123); Secondary Bibliography (p. 124-126); Index (p. 127-135); About Curtis C. Smith (p. 136).

A244. *Laughing Like Hell: The Harrowing Satires of Jim Thompson*, by Gay Brewer. BROWNSTONE MYSTERY GUIDES, Volume 17. A Brownstone Book. 144 p. LC 95-5337. OCLC #31970941. ISBN 0-941028-21-6 cloth $27; ISBN 0-941028-22-4 paper $17. Illustrated with photographs of the author. Cover: standard series design by Highpoint Type & Graphics, using photo of author, black ink on pale green background. First Edition, January 1996 (i.e., December 1995).

BP 300, by Robert Reginald & Mary Wickizer Burgess

A critique on the works of the late American writer, Jim Thompson (1906-1977).

CONTENTS: Dedication (p. 4); About Gay Brewer (p. 4); Foreword: A Careening Bandwagon (p. 5-7); A Jim Thompson Chronology (p. 8-18); 1. *The Killer Inside Me*: Community and Negation (p. 19-42); 2. *Pop. 1280*: The Risible Christ (p. 43-67); 3. *The Getaway*: Monsters and Kings (p. 68-90); 4. *The Grifters*: Blood Money (p. 91-112); Notes (p. 113-123); Primary Bibliography (p. 124-125); Secondary Bibliography (p. 126-138); Index (p. 138-144).

A245. *The Work of Stephen King: An Annotated Bibliography & Guide*, by Michael R. Collings, edited by Boden Clarke. BIBLIOGRAPHIES OF MODERN AUTHORS, Number 25. 480 p. LC 93-16091. OCLC #27683725. ISBN 0-8095-0520-7 cloth $49; ISBN 0-8095-1520-2 paper $39. Cover: standard series design by Highpoint Type & Graphics, photo of author by George Beahm, black ink on gray background. First Edition, January 1996.

b. Second Printing, February 1996. This printing corrects a typographical error that appeared on the spine of the first edition.

A bibliography of and literary guide to the modern American writer, Stephen King (1947-).

CONTENTS: Dedication (p. 4); Introduction: "Not So Much to Tell, as to Let the Story Flow Through" (p. 5-8); A Stephen King Chronology (p. 9-15); About Michael R. Collings (p. 16).

Part One: Primary Sources. A. Books (p. 19-125); B. Short Fiction (p. 126-154); C. Short Nonfiction (p. 155-179); D. Poetry (p. 180-182); E. Screenplays (p. 183-184); F. Public and Screen Appearances (p. 185-188); G. Visual Adaptations of King Materials (p. 189-235); H. Audio Adaptations of King Materials (p. 236-243).

Part Two: Secondary Sources. I. Books and Book-Length Studies (p. 247-281); J. Newsletters (p. 282-284); K. Bibliographies and Filmographies (p. 285-289); L. Profiles and Bio-Bibliographical Sketches (p. 290-297); M. Interviews (p. 298-326); N. Scholarly Essays (p. 327-356); O. Popular and News Magazines (p. 357-360); P. Media Magazines, Speciality Magazines, Fan Publications (p. 361-374); Q. *Castle Rock: The Stephen King Newsletter* (1985-1989) (p. 375-394); R. Newspaper Articles (p. 395-406); S. Articles in Professional and Trade Journals (p. 407-408); T. Selected Reviews of King Works (p. 409-425); U. Stephen King Archives, University of Maine, Orono (p. 426-427); V. Unpublished Works (p. 428-429); W. Parodies, Pastiches, Etc. (p. 430-438); X. Honors and Awards (p. 439-440); Y. Miscellanea (p. 441).

Quoth the Critics (p. 442-449); Index (p. 450-480).

A246. *Murder Most Poetic: The Mystery Novels of Ngaio Marsh*, by Mary S. Weinkauf, edited by Mary A. Burgess. BROWNSTONE MYSTERY GUIDES, Volume 14. A Brownstone Book. 144 p. LC 95-5336. OCLC #31970935. ISBN 0-89370-197-1 cloth $27; ISBN 0-89370-297-8 paper $17. Cover: standard series design by Highpoint Type & Graphics, black ink on lemon background. First Edition, February 1996.

A critique on the works on the late New Zealand author, Ngaio Marsh (1895-1982).

CONTENTS: About Mary S. Weinkauf (p. 4); A Ngaio Marsh Chronology (p. 5-6); 1. The Play's the Thing: Ngaio Marsh as Producer-Director of Classic Mysteries (p. 7-16); 2. A Star Is Born: Inspector Alleyn and His Supporting Cast (p. 17-36); 3. All the World's a Stage: The *Dramatis Personae* in Marsh's Fiction (p. 37-69); Appendix I: Actors and Others Associated with the Theatre Who Are Killers and Victims in Marsh's Fiction (p. 70); 4. As You Like It: Marsh and the Shakespearean Influence (p. 71-101); Appendix II: Shakespearean Plays and the Ngaio Marsh Novels Which Quote Them (p. 102); 5. Back Stage: Theatrical Devices in Marsh's Fiction (p. 103-123); 6. Final Act: Ngaio Marsh and Her Detective Fiction (p. 125-127); Appendix III: Shakespeare's Characters in Marsh's Works (p. 128); Notes (p. 129-134); Selected Primary Bibliography (p. 135-136); Selected Secondary Bibliography (p. 137-138); Index (p. 139-144).

A247. *Islands in the Sky: The Space Station Theme in Science Fiction Literature*, by Gary Westfahl. I.O. EVANS STUDIES IN THE PHILOSOPHY & CRITICISM OF LITERATURE, Number 15. 224 p. LC 95-5024. OCLC #31934215. ISBN 0-89370-307-9 cloth $31; ISBN 0-89370-407-5 paper $21. Cover: modified series design

BP 300, by Robert Reginald & Mary Wickizer Burgess

by Highpoint Type & Graphics with drawing of a space station, black ink on rose background. First Edition, April 1996.

A guide to and critique of the space station theme in modern literature.

CONTENTS: Dedication (p. 4); Preface, by Gregory Benford (p. 5-6); Acknowledgments (p. 7-8).

Part One: Parameters. 1. *Beyond the Planet Earth*: Polemical Introduction (p. 11-24); 2. *Into the Sea of Stars*: Definitions and History of the Space Station in Fiction (p. 25-35); 3. *The Wheel in the Sky*: Space Station Design and Appearance (p. 36-42).

Part Two: Functions. 4. "Factory in the Sky": Space Stations as Businesses (p. 45-65); 5. *Killer Station*: Space Stations as Haunted Houses (p. 66-76); 6. *City in the Sky*: Space Stations as Communities (p. 77-86).

Part Three: Transformations. 7. *Exiled from Earth*: The Traveling Space Station (p. 89-94); 8. "Home on Lagrange": The Space Habitat (p. 95-115); 9. *The Web Between the Worlds*: The Space Elevator—And Beyond (p. 116-122).

Part Four: Iconography. 10. "Stranger Station": Space Stations in the Universe of Science Fiction (p. 125-142); 11. *This Strange Tomorrow*: The Future of Space Stations in Life and Literature (p. 143-150).

Part Five: Applications. 12. *Step to the Stars*: Space Station Freedom in the Context of Science Fiction (p. 153-168); 13. *A Handful of Stars*: Space Stations in Recent Science Fiction (p. 169-175).

Notes (p. 177-188); Primary Bibliography (p. 189-205); Secondary Bibliography (p. 207-208); Index (p. 209-223); About the Author (p. 224).

A248. *Beneath the Red Star: Studies on International Science Fiction*, by George Zebrowski, edited by Pamela Sargent. I.O. EVANS STUDIES IN THE PHILOSOPHY AND CRITICISM OF LITERATURE, Number 9. 120 p. LC 93-331. OCLC #27642972. ISBN 0-89370-350-8 cloth $25; ISBN 0-89370-450-4 paper $15. Cover: standard series design by Highpoint Type & Graphics, black ink on gray background. First Edition, June 1996.

_BP 300_, by Robert Reginald & Mary Wickizer Burgess

A collection of previously-published reviews and essays on the fantastic literature of Eastern Europe, focusing particularly on the fiction of Stanislaw Lem (1921-) and the Strugatsky Brothers.

CONTENTS: Introduction (p. 5-7); 1. Books 1974 (p. 9-17); 2. Books 1977 (p. 19-28); 3. Books 1979 (p. 29-39); 4. Books 1981 (p. 41-51); 5. Books 1982 (p. 53-63); 6. Escape from the Red Star: International Science Fiction 1987 (p. 65-77); 7. Stalkers (p. 79-82); 8. Searching for Asylum (p. 83-84); 9. The Cyberiad (p. 85-93); Notes (p. 95-96); A Checklist of Major Non-English SF Published in English Since 1970 (p. 97-108); Index (p. 109-119); About the Author and Editor (p. 120).

A249. *The Work of George Zebrowski: An Annotated Bibliography and Literary Guide, Third Edition, Revised and Expanded*, by Jeffrey M. Elliot & Robert Reginald, edited by Boden Clarke. BIBLIOGRAPHIES OF MODERN AUTHORS, Number 4. 144 p. LC 96-15694. OCLC #34544361. ISBN 0-89370-392-3 cloth $27; ISBN 0-89370-492-X paper $17. Cover: standard series design by Highpoint Type & Graphics, black ink on gray background, author photo by Jerry Bauer. Third Edition, June 1996.

A bibliography of and literary guide to the works of the American science fiction writer, George Zebrowski (1945-).

CONTENTS: Introduction (p. 5-8); A George Zebrowski Chronology (p. 9-18); A. Books and Monographs (p. 19-42); B. Short Fiction (p. 43-59); C. Short Nonfiction (p. 60-84); D. Short Translations (p. 85); E. Editorial Credits (p. 86-88); F. Juvenilia (p. 89-92); G. Unpublished Works (p. 93); H. Other Media (p. 94); I. Honors and Awards (p. 95-96); J. Public Appearances (p. 97-103); K. Secondary Sources (p. 104-111); L. Miscellanea (p. 112-114); Quoth the Critics (p. 115-134); Afterword: 6,250 Bits of Immortality, by George Zebrowski (p. 135-136); Index (p. 137-143); About Jeffrey M. Elliot & Robert Reginald (p. 144).

A revised and expanded version of **A72** and **A114**.

A250. *The Work of Pamela Sargent: An Annotated Bibliography and Literary Guide, Second Edition, Revised and Expanded*, by Jeffrey M. Elliot, edited by Boden Clarke. BIBLIOGRAPHIES OF MODERN AUTHORS, Number 13. 144 p. LC 96-15693. OCLC #34514643. ISBN 0-89370-396-6 cloth $27; ISBN 0-89370-496-2 paper $17. Cover: standard series design by Highpoint Type &

BP 300, by Robert Reginald & Mary Wickizer Burgess

Graphics, blank ink on pale pink background, author photo by Jerry Bauer. Second Edition, June 1996.

A bibliography of and literary guide to the American writer, Pamela Sargent (1948-).
CONTENTS: Introduction: "What Doesn't Kill You Makes You Stronger" (p. 5-10); A Pamela Sargent Chronology (p. 11-14); A. Books and Monographs (p. 15-43); B. Short Fiction (p. 44-60); C. Short Nonfiction (p. 61-72); D. Unpublished Works (p. 73); E. Editorial Credits (p. 74-75); F. Other Media (p. 76); G. Juvenilia (p. 77); H. Public Appearances (p. 78-85); I. Honors and Awards (p. 86-87); J. Secondary Sources (p. 88-94); K. Miscellanea (p. 95-96); Quoth the Critics (p. 97-113); Three Essays by Pamela Sargent: "Nicotine Fits" (p. 114-123); "Writing, Science Fiction, and Family Values" (p. 124-135); Afterword: "Through the Looking Glass" (p. 136-137); Notes (p. 138-139); Index (p. 140-143); About Jeffrey M. Elliot (p. 144).
See also the First Edition (**A109**).

A251. ***The Genealogical History of Providencia Island***, by J. Cordell Robinson. BORGO FAMILY HISTORIES, Number 5. An Emeritus Enterprises Book. xii+286 p. LC 96-8530. OCLC #34691187. ISBN 0-913960-42-X cloth $43; ISBN 0-913960-43-8 paper $33. Cover: standard series design adapted by Highpoint Type & Graphics, brown ink on teal blue background, displaying a map of Providencia Island on the front cover. Illustrated with photographs of the Robinson Family and a map of the island. First Edition, June 1996.

b. Second Printing, September 1996.

A genealogical guide to the major families residing in La Providencia Island in the Caribbean.
CONTENTS: Author's Note (p. iii-iv); Map of Providencia Island (p. vi); Preface (p. vii-x); Part I: History (p. 1-31); Economic Structure and Activities (p. 32-37); Social Stratification and Social Life (p. 38-49); Education and Language (p. 50-60); Consanguineous Relationships and the Genetic Consequences (p. 61-75); Religious Life (p. 76-89); Outmigration (p. 90-98). Part II. Family Charts: John Robinson (Theodore Birelski) (p. 101-152); Photos (p. 153-164); Capt. Francis Archbold (p. 165-195); Simon

Howard Sr. (p. 197-208); William Newball Sr. (p. 209-226); Thomas Taylor (Tayler) (p. 227-235); James C. Taylor (p. 237-238); John C. Britton Sr. (p. 239-242); Bibliography (p. 243-254); Index of Text (p. 255-257); Index of Names (p. 259-285); About the Author (p. [286])..

A252. *Providencia Island: Its History and Its People*, by J. Cordell Robinson. STOKVIS STUDIES IN HISTORICAL CHRONOLOGY AND THOUGHT, Number 17. x+118 p. LC 96-8531. OCLC #34651372. ISBN 0-8095-0108-2 cloth $25; ISBN 0-8095-1108-8 paper $15. Cover: standard series design adapted by Highpoint Type & Graphics, black ink on light blue background, displaying a map of Providencia Island on the front cover. Illustrated with a map of the island. First Edition, June 1996.

A history of La Providencia Island in the Caribbean, consisting of the first half of **A251** (*q.v.*), plus the bibliography from that book, and a new index.

CONTENTS: Author's Note (p. iii-iv); Map of Providencia Island (p. vi); Preface (p. vii-x); Part I: History (p. 1-31); Economic Structure and Activities (p. 32-37); Social Stratification and Social Life (p. 38-49); Education and Language (p. 50-60); Consanguineous Relationships and the Genetic Consequences (p. 61-75); Religious Life (p. 76-89); Outmigration (p. 90-98); Bibliography (p. 99-110); Index (p. 112-117); About the Author (p. [118]).

A253. *Life Upon the Wicked Stage: A Visit to the American Theatre of the 1860s, 1870s, and 1880s as Seen in the Pages of the New York Clipper*, edited by William L. Slout. CLIPPER STUDIES IN THE THEATRE, Number 14. xii+168 p. LC 96-1562. OCLC #34190958. ISBN 0-89370-363-X cloth $29; ISBN 0-89370-463-6 paper $19. Cover: standard series design by Highpoint Type & Graphics, black ink on green background. Illustrated with reproductions of contemporary woodcuts. First Edition, July 1996.

Reprints of essays on the American nineteenth-century theatre.
CONTENTS: List of Illustrations (p. [v]-vi); Preface (p. [vii]-9); Part I: About Theatre People. "A Little Gossip About Show People," by Ralph Keeler (p. 1-5); "The Stage Grumbler," by

BP 300, by Robert Reginald & Mary Wickizer Burgess

Marcus Moriarty (p. 5-6); "The Actor," by Bambrino (p. 6-9); "Criticism on Acting by Actors and Actresses" (p. 11-13); "The Actor in Society," by Bambrino (p. 13-17); "Actresses," by Bambrino (p. 17-20); "The Actress' Dresser" (p. 20-24); "The Prompter" (p. 25-29); "The Call Boy" (p. 29-35); "The Stage Doorkeeper," by Bambrino (p. 35-41). Part II: Behind the Footlights. "The 'Realistic' on the Stage" (p. 43-46); "Stage Banquets" (p. 46-50); "Stage Mishaps," by Susan Archer Weiss (p. 50-53); "Accidents in Theatres" (p. 53-56); "Behind the Scenes" (p. 57-62). Part III: About Some Audiences. "In the Audience," by W. E. M. (p. 63-66); "The Bower Gods: Their Ways and Favorites," by Frank McHale (p. 66-68); "The 'Gods'," by J. Booth Renauld (p. 69-71); "An East Side Theatre," by "Arab" (p. 72-76); "The Bowery and the Bowery Boy" (p. 76-78). Part IV: About Performance. "Talent and Tact: Hints to a Young Professional," by Bambrino (p. 79-90); "'Indisposition' on the Stage" (p. 91-93); "The Stage in America from an English Point of Observation," by Wardle Corbyn (p. 94-97); "On Stage Management" (p. 97-100); "The Drama," by "a retired actor" (p. 101-108). Part V: About Theatrical Promotion. "On Business Management," by Dramaticus (p. 109-114); "Advertising Amusements" (p. 114-117); "Theatrical Managers and the Press" (p. 117-121); "The Star System" (p. 123-124). Part VI: About the Musical Stage, etc. "Notes of a Leader of Orchestra," by Charles Connolly (p. 125-165); Index (p. 167-168); About William L. Slout (p. [168]).

A254. *Running from the Hunter: The Life and Works of Charles Beaumont*, by Lee Prosser, edited by Miguel Alcalde. THE MILFORD SERIES: POPULAR WRITERS OF TODAY, Volume 68. 136 p. LC 95-5346. OCLC #31971083. ISBN 0-89370-191-2 cloth $27; ISBN 0-89370-291-9 paper $17. Cover: standard series design by Highpoint Type & Graphics, black ink on violet background. First Edition, July 1996.

A critique of the writings of science fiction and television writer, Charles Beaumont (1929-1967).

CONTENTS: A Charles Beaumont Chronology (p. 5-12); 1. Introduction and Interviews (p. 13-24); 2. Autobiographical Sketches (p. 25-27); 3. Nonfiction Works (p. 28-33); 4. Television Scripts (p. 34-35); 5. Motion Picture Screenplays (p. 36-37); 6.

The Intruder (1959) (p. 38-45); 7. *Run from the Hunter* (1957) (p. 46-50); 8. The Short Fiction (p. 51-115); 9. Conclusion (p. 116-118); Primary Bibliography, by William F. Nolan (p. 119-122); Secondary Sources (p. 123-125); Index (p. 126-134); Reflections (p. 135); About Lee Prosser (p. 136).

A255. ***BP 250: An Annotated Bibliography of the First 250 Publications of The Borgo Press, 1975-1996,*** by Robert Reginald and Mary A. Burgess. BORGO LITERARY GUIDES, Number 10. 192 p. LC 96-1744. OCLC #34151781. ISBN 0-8095-0206-2 cloth $29; ISBN 0-8095-1206-8 paper $19. Limited to 110 signed and numbered copies (numbered i-x and 1-100). Cover: standard series design by Highpoint Type & Graphics, black ink on green background. First Edition, June 1996.

An annotated bibliography of the publications of the Borgo Press and its major affiliated lines and imprints.
     CONTENTS: Introduction (p. 5-6); A. Borgo Press Books, 1976-1996 (p. 7-140); B. Xenos Books, 1986-1990 (p. 141); C. Brownstone Books, 1981-1989 (1991) (p. 142-143); D. Starmont Contemporary Writer Series, 1988-1998 (1991) (p. 144); E. Sidewinder Press (Sun Dance Press), 1971 (1991) (p. 145); F. St. Willibrord's Press, 1985-1991 (1991) (p. 146-147); G. Starmont House & FAX Collector's Editions, 1973-1992 (1993) (p. 148-160); H. Miscellaneous Publications, 1973-1994 (p. 161-162); Series Index (p. 163-172); Author Index (p. 173-176); Title Index (p. 177-190); About the Authors (p. 191); Limitation Page (p. 192).

A256. ***The Directory of Autocephalous Bishops of the Churches of the Apostolic Succession, Eighth Edition,*** by Bishop Karl Pruter. THE AUTOCEPHALOUS ORTHODOX CHURCHES, No. 1. A St. Willibrord's Press Book. 104 p. LC 96-28189. OCLC #35001840. ISBN 0-912134-30-5 cloth $23; ISBN 0-912134-31-3 paper $13. Cover: standard series design by Highpoint Type & Graphics, black ink on salmon background. First Edition, August 1996.

BP 300, **by Robert Reginald & Mary Wickizer Burgess**

A guide to the prelates of the independent Old Catholic and Orthodox churches in America. Spine title: *Eighth Directory of Autocephalous Bishops.*

CONTENTS: Preface (p. 7-8); Directory: United States & Canada, Central & South America (p. 9-94); Index of Jurisdictions (p. 95-101); Geographic Index (p. 102-103); About the Author (p. 104).

A257. ***Rubber Dinosaurs and Wooden Elephants: Essays on Literature, Film, and History,*** by L. Sprague de Camp. I.O. EVANS STUDIES IN THE PHILOSOPHY AND CRITICISM OF LITERATURE, No. 26. 144 p. LC 95-5348. OCLC #32203134. ISBN 0-89370-354-0 cloth $29; ISBN 0-89370-454-7 paper $19. Cover: standard series design by Highpoint Type & Graphics, black ink on yellow-orange background. First Edition, August 1996.

Selected essays on science fiction, fantasy, and history by the well-known SF writer.

CONTENTS: Acknowledgments (p. 4); Introduction (p. 5); 1. Silent Specters, Spiders, and Sauropods (p. 7-13); 2. The Con Man from Baghdad (p. 14-21); 3. Three Thirds of a Hero (p. 22-30); 4. Lovecraft: Failed Aristocrat (p. 31-42); 5. Conan, Illusion, and Reality (p. 43-52); 6. Thoats, Tharks, and Thews (p. 53-62); 7. Pseudohistory (p. 63-67); 8. Books That Never Were (p. 68-75); 9. The Man Who Invented R. and D. (p. 76-80); 10. Brachiating in the Family Tree (p. 81-88); 11. Lovecraft and the Aryans (p. 89-102); 12. Howard and the Celts (p. 103-114); 13. The Heroic Barbarian (p. 115-126); Notes (p. 127-129); Index (p. 131-143); About the Author (p. 144).

A258. ***The Ancient Church on New Shores: Antioch in North America,*** by Archpriest Antony Gabriel. THE AUTOCEPHALOUS ORTHODOX CHURCHES, No. 5. A St. Willibrord's Press Book. 240 p., illus. LC 96-8362. OCLC #34651354. ISBN 0-912134-26-7 cloth $35; ISBN 0-912134-27-5 paper $25. Cover: standard series design by Highpoint Type & Graphics, black ink on beige background; cover drawing of St. George Syrian Orthodox Church, Montréal, by R. D. Wilson. First Edition, September 1996.

b.   Second Printing, December 1996 (January 1997).

A history of the Orthodox Church of Antioch's Archdiocese in the United States and Canada.
    CONTENTS: Acknowledgments (p. 5); A Chronology of the Antiochian Church in North America (p. 6-13); Foreword, by P. W. S. Schneirdla (p. 14); Preface (p. 15-16); An Historical Foreword: The Patriarchate of Antioch (p. 17-20); 1. An Historical and Cultural Canvas (p. 21-29); 2. The Church in America (p. 30-38); 3. The Agony Begins (p. 39-55); 4. A Time for Hope, A Time of Troubles (p. 56-73); 5. Changes in the North American Church (p. 74-87); 6. The Clouds Gather in the Midst of a Summer Day (p. 88-117); 7. One Chapter Closes, Another Begins (p. 118-130); 8. Relations Between the Churches in the Middle East and North America (p. 131-140); 9. The Church of Antioch Turns to the Future (p. 141-159); Epilogue/Reflections (p. 160-162); Appendix 1: Three Pioneer Priests in North America (p. 163-164); Appendix 2: A Profile of Four Parishes (p. 165-170); Appendix 3: Constitutional Documents Relating to the Archdiocese of New York and All the Americas (p. 171-189); Appendix 4: Hierarchs Who Exercised Authority in the Antiochian Church of North America (p. 190-191); Appendix 5: Original Petition (p. 192-194); Notes (p. 195-214); Bibliography (p. 215-228); Index (p. 229-240).

A259. *Discovering Classic Fantasy Fiction: Essays on the Antecedents of Fantastic Literature*, edited by Darrell Schweitzer. I.O. EVANS STUDIES IN THE PHILOSOPHY AND CRITICISM OF LITERATURE, No. 23. A Thaddeus Dikty Book. 176 p. LC 95-5347. OCLC #31971087. ISBN 1-55742-086-6 cloth $31; ISBN 1-55742-087-4 paper $21. Cover: standard series design by Highpoint Type & Graphics, black ink on teal blue background. First Edition, September 1996.

An anthology of essays on fantastic literature.
    CONTENTS: Introduction (p. 5); Acknowledgments (p. 6); 1. "Lord Dunsany: The Career of a Fantaisiste," by S. T. Joshi (p. 7-48); 2. "James Branch Cabell: No Fit Employment for a Grown Man," by Don D'Ammassa (p. 49-55); 3. "Mervyn Wall and the Comedy of Despair," by Darrell Schweitzer (p. 56-67); 4. "John Collier, Fantastic Miniaturist," by Alan Warren (p. 68-75); 5. "A.

BP 300, by Robert Reginald & Mary Wickizer Burgess

Merritt: A Reappraisal," by Ben P. Indick (p. 76-87); 6. "Villains of Necessity: The Works of E. R. Eddison," by Don D'Ammassa (p. 88-93); 7. "Subtle Perceptions: The Fantasy Novels of Algernon Blackwood," by Jeffrey Goddin (p. 94-103); 8. "David Lindsay and the Quest for Muspel-Fire," by Galad Elflandsson (p. 104-112); 9. "Classic American Fairy Tales: The Fantasies of L. Frank Baum," by Neal Wilgus (p. 113-121); 10. "Henry Kuttner: Man of Many Virtues," by Don D'Ammassa (p. 122-125); 11. "Of the Master, Merlin, and H. Warner Munn," by Don Herron (p. 126-150); Notes (p. 151-154); Bibliography (p. 155-162); About the Contributors (p. 163-164); Index (p. 165-176).

A260. *Seven by Seven: Interviews with American Science Fiction Writers of the West and Southwest*, by Neal Wilgus. THE MILFORD SERIES: POPULAR WRITERS OF TODAY, Vol. 44. 136 p. LC 87-814. OCLC #15164305. ISBN 0-89370-173-4 cloth $29; ISBN 0-89370-273-0 paper $19. Cover: standard series design by Highpoint Type & Graphics, black ink on pink background. First Edition, September 1996.

Interviews with American science fiction writers of the West.
CONTENTS: Introduction (p. 5-7); Acknowledgments (p. 8); A Robert Anton Wilson Chronology (p. 9-10); 1. Robert Anton Wilson: The Man with the Cosmic Triggerfinger (p. 11-28; A Robert Shea Chronology (p. 29-30); 2. Robert Shea: Illuminated Co-Conspirator (p. 31-44); A Suzy McKee Charnas Chronology (p. 45-46); 3. Suzy McKee Charnas: Walk to the End of the *Motherlines* (p. 47-64); A Stephen R. Donaldson Chronology (p. 65-66); 4. Stephen R. Donaldson: Chronicles of the Unbeliever (p. 67-81); A Fred Saberhagen Chronology (p. 82-83); 5. Fred Saberhagen: Berserkers and Vampires (p. 84-92); A Roger Zelazny Chronology (p. 93-94); 6. Roger Zelazny: Lord of Shadows, Jack of Light (p. 95-107); A Jack Williamson Chronology (p. 108-109); 7. Jack Williamson: Grand Master (p. 110-121); About Neal Wilgus (p. 122); Index (p. 123-127); Character Index (p. 128).

A261. *The Priest's Handbook, Second Edition, Revised and Expanded*, by Bishop Karl Pruter. ST. WILLIBRORD STUDIES IN PHILOSOPHY AND RELIGION, No. 4. A St. Willibrord's Press Book. 62 p. LC 96-25022. OCLC #35008104. ISBN 0-912134-28-3 cloth $23;

BP 300, by Robert Reginald & Mary Wickizer Burgess

ISBN 0-912134-29-1 paper $13. Cover: standard series design by Highpoint Type & Graphics, black ink on olive green background. Second Edition, October 1996.

A guide for priests of the Old Catholic Church.
CONTENTS: Foreword (p. 5-6); 1. The Rights and Duties of Pastors (p. 7-11); 2. The Divine Services (p. 13-14); 3. Sacraments of Penance/Confession and Communion (p. 15-16); 4. The Sacrament of Holy Baptism (p. 17-18); 5. The Sacrament of Confirmation (p. 19-20); 6. The Reception of Converts (p. 21); 7. The Sacrament of Holy Matrimony (p. 23-24); 8 The Sacrament of Holy Unction (p. 25); 9. The Funeral Service (p. 27-29); 10. Some Priestly Disciplines (p. 31-33); 11. Unassigned and Non-Parochial Clergy (p. 35); 12. Regarding Visits by the Bishop (p. 37); 13. Parochial Financial Obligation to the Diocese (p. 39); 14. Deaneries (p. 41-44); 15. Ecumenical Guidelines (p. 45-48); 16. Relations with Non-Christians (p. 49-50); Bibliography (p. 51); Index (p. 53-61); About the Author (p. 62).

A262. *A Subtler Magick: The Writings and Philosophy of H.P. Lovecraft, Second Edition, Revised and Expanded*, by S. T. Joshi. THE MILFORD SERIES: POPULAR WRITERS OF TODAY, Vol. 62. A Thaddeus Dikty Book. 312 p. LC 95-5026. OCLC #31934230. ISBN 0-916732-58-4 cloth $39; ISBN 0-916732-59-2 paper $29. Cover: standard series design by Highpoint Type & Graphics, black ink on beige background. First Edition, October 1996.

A critique of the writing of American horror writer, H. P. Lovecraft (1890-1937).
CONTENTS: Introduction (p. 5-6); An H. P. Lovecraft Chronology (p. 7-11); 1. Life and Thought (p. 13-50); 2. Early Fiction (1905-1921) (p. 51-69); 3. The "Dunsanian" Tales (1919-1921) (p. 70-84); 4. Regional Horror (1921-1926) (p. 85-111); 5. The Major Fiction: First Stage (1926-1930) (p. 112-149); 6. Major Fiction: Second Stage (1931-1935) (p. 150-184); 7. Revisions and Collaborations (p. 185-205); 8. Essays (p. 206-219); 9. Poetry (p. 220-235); 10. Letters (p. 236-249); 11. Conclusion (p. 250-268); Notes (p. 269-283); Annotated Primary Bibliography (p. 284-287); Annotated Secondary Bibliography (p. 288-293); Index (p. 294-312); About S. T. Joshi (p. 312).

BP 300, by Robert Reginald & Mary Wickizer Burgess

A263. *Confessions of a Trekoholic: A New Look at The Next Generation*, by Hilary Palencar. MALCOLM HULKE STUDIES IN CINEMA AND TELEVISION, No. 1. 120 p. LC 96-6740. OCLC #34281585. ISBN 0-8095-10001-9 cloth $25; ISBN 0-8095-1001-4 paper $15. Cover: standard series design by Highpoint Type & Graphics, First Edition, black ink on pink background. November 1996.

A critique of the popular American television series, *Star Trek: The Next Generation*.

CONTENTS: Acknowledgments (p. 4); Warning (p. 5); Preface (p. 6); 1. Introduction (p. 7-13); 2. "Darmok" (p. 14-21); 3. Data and the Disappearance of the Hero, Part One (p. 22-37); 4. Data and the Disappearance of the Hero, Part Two (p. 38-48); 5. Wesley's Not-So-Excellent Adventure (p. 49-57); 6. Women and Sexuality in *The Next Generation* (p. 48-76); 7. Klingons, Honor, and Traditional Family Values in *The Next Generation* (p. 77-87); 8. Two Episodes: "I, Borg" and "Ship in a Bottle" (p. 88-95); 9. The Holodeck, Time Travel, Q, and Rewriting Reality (p. 96-107); 10. Conclusion (p. 108-109); Index (p. 110-112); Title Index (p. 113-116); Character Index (p. 117-119); About the Author (p. 120).

A264. *Xenograffiti: Essays on Fantastic Literature*, by Robert Reginald. I.O. EVANS STUDIES IN THE PHILOSOPHY AND CRITICISM OF LITERATURE, No. 33. 224 p. LC 96-35246. OCLC #35548797. ISBN 0-8095-0900-8 cloth $33; ISBN 0-8095-1900-3 paper $23. Cover: standard series design by Highpoint Type & Graphics, black ink on red background. First Edition, December 1996.

A collection of essays on science fiction and fantasy.

CONTENTS: Introduction (p. 5); 1. Languid Dreams: Andrew Lang and *The Book of Dreams and Ghosts* (1972) (p. 7-9); 2. "They" Live! The Parodies of H. Rider Haggard (1978) (p. 10-13); 3. Dance of the Spheres: Keith Roberts and the *Pavane* of History (1979) (p. 14-18); 4. A Stitch in Time: Free Will in Ward Moore's *Bring the Jubilee* (1979) (p. 19-23); 5. Beware of the House: The Nature of Reality in Daphne du Maurier's Fantasy (1983) (p. 24-26); 6. Comeau's *Magic* (1983) (p. 27-29); 7.

161

Curious Things: The Horror Fiction of Eleanor M. Ingram (1983) (p. 30-32); 8. The Devil Took Her! Charlotte Haldane's *Melusine* (1983) (p. 33-35); 9. Gory Interludes: John Norman and the Ennui of Sexual Fantasy (1983) (p. 36-39); 10. Jewels of Fantasy: The Dunsanian Pastiches of Vernon Knowles (1983) (p. 40-42); 11. The Life of Death: Robert Nathan and the Necessity of Love (1983) (p. 43-45); 12. Merovingian Dreams: The Neustrian Fantasies of Leslie Barringer (1983) (p. 46-50); 13. One Is One and All Alone: Fritz Leiber's Solipsistic Fantasy (1983) (p. 51-53); 14. Paladorean Idylls: Sir Henry Newbolt's *Aladore* (1983) (p. 54-56); 15. Prospero Updated: The Fantasy of John Bellairs (1983) (p. 57-59); 16. Strange Lessons: Edward Heron-Allen's Cosmopoli Tales (1983) (p. 60-62); 17. Styx Tryx: The Humorous Fantasies of John Kendrick Bangs (1983) (p. 63-67); 18. A Thousand Nights in Serendip: Piers Anthony's *Hasan* (1983) (p. 68-70); 19. Vivo, Ergo Sum: The Problem of Immortality in Edwin Lester Arnold's *Phra the Phoenician* (1983) (p. 71-73); 20. Between Order and Chaos: The Fiction of Bruce McAllister (1986) (p. 74-76); 21. Moral/Immoral: The Fictional Universe of Michael Reaves (1986) (p. 77-79); 22. Teacher-Preacher: R. Lionel Fanthorpe and the Literature of Abundity (1986) (p. 80-82); 23. The Brush of Æons: George Zebrowski's Fictional Universe (1991) (p. 83-86); 24. Derynian Dreams: The Fantasy Worlds of Katherine Kurtz (1991) (p. 87-90); 25. The Fat Man, the Consulting Detective, and the Seller of Speculations: The Curious World of Arthur Byron Cover (1991) (p. 91-93); 26. Slicing Away at Suburbia: The Fantastic Fiction of William F. Nolan (1991) (p. 94-96); 27. Pilgrim Award Acceptance Speech (1993) (p. 97-100); 28. A Requiem for Starmont House and FAX Collector's Editions, 1972-1993: A History and Bibliography (1993) (p. 101-127); 29. Laughing Like Hell: Brian Stableford's World of Agony (1995) (p. 128-130); 30. Margaret Atwood: The Young Woman in Agony (1996) (p. 131-134); 31. A Turbot at a Time: The Mystery Novels of Lindsey Davis (p. 135-137); 32. Selected Reviews (1971-1993) (p. 138-165); 33. Selected Obituaries (1983-1996) (p. 166-179); Bibliography (p. 180-186); Index (p. 187-198); Title Index (p. 199-219); Character Index (p. 220-223); About the Author (p. 224).

A265. *Motherless Children, Fatherless Waifs: Modern Fictional Protagonists and the Artist's Search for the Real Self*, by Leo

BP 300, by Robert Reginald & Mary Wickizer Burgess

Schneiderman. I.O. EVANS STUDIES IN THE PHILOSOPHY AND CRITICISM OF LITERATURE, No. 12. 232 p. LC 95-5021. OCLC #31901566. ISBN 0-89370-306-0 cloth $35; ISBN 0-89370-406-7 paper $25. Cover: standard series design by Highpoint Type & Graphics, black ink on off white background. First Edition, December 1996.

A psychological critique of parentless children in literature.
    CONTENTS: Acknowledgments (p. 4); Glossary of Psychoanalytic Terms (p. 5-7); 1. The Real Self: Universal Significance of Personal Experience (p. 9-23); 2. Arthur Miller: Drama from the Standpoint of Self Psychology (p. 24-44); 3. John Steinbeck: A Study of Identity Diffusion and Ambivalence (p. 45-67); 4. John Updike: Fiction and the Writer's Access to Contradictory Ego States (p. 68-77); 5. Georges Simenon: Self-Theory and Impulse-Regulation (p. 78-92); 6. Eugene Ionesco: Anger as Despair, Pity as Scorn (p. 93-115); 7. Hermann Hesse: Conflict Resolution in His Fiction (p. 116-128); 8. E. T. A. Hoffmann: Ego-Ideal and Parental Loss (p. 129-145); 9. D. H. Lawrence: Fear of Fusion (p. 146-162); 10. Jean-Paul Sartre: Ego and Superego Functions in Fiction and Ideology (p. 163-183); 11. Tom Stoppard: What Passion Weaves by Reason is Undone (p. 184-196); Notes (p. 197-205); Selected Primary Bibliography (p. 206-211); Selected Secondary Bibliography (p. 212-216); Index (p. 217-221); Title Index (p. 222-228); Character Index (p. 229-231); About the Author (p. 232).

A266. *The Cape of Don Francisco Torquemada*, by Benito Pérez Galdós, translated from the Spanish by Robert G. Trimble. An Emeritus Enterprises Book. vi+626 p. LC 96-38812. OCLC #355867677. ISBN 0-913960-46-2 cloth $59; ISBN 0-913960-47-0 paper $49. Cover: standard series design by Highpoint Type & Graphics, black ink on red background. First Edition, November 1996.

b.   [Second Printing, March 1997.]

An original translation of a novel by Spanish writer Pérez Galdós. The first printing was scrapped, and the book was reprinted with the background cover color in pink in March 1997.

BP 300, by Robert Reginald & Mary Wickizer Burgess

CONTENTS: Preface: Benito Pérez Galdós, by Robert G. Trimble (p. [iv]); Book I: Torquemada in the Bonfire (p. 1-64); Book II: Torquemada on the Cross (p. 65-239); Book III: Torquemada in Purgatory (p. 241-444); Book IV: Torquemada and Saint Peter (p. 445-625); About the Translator (p. 626).

A267. *The Old Catholic Church: A History and Chronology, Second Edition, Revised and Expanded*, by Bishop Karl Pruter. THE AUTOCEPHALOUS ORTHODOX CHURCHES, No. 3. A St. Willibrord's Press Book. 96 p., illus. LC 95-3866. OCLC #31934090. ISBN 0-912134-18-6 cloth $27; ISBN 0-912134-19-4 paper $17. Cover: standard series design by Highpoint Type & Graphics, black ink on pale pink background. Second Edition, December 1996.

A history of the Old Catholic Church.
CONTENTS: About the Author (p. 4); Preface to the Second Edition (p. 5-6); Old Catholic Church Chronology (p. 7-9); List of Illustrations (p. 10); 1. The Early Church (p. 11-14); 2. The Reformation (p. 15-18); 3. The Old Catholic Church in Europe (p. 19-21); 4. The Oxford Movement (p. 23-26); 5. The Autocephalous Orthodox Churches (p. 27-30); 6. The Old Catholic Church of England (p. 31-35); 7. The Roman Catholic Church in America (p. 37-41); 8. Joseph René Vilatte (p. 43-48); 9. Carmel Henry Carfora (p. 49-52); 10. The Polish National Catholic Church (p. 53-58); 11. The African Orthodox Church (p. 59-62); 12. The Free Catholic Movement (p. 63-66); 13. Christ Catholic Church (p. 67-72); 14. Christ Catholic Church International (p. 73-77); 15. Other Old Catholic Bodies in America (p. 79-81); Notes (p. 82-83); Bibliography (p. 84-86); Index (p. 87-96).

A268. *Fidel by Fidel: An Interview with Dr. Fidel Castro Ruz, President of the Republic of Cuba*, conducted by Rep. Mervyn M. Dymally and Dr. Jeffrey M. Elliot. GREAT ISSUES OF THE DAY, No. 3. 120 p. LC 85-25551. OCLC #12752398. ISBN 0-89370-330-3 cloth $27; ISBN 0-89370-430-X paper $17. Cover: standard series design by Highpoint Type & Graphics, black ink on beige background. First Edition, December 1996.

An interview with Cuban President Fidel Castro.

BP 300, by Robert Reginald & Mary Wickizer Burgess

CONTENTS: Introduction, by Boden Clarke (p. 5-7); A Fidel Castro Chronology (p. 8-14); 1. The Economic Crisis in Latin America and the Third World (p. 15-80); 2. The Political Crisis in Central America (p. 81-111); Index (p. 112-119); About the Authors (p. 120).

A269. *Cat'spaw Utopia: Albert K. Owen, the Adventurer of Topolobampo Bay, and the Last Great Utopian Scheme, Second Edition, Revised and Expanded*, by Ray Reynolds. WEST COAST STUDIES, No. 4. 160 p., illus. LC 93-12180. OCLC #27429247. ISBN 0-8095-2803-7 cloth $31; ISBN 0-8095-3803-2 paper $21. Cover: standard series design by Highpoint Type & Graphics, black ink on brown background, photos of Topolobampo Bay and Albert Owen courtesy of the author. Second Edition, December 1996 (January 1997).

An historical account of the building of a utopian colony on the West Coast of México.
CONTENTS: Acknowledgments (p. 4); Preface (p. 5-6); About the Author (p. 6); 1. One Man's Railroad (p. 7-17); 2. Paradise Incorporated (p. 18-29); 3. The Terrible Tales (p. 30-43); 4. Enter the Kansas Element (p. 44-54); 5. Scandalous Women (p. 55-68); 6. Ira Kneeland Writes Home (p. 69-84); 7. The Dividing Ditch (p. 85-95); 8. Crack-Up (p. 96-106); 9. Afterwards (p. 107-116); 10. Conclusion (p. 117); Appendices (p. 118-139); Selected Bibliography (p. 140-144); Index (p. 153-160).

A270. *Outposts: Literatures of Milieux*, by Algis Budrys. I.O. EVANS STUDIES IN THE PHILOSOPHY AND CRITICISM OF LITERATURE, No. 28. 144 p. LC 95-5345. OCLC #31971079. ISBN 0-89370-347-8 cloth $29; ISBN 0-89370-447-4 paper $19. Cover: standard series design by Highpoint Type & Graphics, black ink on olive green background. First Edition, December 1996 (January 1997).

A collection of essays on SF and fantasy by a well-known American critic.
CONTENTS: About the Author (p. 4); Introduction (p. 5-6); 1. Beyond Rayguns and Godzilla (p. 7-17); 2. Paradise Charted (p. 18-68); 3. Literatures of Milieux (p. 69-85); 4. Foundation and Asimov (p. 86-92); 5. Non-Literary Influences on Science Fiction

(p. 93-114); Notes (p. 115-127); A Science Fiction Glossary (p. 128-130); Fan Terms (p. 131-132); Index (p. 133-144).

A271. *Clowns and Cannons: The American Circus During the Civil War*, by William L. Slout. CLIPPER STUDIES IN THE THEATRE, No. 16. xii+247 p., illus. LC 96-36573. OCLC #35593540. ISBN 0-8095-0304-2 cloth $37; ISBN 0-8095-1304-8 paper $27. Cover: standard series design by Highpoint Type & Graphics, black ink on bright pink background. First Edition, April 1997.

An account of the development of the American circus during the 1860s.
CONTENTS: Preface (p. vii-xii); 1860 (p. 3-38); 1861 (p. 39-79); 1862 (p. 83-122); 1863 (p. 125-154); 1864 (p. 155-180); 1865 (p. 181-219); Bibliography (p. 221-230); Index (p. 231-247).

A272. *Detective and Mystery Fiction: An International Bibliography of Secondary Sources, Second Edition, Revised and Expanded*, by Walter Albert. BROWNSTONE MYSTERY GUIDES, Vol. 10. A Brownstone Book. 672 p., 8.5 x 11". LC 95-5335. OCLC #31970930. ISBN 0-941028-15-1 cloth $100; ISBN 0-941028-16-X paper $80. Cover: standard series design by Highpoint Type & Graphics, black ink on beige background. Second Edition, June 1997.

A bibiography of secondary sources relating to mystery and detective fiction.
CONTENTS: Introduction (p. 5-7); Abbreviations (p. 8-10); A. Reference Works: Bibliographies, Dictionaries, Encyclopedias, and Checklists (p. 11-41); B. General Historical and Critical Works: Books (p. 42-130); C. General Historical and Critical Works:Articles (p. 131-241); D. Dime Novels, Juvenile Series, and the Pulps (p. 242-306); E. Works About Specific Authors (p. 307-612); F. Magazines (p. 613-620); About the Contributors (p. 621-622); Author Index (p. 623-672).

A273. *Periodic Stars: An Overview of Science Fiction Literature in the 1980s and '90s*, by Tom Easton. I.O. EVANS STUDIES IN THE PHILOSOPHY AND CRITICISM OF LITERATURE, No. 24. 264 p. LC 95-3914. OCLC #31969747. ISBN 0-8095-0202-X cloth $37; ISBN 0-8095-1202-5 paper $27. Cover: standard series design

BP 300, by Robert Reginald & Mary Wickizer Burgess

by Highpoint Type & Graphics, black ink on gray background. First Edition, July 1997.

Selected book reviews on science fiction by well-known critic Tom Easton (1944-).
CONTENTS: Preface (p. 5-6); Introduction (p. 7-11); Periodic Stars (p. 13-253); Notes (p. 254); Index (p. 255-263); About the Author (p. 264).

A273. *Comic Inferno: The Satirical World of Robert Sheckley*, by Gregory Stephenson, edited by Roger C. Schlobin. THE MILFORD SERIES: POPULAR WRITERS OF TODAY, Vol. 66. A Thaddeus Dikty Book. 144 p. LC 95-5025. OCLC #31934224. ISBN 0-916732-60-6 cloth $29; ISBN 0-916732-61-4 paper $19. Cover: standard series design by Highpoint Type & Graphics, black ink on gray-green background. First Edition, July 1997.

A critique of American SF writer, Robert Sheckley (1928-).
CONTENTS: A Robert Sheckley Chronology (p. 5-7); About Gregory Stephenson (p. 8); 1. The Fantasist in Quest of the Marvelous (p. 9-13); 2. Decade the 1950s: *Untouched by Human Hands, Citizen in Space, Pilgrimage to Earth, Immortality, Inc., Notions: Unlimited, Store of Infinity, Shards of Space* (p. 14-38); 3. Decade the 1960s: *The Status Civilization, Journey Beyond Tomorrow, Mindswap, Dimension of Miracles, The People Trap* (p. 39-61); 4. Decade the 1970s: *Can You Feel Anything When I Do This?, Options, Crompton Divided* (p. 62-75); 5. Decade the 1980s: *The Robot Who Looked Like Me, Is That What People Do?, Dramocles, The 10th Victim, Victim Prime, Hunter/Victim* (p. 76-98); 6. Into the 1990s: *Bill the Galactic Hero on the Planet of Bottled Brains, Bring Me the Head of Prince Charming, If at Faust You Don't Succeed, The Collected Short Stories, The Alternative Detective, A Farce to Be Reckoned With, Draconian New York, Soma Blues* (p. 99-104); 7. Other Facets of a Fantasist: *The Man in the Water, Calibre .50, Dead Run, Live Gold, White Death, Time Limit, The Game of X* (p. 105-122); 8. The Comic Inferno of Robert Sheckley (p. 123-128); Notes (p. 129); Annotated Primary Bibliography (p. 130-133); Annotated Secondary Bibliography (p. 134-137); Index (p. 138-144).

A274. *Chicago Ain't No Sissy Town!: The Regional Detective Fiction of Howard Browne*, by John A. Dinan. BROWNSTONE MYSTERY GUIDES, Vol. 18. A Brownstone Book. 96 p., illus. LC 95-5338. OCLC #32012828. ISBN 0-941028-23-2 cloth $25; ISBN 0-941028-24-0 paper $15. Cover: standard series design by Highpoint Type & Graphics, black ink on pale pink background. First Edition, August 1997.

A guide to the mystery fiction of American writer Howard Browne (1907-1999).

CONTENTS: About John A. Dinan (p. 4); A Howard Browne Chronology (p. 5-6); Introduction (p. 7-12); 1. The Ziff-Davis Years (p. 13-20); 2. The Pulp Years (p. 21-34); 3. Film and Television Work (p. 35-38); 4. Browne's Novels (p. 39-44); 5. The Regional P.I. (p. 45-58); 6. The Paul Pine Novels (p. 59-74); 7. Howard Browne's Chicago (p. 75-77); Primary Bibliography (p. 78-82); Secondary Bibliography (p. 83-85); Appendix (p. 86-88); Index (p. 89-96).

A275. *Lemady: Episodes of a Writer's Life*, by Keith Roberts. BORGO BIOVIEWS, No. 9. 168 p. LC 96-30728. OCLC #35183959. ISBN 0-8095-2101-6 cloth $29; ISBN 0-8095-3101-1 paper $19. Cover: standard series design by Highpoint Type & Graphics, black ink on beige background, cover illustration by Keith Roberts. First Edition, August 1997.

A loosely fictionalized autobiography of British SF writer, Keith Roberts (1935-2000).

CONTENTS: Chapter I (p. 5-19); Chapter II (p. 20-30); Chapter III (p. 31-42); Chapter IV (p. 43-55); Chapter V (p. 56-79); Chapter VI (p. 80-101); Chapter VII (p. 102-124); Chapter VIII (p. 125-146); Chapter IX (p. 147-156); Index (p. 157-168).

A276. *Scaring Us to Death: The Impact of Stephen King on Popular Culture, Second Edition, Revised and Expanded*, by Michael R. Collings. THE MILFORD SERIES: POPULAR WRITERS OF TODAY, Vol. 63. A Thaddeus Dikty Book. 168 p. LC 95-5023. OCLC #31934211. ISBN 0-930261-37-2 cloth $31; ISBN 0-930261-38-0 paper $21. Original title: *The Stephen King Phenomenon*. Cover: standard series design by Highpoint Type & Graphics, black ink on gray-green background. Second Edition, August 1997.

A critique of American horror writer, Stephen King (1947-).
CONTENTS: "You, Stephen King" (poem) (p. 4-5); A Stephen King Chronology (p. 6-14); 1. A Concatenation of Monsters: Stephen King's *IT* (p. 15-32); 2. Stephen King, Science Fiction, and *The Tommyknockers* (p. 33-43); 3. A Bestselling Bestseller (p. 44-54); Table I: Stephen King Bestsellers (p. 55-77); 4. King and the Critics (p. 78-94); 5. King and the Schoolmasters: A Personal Perspective (p. 95-101); 6. Acorns to Oaks: Explorations of Theme, Image, and Character in the Early Works of Stephen King (p. 102-114); 7. Beginnings: "King's Garbage Truck" (p. 115-128); 8. The World-Wide King: Some Notes on Non-English Publications (p. 129-143); Notes (p. 144-147); Selected Bibliography (p. 148-153); Index (p. 154-167); About Michael R. Collings (p. 168).

A277. *Ghetto, Shtetl, or Polis? The Jewish Community in the Writings of Karl Emil Franzos, Sholom Aleichem, and Shmuel Yosef Agnon*, by Miriam Roshwald. I.O. EVANS STUDIES IN THE PHILOSOPHY AND CRITICISM OF LITERATURE, No. 30. 192 p. LC 95-924. OCLC #31970978. ISBN 0-89370-145-9 cloth $31; ISBN 0-89370-245-5 paper $21. Cover: standard series design by Highpoint Type & Graphics, black ink on brown background. First Edition, September 1997.

Critiques of three major Yiddish writers of Eastern Europe.
CONTENTS: Introduction (p. 5-18); A Karl Emil Franzos Chronology (p. 19-20); A Sholom Aleichem Chronology (p. 21-23); A Shmuel Yosef Agnon Chronology (p. 24-25); Acknowledgments (p. 26); 1. The Physical Setting of the Shtetl: The Region; The Town; The Marketplace; The Cemetery (p. 27-68); 2. The Major Characters: Old Community: Reb Yubel; Tevye; Türkischgelb (p. 69-105); 3. The Major Characters: Changing Community: Hershl Hurwitz; Sender; Menahem Mendl (p. 106-139); 4. Holidays and Sabbath: Holidays; Sabbath (p. 140-165); Notes (p. 166-174); Bibliography (p. 175-178); Index (p. 179-191); About Miriam Roshwald (p. 192).

BP 300, by Robert Reginald & Mary Wickizer Burgess

A278. *The Woman in the Portrait: The Transfiguring Female in James Joyce's A Portrait of the Artist as a Young Man*, by Julienne H. Empric. THE MILFORD SERIES: POPULAR WRITERS OF TODAY, Vol. 59. 200 p. LC 95-5116. OCLC #31970360. ISBN 0-89370-193-9 cloth $33; ISBN 0-89370-293-5 paper $23. Cover: standard series design by Highpoint Type & Graphics, black ink on green background. First Edition, October 1997.

A critique of Irish writer, James Joyce (1882-1941).
CONTENTS: Acknowledgments (p. 5); A James Joyce Chronology (p. 7-10); Introduction (p. 11-13); 1. Stephen and M/Other (p. 15-26); 2. Lady of Transfiguration (p. 27-47); 3. Eve—Mary—Emma (p. 48-54); 4. An Earthly Muse (p. 55-70); 5. Temptress (p. 71-97); 6. Writing the Woman: The Villanelle (p. 98-120); 7. Hidden Redemptress (p. 121-153); Notes (p. 154-182); Selected Bibliography (p. 183-193); Index (p. 195-199); About Julienne H. Empric (p. 200).

A279. *The Work of William F. Nolan: An Annotated Bibliography & Guide, Second Edition, Revised and Expanded*, by Boden Clarke and James Hopkins. BIBLIOGRAPHIES OF MODERN AUTHORS, No. 14. 256 p. LC 95-2762. OCLC #31970421. ISBN 0-8095-0518-5 cloth $35; ISBN 0-8095-1518-0 paper $25. Cover: standard series design by Highpoint Type & Graphics, black ink on brown-orange background. Second Edition, November 1997.

A bibliography of the American writer of the fantastic, William F. Nolan (1928-).
CONTENTS: Preface to the Second Edition (p. 5-6); Introduction to the First Edition: "The Multi-Media Man," by Jeffrey M. Elliot (p. 7-10); A William F. Nolan Chronology (p. 11-19); Note (p. 20); A. Books and Monographs (p. 21-54); B. Short Fiction (p. 55-87); C. Verse (p. 88-91); D. Personality Profiles (p. 92-112); E. Reviews (p. 113-116); F. Other Nonfiction (p. 117-142); G. Screenplays (p. 143-144); H. Teleplays (p. 145-148); I. Film and Television Outlines (p. 149-153); J. Radio (p. 154); K. Stage (p. 155); L. Comics (p. 156-158); M. Letters (p. 159-162); N. Juvenilia (p. 163-168); O. Interviews with William F. Nolan (p. 169-172); P. Speeches and Public Appearances (p. 173-180); Q. Television and Radio Appearances (p. 181-184); R.

BP 300, by Robert Reginald & Mary Wickizer Burgess

Other Media (p. 185); S. Artwork (p. 186-193); T. Editorial Posts (p. 194); U. Honors and Awards (p. 195-196); V. Secondary Sources (p. 197-206); W. Unpublished Works (p. 207-213); X. Miscellanea (p. 214-223); Quoth the Critics (p. 224-232); "Preface: A Man Remembers," by William F. Nolan (p. 233); "A Year of Yesterdays: An Essay," by William F. Nolan (p. 234-240); "Preface: Simply a Beginning," by William F. Nolan (p. 241); "Simply an Ending: A Short Story," by William F. Nolan (p. 242-243); Title Index (p. 244-256).

See also the First Edition (**A90**).

A280. *Legends and Lovers: Fourteen Profiles*, by William F. Nolan. BORGO BIOVIEWS, No. 4. 152 p. LC 88-36791. OCLC #18960798. ISBN 0-89370-340-0 cloth $29; ISBN 0-89370-440-7 paper $19. Cover: standard series design by Highpoint Type & Graphics, black ink on red background. Originally published in 1965 as *Sinners and Supermen*. First Borgo Edition, December 1997.

A collection of fourteen interviews and profiles with well-known writers, actors, other personalities.

CONTENTS: Preface (p. 5); Introduction (p. 7-8); 1. Marlon Brando: Rebel on the Run (p. 9-20); 2. Ian Fleming: The Man Behind 007 (p. 21-29); 3. Otto Preminger: The Outrageous Mr. P. (p. 30-39); 4. Ray Bradbury: Space Age Storyteller (p. 40-50); 5. Louis Miguel Dominguín: The Number One (p. 51-62); 6. Orson Welles: Citizen Wild (p. 63-75); 7. Rod Serling: TV's Top Sword (p. 76-85); 8. Lance Reventlow: High Speed Millionaire (p. 86-93); 9. Raymond Chandler: Epitaph for a Tough Guy (p. 94-103); 10. Peter Sellers: England's Master Mimic (p. 104-107); 11. Ben Hecht: Hollywood's Last Hurrah (p. 108-115); 12. Dean Martin: The New Dino (p. 116-123); 13. Howard Hughes: The Phantom Tycoon (p. 124-134); 14. James Thurber: The Gentle Man (p. 135-141); Index (p. 142-152).

A281. *The Mystic Path*, by Karl Pruter. ST. WILLIBRORD STUDIES IN PHILOSOPHY AND RELIGION, No. 5. A St. Willibrord's Press Book. 80 p. LC 96-48219. OCLC #35814881. ISBN 0-912134-32-1 cloth $23; ISBN 0-912134-33-X paper $13. Cover: standard series design by Highpoint Type & Graphics, black ink on light blue background. First Edition, December 1997.

A discourse on mysticism as a part of the individual's everyday spiritual life.

CONTENTS: Introduction (p. 5-6); 1. Mysticism (p. 7-20); 2. The Awakening (p. 21-34); 3. Purgation (p. 35-44); 4. Illumination (p. 45-50); 5. Union with God (p. 51-57); 6. Prayers for the Mystic Way (p. 58-75); Notes (p. 76); Bibliography (p. 77-78); Index (p. 79-80).

A282. *The Steadfast James Joyce: A Social Context for the Early Joyce*, by Grace Eckley. THE MILFORD SERIES: POPULAR WRITERS OF TODAY, Vol. 74. x+222 p. LC 97-40327. OCLC #37594263. ISBN 0-89370-550-0 cloth $35; ISBN 0-89370-551-9 paper $25. Cover: standard series design by Highpoint Type & Graphics, black ink on off-white background. First Edition, December 1997.

A critique on Irish writer James Joyce (1882-1941).

CONTENTS: Preface (p. i-vi); 1. Ghostly Facts and Factual Ghosts (p. 1-20); 2. The Absent Presence in *Dubliners*: "The Sisters," "An Encounter," "Araby," "Eveline," Interlude: Children's Games, "After the Race," "Two Gallants," "The Boarding House," "A Little Cloud," "Counterparts," "Clay," "A Painful Case," "Ivy Day," "A Mother," "Grace," "The Dead" (p. 21-92); 3. Ghostwriting Ibsen and *Exiles* (p. 93-109); 4. The Artist as Medium (p. 111-138); 5. The Ghostly Artificer of the *Portrait* (p. 139-166); 6. Aquinas Applied (p. 167-191); 7. "Old Father, Old Artificer" (p. 192-199); Works Cited (p. 201-208); Index (p. 209-221).

A283. *Knight with Quill: Essays on British and European Literature and Littérateurs*, by Charles Whibley, edited and with an introduction by Frederick Rankin MacFadden, Jr. THE MILFORD SERIES: POPULAR WRITERS OF TODAY, Vol. 67. 240 p. LC 95-5117. OCLC #31899988. ISBN 0-89370-968-9 cloth $35; ISBN 0-89370-969-7 paper $25. Cover: standard series design by Highpoint Type & Graphics, black ink on beige background. First Edition, December 1997.

A selection of literary essays by well-known British critic, Charles Whibley (1859-1930).

BP 300, by Robert Reginald & Mary Wickizer Burgess

CONTENTS: Acknowledgments (p. 5-6); Preface (p. 7-9); A Charles Whibley Chronology (p. 10-12); Charles Whibley: A Brief Biography (p. 13-32); Part I: Interchapter. Backgrounds: May 1900-March 1901 (p. 33-35); 1. *Lawless Biographers* (p. 36-38); 2. *Victoria* (p. 39-48). Part II: Interchapter. Backgrounds: April 1901-August 1901 (p. 49-55); 3. *Literature Is Unteachable* (p. 56-61); 4. *The Upholstered Theatre* (p. 62-70); 5. *Sports Destandardized* (p. 71-75). Part III: Interchapter. Backgrounds: September 1902-November 1904 (p. 76-86); 6. *Belgian Art* (p. 87-90); 7. *Pinero* (p. 91-94); 8. *Literature Is Its Own Reward* (p. 95-97); 9. *The Music Halls* (p. 98-100). Part IV: Interchapter. Backgrounds: August 1905-March 1909 (p. 101-110); 10. *Mezzotints* (p. 111-114); 11. *The Decline of French Journalism* (p. 115-117); 12. *Coleridge* (p. 118-122); 13. *Coquelin* (p. 123-127). Part V: Interchapter. Backgrounds: May 1909-January 1914 (p. 128-132); 14. *The FitzGerald Cult* (p. 133-137); 15. *Commercialized Letters* (p. 138-139); 16. *The Essence of the Drama* (p. 140-142); 17. *George Wyndham* (p. 143-148); 18. *The Futurists* (p. 149-153). Part VI: Interchapter. Backgrounds: April 1917-August 1918 (p. 154-161); 19. *Harry Cust* (p. 162-166); 20. *A Definition of Poetry* (p. 167-172); 21. *The Victorian Age* (p. 173-176). Part VI: Interchapter. Backgrounds: September 1921-February 1929 (p. 177-183); 22. *A Post-Mortem on Greek* (p. 184-191); 23. *Literary Inspiration* (p. 192-195); 24. *Boosters* (p. 196-197); 25. *English Is Ungovernable* (p. 198-203); 26. *Andrew Lang* (p. 204-209); 27. *Dutch Painters* (p. 210-215); Notes (p. 216-219); Selected Background Sources (p. 220-225); Bibliography (p. 226-228); Index (p. 229-240).

A284. ***Grand Entrée: The Birth of the Greatest Show on Earth, 1870-1875,*** by Stuart Thayer and William L. Slout. CLIPPER STUDIES IN THE THEATRE, No. 17. x+182 p., ill. LC 97-36042. OCLC #37426474. ISBN 0-8095-0309-3 cloth $31; ISBN 0-8095-1309-9 paper $21. Cover: standard series design by Highpoint Type & Graphics, black ink on beige background. First Edition, March 1998.

A history of the Ringling Brothers Barnum & Bailey circus.

CONTENTS: Introduction (p. vii-viii); Chapter I: Prelude to Barnum, the Coup and Castello Show, 1870 (p. 1-14); Chapter II: P. T. Barnum's Great Travelling Museum, Menagerie, Caravan and Hippodrome, 1871 (p. 15-32); Chapter III: P. T. Barnum's Travelling Exposition and World's Fair, 1872 (p. 33-46); Chapter IV: P. T. Barnum's Great Museum, Menagerie, Hippodrome, and Traveling World's Fair, 1873 (p. 47-64); Chapter V: Formation of P. T. Barnum's Great Roman Hippodrome, 1874 (p. 65-81); Chapter VI: First New York Engagement of Barnum's Roman Hippodrome, 1874 (p. 83-100); Chapter VII: Road Engagements, Barnum's Roman Hippodrome, 1874 (p. 101-122); Chapter VIII: Winter Season, Barnum's Roman Hippodrome, 1874-1875 (p. 123-134); Chapter IX: Final Tour, Barnum's Roman Hippodrome, 1875 (p. 135-157); Conclusions and Speculations (p. 159-163); The Barnum Route from 1871 Through 1875 (p. 165-172); Bibliography (p. 173-175); Index (p. 177-182).

A285. *A Triumph of the Spirit: Thirteen Stories of Holocaust Survivors, Second Edition, Revised and Expanded*, edited by Jacob Biber, additional editing by Mary A. Burgess. STUDIES IN JUDAICA AND THE HOLOCAUST, No. 9. 216 p. LC 95-19141. OCLC #35509226. ISBN 0-8095-0410-3 cloth $33; ISBN 0-8095-1410-9 paper $23. Cover: standard series design by Highpoint Type & Graphics, black ink on white background. Second Edition, March 1998.

Interviews with survivors of the Jewish Holocaust.
CONTENTS: *My Days and Nights*, by Jacob Biber (poem) (p. 5-6); Introduction: "Survivors," by Jacob Biber (p. 7-21); 1. Itzchok "Ike" Gochman (p. 23-29); 2. Halina Zemanska Laster (p. 31-38); 3. Yechiel M. Strohly (p. 39-49); 4. Harry Parzen (Shewski) (p. 51-56); 5. Ruth Josovitz Rosenblum (p. 57-63); 6. Rose Milder (p. 65-70); 7. Leon Faigenbam (p. 71-82); 8. Abraham Mahler (p. 83-90); 9. Selig Schwitzer (p. 91-96); 10. Eva Cherniak Biber (p. 97-122); 11. Paul Blank (p. 123-139); 12. Joseph C. Rosenbaum (p. 140-178); 13. Evelyn Romanowski-Ripp (p. 179-208); Index (p. 209-216).
See also the First Edition (**A181**).

A286. *Codex Derynianus: Being a Comprehensive Guide to the Peoples, Places, & Things of the Derynye & the Human Worlds of the XI Kingdoms: Including Historyes of the Major & Minor States & the Occurrences Which Have Been of Most Importance to Them: With Compleat Biographyes of the*

BP 300, by Robert Reginald & Mary Wickizer Burgess

Prominent Personages & Holy Saints of Gwynedd, Torenth, Meara, Bremagne, Mooryn, Howicce, Llannedd, The Connait, R'Kassi, Orsal & Tralia, Fallon, Byzantyun, The Forcinn Buffer States, & the Other Countryes of This Region from the Birth of Our Lord Jesus Christ unto Anno Domini 1126: Together with a Detail'd Chronological Historye of the Great Sovereign Kingdom of Gwynedd and All Her Neighbours: Also Including a Liturgical Calendar of the Saints of Gwynedd: With Many Lists of the Patriarchs, Primates, Kings, Princes, Dukes, Earls, Counts, & Other Nobles & Notables of These States: With Much True Opinions & Observations Regarding Same, by Katherine Kurtz and Robert Reginald. A Borgo Press/Underwood Book. 344 p., 8.5 x 11", maps, charts. LC 96-44355. OCLC #35686123. ISBN 0-89370-011-8 signed, limited cloth of 500 copies $50; ISBN 1-887424-33-4 Underwood edition. Cover art by Hannah Shapero; maps by Charles Morehead. First Edition, April 1998.

A guide to the fictional universe of Katherine Kurtz, 99% of which was written by Reginald. The book sold out within three months of publication, and has since become a high-priced collector's item, with copies fetching as much as $2,905 each on eBay.
 CONTENTS: Dedicatio (p. 6); Introductio: Uncovering the Codex (p. 7-8); Præfatio: Gaudeamus! (p. 10); Codex Derynianus (p. 11-246); Ordo Temporum: A Chronology of the XI Kingdoms (p. 247-325); Calendarium Liturgicum XI Regnorum: A Liturgical Calendar of the XI Kingdoms (p. 327-329); Genealogiæ Familiarum Regiarum XI Regnorum: Genealogies of the Royal Families of the XI Kingdoms (p. 330-335); Tabulæ XI Regnorum: Maps of the XI Kingdoms, by Charles Morehead (p. 336-342); De Auctoribus et Bibliographia Librorum (p. 343-344).

A287. *Mystic Rhythms: The Philosophical Vision of Rush*, by Carol Selby Price with Robert M. Price. THE WOODSTOCK SERIES: POPULAR MUSIC OF TODAY, Vol. 2. 160 p. LC 95-2218. OCLC #31969633. ISBN 0-8095-0800-1 cloth $29; ISBN 0-8095-1800-7 paper $19. Cover: standard series design by Highpoint Type & Graphics, black ink on bright green background. First Edition, May 1998.

BP 300, by Robert Reginald & Mary Wickizer Burgess

b. Second Printing, August 1998.
c. [Third Printing], September 1998. Printing information not specifically marked in book.

A critical guide to the music of the pop group, Rush.
CONTENTS: Dedication and Acknowledgments (p. 4); Introduction (p. 5-10); A Rush Chronology (p. 11-12); 1. Fear (p. 13-24); 2. The Mass Production Zone (p. 25-47); 3. In Touch with Some Reality (p. 48-67); 4. Castles in the Distance (p. 68-81); 5. The Sounds of Salesmen (p. 82-102); 6. The Fabric of Their Dreams (p. 103-123); 7. Machine and Man (p. 124-143); 8. Conclusion: Not Looking Back (p. 144-145); A Rush Discography (p. 146-150); A Rush Videography (p. 151); Selected Bibliography (p. 152-154); Index (p. 155-160).

A288. *Yesterday's Bestsellers: A Voyage Through Literary History*, by Brian Stableford. I.O. EVANS STUDIES IN THE PHILOSOPHY AND CRITICISM OF LITERATURE, No. 34. 160 p. LC 98-6941. OCLC #38884201. ISBN 0-8095-0906-7 cloth $29; ISBN 0-8095-1906-2 paper $19. Cover: standard series design by Highpoint Type & Graphics, black ink on pale pink background. First Edition, May 1998.

A collection of literary essays on bestseller writers of the nineteenth and early twentieth centuries.
CONTENTS: Introduction (p. 5-7); Part 1: Getting Away from It All: Odysseys in Exotica. 1. The Descendants of Robinson Crusoe (p. 11-19); 2. *She* (p. 20-28); 3. *Alice in Wonderland* (p. 29-37); 4. *Green Mansions* (p. 38-46); 5. *Lost Horizon* (p. 47-54). Part 2: How Different It Seems Now: The Past and Other Foreign Countries; 6. *The Last Days of Pompeii* (p. 57-66); 7. *Vice Versa* (p. 67-74); 8. Marie Corelli (p. 75-83); 9. *The Garden of Allah* (p. 84-91); 10. *I, Claudius* (p. 92-100). Part 3: Passing Judgment: Assorted Crimes and Punishments; 11. *The Mysteries of Paris* (p. 103-111); 12. *Beau Geste* (p. 112-120); 13. Raymond Chandler (p. 121-129); 14. *No Orchids for Miss Blandish* (p. 130-138); 15. The Trials of Hank Janson (p. 139-147); Index (p. 148-160).

A289. *Glorious Perversity: The Decline and Fall of Literary Decadence*, by Brian Stableford. I.O. EVANS STUDIES IN THE PHILOSOPHY AND CRITICISM OF LITERATURE, No. 35. 152 p. LC

BP 300, by Robert Reginald & Mary Wickizer Burgess

98-6940. OCLC #38884190. ISBN 0-8095-0908-3 cloth $30; ISBN 0-8095-1908-9 paper $20. Cover: standard series design by Highpoint Type & Graphics, black ink on violet background. First Edition, July 1998.

A critical history of the Literary Decadence Movement.
CONTENTS: Acknowledgments (p. 4); Part One: The Origins of the Decadent Worldview. 1. Civilization Grown Old: The Idea of Decadence (p. 6-14); 2. *Le Spleen de Paris*: Charles Baudelaire and the Decadent Style (p. 15-25); 3. The Cult of Artificiality: The Development of Decadent Consciousness (p. 26-40); 4. *A Rebours*: Joris-Karl Huysmans and the Decadent Manifesto (p. 41-53); 5. Extraordinary Sensations: Disease, Disorder, and Decadence (p. 54-66). Part Two: Case Studies from the Decadent Movement; 6. *Masques*: Jean Lorraine and the Decadent Quest (p. 68-83); 7. Angels of Perversity: Rémy de Gourmont's Retreat from the World (p. 84-96); 8. *The Torture Garden*: Octave Mirbeau and the Politics of Decadence (p. 97-107); 9. The Decay of Lying: Oscar Wilde and the English Decadent Movement (p. 108-123); 10. *Fin de Siècle*: The Decadent Heritage (p. 124-137); Notes (p. 138-139); Selected Bibliography (p. 140-143); Index (p. 144-152).

A290. *The Presidential-Congressional Political Dictionary*, by Jeffrey M. Elliot and Sheikh R. Ali. BORGO REFERENCE GUIDES, No. 3. x+366 p. LC 98-18705. OCLC #39002581. ISBN 0-8095-0706-4 cloth $41; ISBN 0-8095-1706-X paper $31. Cover: standard series design by Highpoint Type & Graphics, black ink on gray background. First Borgo Edition, August 1998.

A reprint of a political guide to the powers of the American President and American Congress.
CONTENTS: Preface (p. vii-viii); How to Use This Book (p. ix-x); 1. The President and the Electorate (p. 3-25); 2. Powers of the President (p. 27-50); 3. The Presidents (p. 51-95); 4. Presidential Leadership (p. 97-116); 5. The Presidential Establishment (p. 117-139); 6. Agencies, Bureaus, and Commissions (p. 141-158); 7. The Congress and the Electorate (p. 159-183); 8. Powers of Congress (p. 185-212); 9. Congressional Leadership (p. 213-232); 10. The Committee Structure (p. 233-253); 11. Rules and Procedures (p. 255-305); 12. Congressional

BP 300, by Robert Reginald & Mary Wickizer Burgess

Staffs and Specialized Offices (p. 307-326); Appendix (p. 327-339); Notes (p. 341-342); Index (p. 343-365).

A291. ***World War II: A Cataloging Reference Guide***, by Buckley Barry Barrett. [An Emeritus Enterprises Book.] BORGO CATALOGING GUIDES, No. 5. vi+536 p. LC 98-39000. OCLC #39655076. ISBN 0-89370-839-9 cloth $53; ISBN 0-89370-939-5 paper $43. Cover: standard series design by Highpoint Type & Graphics, black ink on yellow-orange background. First Edition, September 1998.

A guide to cataloging materials on World War II in the Library of Congress cataloging system.
  CONTENTS: Acknowledgments (p. v); Introduction (p. 1-2); 1. Library of Congress Classification Numbers (p. 3-144); 2. Dewey Decimal Classification Numbers (p. 145-197); 3. Index to Classification Numbers (p. 198-380); 4. Library of Congress Subject, Corporate, and Biographical Headings (p. 381-529); About the Author (p. 530).

A292. ***Discovering Stephen King's The Shining: Essays on the Bestselling Novel by America's Premier Horror Writer, Second Edition, Revised and Expanded***, edited by Tony Magistrale. I.O. EVANS STUDIES IN THE PHILOSOPHY AND CRITICISM OF LITERATURE, No. 36. 144 p. LC 98-38108. OCLC #39627598. ISBN 1-55742-132-3 cloth $30; ISBN 1-55742-133-1 paper $20. Cover: standard series design by Highpoint Type & Graphics, black ink on beige background. New version of *The Shining Reader*. Second Edition (listed as First Edition in the book), October 1998.

An anthology of essays on the American horror writer, Stephen King (1947-).
  CONTENTS: Introduction (p. 5-6); A Stephen King Chronology (p. 7-9); Note (p. 10); 1. "Once Out of Nature: The Topiary," by Michael N. Stanton (p. 11-18); 2. "And We All Shine On: Stephen King's *The Shining* as 'Stream of Non-Consciousness'," by Brian Kent (p. 19-38); 3. "'Truth Comes Out': The Scrapbook Chapter," by Tony Magistrale (p. 39-46); 4. "Character Transformations in *The Shining*," by Sidney Poger (p. 47-53); 5. "The Thousand Faces of Danny Torrance," by

Samantha Figliola (p. 54-61); 6. "Poe's 'The Masque of the Red Death' and King's *The Shining*: Echo, Influence, and Deviation," by Leonard Mustazza (p. 62-73); 7. "'Orders from the House': Kubrick's *The Shining* and Kafka's *The Metamorphosis*," by Mark J. Madigan (p. 74-81); 8. "What About Jack? Another Perspective on Family Relationships in Stanley Kubrick's *The Shining*," by Frank Manchel (p. 82-94); 9. "*The Shining* as Postmodern Horror," by Edward A. Gamarra Jr. (p. 95-106); 10. "Sit and Shine," by Lynda and Bob Haas and Mary and Donald Pharr (p. 107-121); Notes (p. 123-128); Works Cited (p. 129-132); About the Contributors (p. 133-134); Index (p. 135-143); Other Books by Tony Magistrale (p. 144).

A293. *Olympians of the Sawdust Circle: A Biographical Dictionary of the Nineteenth-Century American Circus*, by William L. Slout. [An Emeritus Enterprises Book.] CLIPPER STUDIES IN THE THEATRE, No. 18. iv+344 p., 8.5 x 11", illus. LC 97-36043. OCLC #37432095. ISBN 0-8095-0310-7 cloth $70. ISBN 0-8095-1310-2 paper $50. Cover: standard series design by Highpoint Type & Graphics, black ink on gray background. First Edition, November 1998.

A biographical directory to performers and producers of the nineteenth-century American circus.
CONTENTS: Introduction (p. iii); Olympians of the Sawdust Circle (p. 1-344).

A294. *Below the Iceberg: Anti-Sartre and Other Essays, Second Edition, Revised and Expanded*, by Colin Wilson. THE MILFORD SERIES: POPULAR WRITERS OF TODAY, Vol. 34. 152 p. LC 96-2246. OCLC #34149771. ISBN 0-89370-997-2 cloth $30; ISBN 0-89370-998-0 paper $20. Cover: standard series design by Highpoint Type & Graphics, black ink on gray background. Second Edition, November 1998.

A second edition of *Anti-Sartre*, being a critique of Jean-Paul Sartre and Albert Camus (see **A42**).
CONTENTS: Introduction (p. 5-14); 1. Anti-Sartre (p. 15-60); 2. A Sartre Obituary (p. 61-63); 3. Albert Camus (p. 64-80); 4. Michel Foucault (p. 81-91); 5. A Brief History of French Philosophy (p. 92-106); 6. Derrida and Reconstruction (p. 107-

110); 7. Notes on Derrida for Rowan (p. 111-117); 8. Rediscovering a Masterpiece: Whitehead's *Rediscovering Symbolism: Its Meaning and Effect* (p. 118-125); 9. Below the Iceberg (p. 126-142); Notes (p. 143); Index (p. 144-152).

A295. *Windows of the Imagination: Essays on Fantastic Literature*, by Darrell Schweitzer. I.O. EVANS STUDIES IN THE PHILOSOPHY AND CRITICISM OF LITERATURE, No. 22. 208 p. LC 98-18704. OCLC #38976218. ISBN 0-8095-0921-0 cloth $33; ISBN 0-8095-1921-6 paper $23. Cover: standard series design by Highpoint Type & Graphics, black ink on beige background. First Edition, November 1998.

A collection of essays by a well-known American critic.

CONTENTS: Introduction: Notes from Notes from Beyond the Fields We Know (p. 5-8); My Skeptical Self & Other Evasions of Autobiography: 1. The Necessity of Skepticism (p. 9-25); 2. The Cost of Credulity (p. 26-32); 3. The Layercake of History (p. 33-41); 4. My Career as a Hack Writer (p. 42-48). Writing Fantasy: 5. The Lands That Clearly Pertain to Faery (p. 49-56); 6. Uttering the P-Word (p. 57-63); 7. Why Horror Fiction? (p. 64-68); 8. Intimate Horror (p. 69-72); 9. Horror Beyond New Jersey (p. 73-78); 10. The Limits of Craziness (p. 79-84). H. P. Lovecraft and Others: 11.H. P. Lovecraft: Still Eldritch After All These Years (p. 85-95); 12. About "The Whisperer in Darkness" (p. 96-101); 13. H. P. Lovecraft's Favorite Movie (p. 102-107); 14. M. R. James and H. P. Lovecraft: The Ghostly and the Comic (p. 108-114); 15. Richard Middleton: Beauty, Sadness, and Terror (p. 115-120); 16. How Much of Dunsany Is Worth Reading? (p. 121-128); 17. Count Dracula and His Adapters (p. 129-142). Reviews: 18. Philip K. Dick: Absurdist, Visionary (p. 143-146); 19. *Kipling's Science Fiction* (p. 147-149); 20. *The Black Flame*, by Stanley G. Weinbaum (p. 150-154); 21. On Brian Aldiss's *Barefoot in the Head* (p. 155-157); 22. *A Fisherman of the Inland Sea*, by Ursula K. Le Guin (p. 158-160); 23. *Lexicon Urthus*, by Michael André-Drussi (p. 161-164); 24. Prospero's Dracula (p. 165-167); 25. *Cthulhu 2000*, edited by James Turner (p. 168-171); 26. *The Dragon Path: Collected Stories of Kenneth Morris* (p. 172-176). Loose Cannonfire: 27. An Interview with Edgar Allan Poe (p. 177-180); 28. One Fine Day in the Stygian Haunts of Hell: Being the Lore and Legend of the Fabled "Eye of Argon" (p. 181-

186); 29. Creating Frivolous Literary Theories (p. 187-192); Notes (p. 193-194); Selected Bibliography (p. 194-195); Acknowledgments (p. 196-197); Index (p. 198-208).

A296. *Discovering Dean Koontz: Essays on America's Bestselling Writer of Suspense and Horror Fiction, Second Edition, Revised and Expanded*, edited by Bill Munster. I.O. EVANS STUDIES IN THE PHILOSOPHY AND CRITICISM OF LITERATURE, No. 19. A Thaddeus Dikty Book. 184 p. LC 95-5206. OCLC #31934547. ISBN 1-55742-144-7 cloth $31; ISBN 1-55742-145-5 paper $21. Cover: standard series design by Highpoint Type & Graphics, black ink on pale pink background. Original title: *Sudden Fear*. Second Edition, November 1998.

A collection of essays on American horror writer, Dean Koontz.
   CONTENTS: Introduction, by Tim Powers (p. 5-6); Foreword, by Bill Munster (p. 7-9); A Dean Koontz Chronology (p. 10-14); 1. "*Midnight*: Anatomy of a Thriller," by Bill Munster (p. 15-38); 2. "Not Necessarily Cheaper by the Dozen," by James T. Seels (p. 39-42); 3. "A Dean Koontz Interview," by Bill Munster (p. 43-63); 4. "Dean Koontz and Stephen King: Style, *Invasion*, and the Aesthetics of Terror," by Michael R. Collings (p. 64-79); 5. "In the Midst of Life," by Richard Laymon (p. 80-84); 6. "The Mutation of a Science Fiction Writer," by Stan Brooks (p. 85-96); 7. "Mainstream Horror in *Whispers* and *Phantoms*," by D. W. Taylor (p. 97-111); 8. "Dark Genesis: *Watchers* and *Shadowfires*," by Stan Brooks (p. 112-119); 9. "The Three Faces of Evil: The Monsters of *Whispers*, *Phantoms*, and *Darkfall*," by Michael A. Morrison (p. 120-143); 10. "Dean Koontz's *Twilight Eyes*: Art and Artifact," by Michael R. Collings (p. 144-151); 11. "*Femmes Fatales?* The Woman Protagonists in Four Koontz Novels," by Elizabeth Massie (p. 152-167); 12. "Afterword," by Joe R. Lansdale (p. 168-169); About the Contributors (p. 170-171); Acknowledgments (p. 172); Notes (p. 173); Works Cited (p. 174-175); Bibliography (p. 176-177); Index (p. 178-184).

A297. *Ray Bradbury and the Poetics of Reverie: Gaston Bachelard, Wolfgang Iser, and the Reader's Response to Fantastic Literature, Second Edition, Revised and Expanded*, by William F. Touponce. I.O. EVANS STUDIES IN THE PHILOSOPHY AND

BP 300, by Robert Reginald & Mary Wickizer Burgess

CRITICISM OF LITERATURE, No. 32. 168 p. LC 96-37225. OCLC #35832093. ISBN 0-8095-2005-2 cloth $31; ISBN 0-8095-3005-8 paper $21. Cover: standard series design by Highpoint Type & Graphics, black ink on deep blue background. Second Edition, November 1998.

A critique of American SF and fantasy writer, Ray Bradbury (1920-).

CONTENTS: Introduction (p. 5-18); A Ray Bradbury Chronology (p. 19-20); 1. Wolfgang Iser and the Cognitive Process (p. 21-30); 2. Gaston Bachelard and the Sublimative Reader (p. 31-39); 3. Reverie and the Marvelous (p. 40-63); 4. Reverie and the Gothic (p. 64-76); 5. Reverie and Science Fiction (p. 77-101); 6. Reverie and the Utopian Novel (p. 102-137); 7. Conclusion (p. 138-144); Notes (p. 145-150); Bibliography (p. 151-162); Index (p. 163-168).

A298. *Masters of Evil: A Viewer's Guide to Cinematic Archvillains*, by Georgette S. Fox. MALCOLM HULKE STUDIES IN CINEMA AND TELEVISION, No. 2. 184 p. LC 96-41059. OCLC #35317423. ISBN 0-8095-0003-5 cloth $31; ISBN 0-8095-1003-0 paper $21. Cover: standard series design by Highpoint Type & Graphics, black ink on light gray background. First Edition, November 1998.

An A-Z dictionary of major archvillains in motion pictures.

CONTENTS: Acknowledgments (p. 5); Introduction (p. 6); *The Masters of Evil*, A-to-Z (p. 7-165); Notes (p. 167); Selected Annotated Bibliography (p. 169-173); Index: Films, Directors, Actors (p. 174-183); About the Author (p. 184).

A299. *Sansato*, by William F. Temple, introduction by Mike Ashley. CLASSICS OF FANTASTIC LITERATURE, No. 2. A Unicorn & Son Book. 160 p. LC 96-24044. OCLC #34943230. ISBN 0-913960-38-1 cloth $30; ISBN 0-913960-39-X paper $20. Cover: standard series design by Highpoint Type & Graphics, black and red ink on gray background. Original title: *The Fleshpots of Sansato*. First Borgo Edition, November 1998.

A reprint of an SF novel originally published in 1968.

BP 300, by Robert Reginald & Mary Wickizer Burgess

CONTENTS: Foreword, by Mike Ashley (p. 5-7); *Sansato* (p. 9-159); The Books of William F. Temple (p. 160).

A300. *The Mystery Scene Movie Guide: A Personal Filmography of Modern Crime Pictures*, by Max Allan Collins. BROWNSTONE MYSTERY GUIDES, Vol. 16. A Brownstone Book. 192 p. LC 95-3372. OCLC #31971390. ISBN 0-941028-19-4 cloth $31; ISBN 0-941028-20-8 paper $21. Cover: standard series design by Highpoint Type & Graphics, black ink on pale pink background. First Edition, December 1998.

A critique of modern crime pictures by a well-known mystery writer; the last book issued by The Borgo Press.

CONTENTS: Introduction (p. 5-7); "Mystery Seen" Rating System (p. 7); About the Author (p. 8); *The Mystery Scene Movie Guide* (p. 9-166); Appendix: An Annotated Guide to Mail-Order Video Tape Outlets (p. 167-174); Index (p. 175-192).

B.

XENOS BOOKS
(An Associated Imprint, 1986-1990)

B1. ***Orgy & Other Things***, by Gary Kern. 1986. 216 p. LC 85-29527. OCLC #12977096. ISBN 0-89370-843-7 cloth $19.95; ISBN 0-89370-943-3 paper $9.95.

B2. ***The Mad Kokoschka: A Play in 3 Acts***, by Gary Kern. 1986. 87 p. LC 86-15870. OCLC #13860474. ISBN 0-89370-844-5 cloth $17.95; ISBN 0-89370-944-1 paper $7.95.

B3. ***Anti-Posters: Soviet Icons in Reverse***, by Boris Mukhametshin. 1987. 164 p., 8.5 x 11". LC 86-28104. OCLC #14692814. ISBN 0-89370-842-9 cloth $19.95; ISBN 0-89370-942-5 paper $9.95.

B4. ***Misfortune***, by Gary Kern. Winter 1990. 177 p. LC 88-28071. OCLC #18557521. ISBN 0-89370-841-0 cloth $19.95; ISBN 0-89370-941-7 paper $9.95.

B5. ***The Poet Is a Little God: Creationist Verse of Vicente Huidobro***, translated by Jorge García-Gómez. October 1990. xxxii+180 p. LC 89-24984. OCLC #20594197. ISBN 0-89370-845-3 cloth $19.95; ISBN 0-89370-945-X paper $9.95.

HEREAFTER XENOS BOOKS ASSIGNED ITS OWN ISBNS

C.

BROWNSTONE BOOKS
(Acquired 1 January 1991)
ISBN Prefix 0-941028-

C1. *The Armchair Detective, Volume One*, edited by Allen J. Hubin. 1981. viii+158 p. LC 82-643921. OCLC #8556372. ISBN 0-941028-00-3 cloth $24.95.

C2. *The Sound of Detection: Ellery Queen's Adventures in Radio*, by Francis M. Nevins, Jr. & Ray Stanich. 1983. viii+109 p. LC 85-25462. OCLC #12724167. ISBN 0-89370-556-X cloth $19.95; ISBN 0-941028-01-1 paper $9.95.

C3. *Detective and Mystery Fiction: An International Bibliography of Secondary Sources*, by Walter Albert. 1984. xii+781 p. LC 89-140438. OCLC #11941061. ISBN 0-941028-02-X cloth $60.00.

C4. *Hardboiled Burlesque: Raymond Chandler's Comic Style*, by Keith Newlin. BROWNSTONE CHAPBOOK SERIES, Volume 1. 1984. 50 p. LC 85-25473. OCLC #12724178. ISBN 0-89370-555-1 cloth $19.95; ISBN 0-941028-04-6 paper $9.95.

C5. *The New Hard-Boiled Dicks: A Personal Checklist*, by Robert E. Skinner. BROWNSTONE CHAPBOOK SERIES, Volume 2. 1987. 60 p. LC 87-29791. OCLC #17107233. ISBN 0-8095-6400-9 cloth $19.95; ISBN 0-941028-04-6 paper $9.95. See also the Second Edition (**A228**).

C6. *TAD-Schrift: Twenty Years of Mystery Fandom in The Armchair Detective*, edited by J. Randolph Cox. 1987. viii+111 p. LC 87-36810. OCLC #17298903. ISBN 0-8095-6401-7 cloth $24.95; ISBN 0-941028-05-4 paper $12.95.

BP 300, by Robert Reginald & Mary Wickizer Burgess

C7. *John Nieminski: Somewhere a Roscoe*, by John Nieminski, edited by Ely Liebow and Art Scott. BROWNSTONE CHAPBOOK SERIES, Volume 3. 1987. 61 p. LC 87-36833. OCLC #17299050. ISBN 0-8095-6402-5 cloth $19.95; ISBN 0-941028-06-2 paper $9.95.

C8. *Frederick Irving Anderson (1877-1947): A Biobibliography*, by Benjamin Franklin Fisher IV. BROWNSTONE CHAPBOOK SERIES, Volume 4. 1987. 43 p. LC 88-34112. OCLC #18723806. ISBN 0-8095-6403-3 cloth $19.95; ISBN 0-941028-07-0 paper $9.95.

C9. *A Detective in Distress: Philip Marlowe's Domestic Dream*, by Gay Brewer. BROWNSTONE CHAPBOOK SERIES, Volume 5. 1989. 68 p. LC 90-35522. OCLC #21407579. ISBN 0-8095-6404-1 cloth $19.95; ISBN 0-941028-08-9 paper $9.95.

D.

STARMONT CONTEMPORARY WRITERS SERIES
(Acquired 1 January 1991)

D1.   *Roald Dahl*, by Alan Warren. STARMONT CONTEMPORARY WRITER SERIES, Number 1. 1988. vi+105 p. LC 88-33743. OCLC #18767824. ISBN 0-8095-5200-0 cloth $19.95 (old Starmont ISBN 1-55742-013-0); ISBN 0-8095-5225-6 paper $9.95 (old Starmont ISBN 1-55742-012-2). Became THE MILFORD SERIES: POPULAR WRITERS OF TODAY, Volume 57 (see **A187**).

D2.   *Margaret Drabble, Symbolic Moralist*, by Nora Foster Stovel. STARMONT CONTEMPORARY WRITER SERIES, Number 2. 1989. vii+224 p. LC 88-1079. OCLC #17439497. ISBN 0-8095-5201-9 cloth $24.95 (old Starmont ISBN 1-55742-035-1); ISBN 0-8095-5226-4 paper $14.95 (old Starmont ISBN 1-55742-034-3). Will become part of THE MILFORD SERIES: POPULAR WRITERS OF TODAY.

E.

SIDEWINDER PRESS
(Ex-Sun Dance Press)
(Acquired 1 July 1991)
ISBN Prefix 0-913330-

E1. *Heroes and Incidents of the Mexican War*, by Isaac George. 1971. 296 p. LC 85-4693. OCLC #11785174. ISBN 0-89370-718-X cloth $29.95.

E2. *The Life and Struggles of Negro Toilers*, by George Padmore. 1971. 126 p. LC 85-4221. OCLC #11783224. ISBN 0-89370-721-X cloth $22.95.

F.

ST. WILLIBRORD'S PRESS
(Acquired 1 September 1991)
ISBN prefix 0-912134-

F1. *Bishops Extraordinary*, by Karl Pruter. 1985. 58 p. LC 86-2284. OCLC #13123409. ISBN 0-89370-544-6 cloth $19.95; ISBN 0-912134-04-6 paper $7.95.

F2. *A Directory of Autocephalous Anglican, Catholic, and Orthodox Bishops, Fifth Edition*, by Karl Pruter. 1989. 65 p. LC 88-34593. OCLC #18948621. ISBN 0-8095-6604-4 cloth $19.95; ISBN 0-912134-05-4 paper $9.95. See also the Sixth Edition (**A146**) and Seventh Edition (**A224**).

F3. *Episcopi Vagantes and the Anglican Church*, by George Brandreth. 1987. xix+79 p. LC 87-29809. OCLC #17258289. ISBN 0-89370-558-6 cloth $19.95; ISBN 0-912134-06-2 paper $9.95.

F4. *A History of the Old Catholic Church*, by Karl Pruter. 1985. 76 p. LC 85-13418. OCLC #12162745. ISBN 0-89370-594-2 cloth $19.95; ISBN 0-912134-01-1 paper $9.95. Second Edition pending.

F5. *Neo-Congregationalism*, by Karl Pruter. 1985. 90 p. LC 85-13416. OCLC #12162686. ISBN 0-89370-598-5 cloth $19.95; ISBN 0-912134-02-X paper $9.95.

F6. *The People of God*, by Karl Pruter. 1985. v+162 p. LC 85-13417. OCLC #12162694. ISBN 0-89370-596-9 cloth $19.95; ISBN 0-912134-03-8 paper $9.95.

BP 300, by Robert Reginald & Mary Wickizer Burgess

F7.   *The Priest's Handbook*, by Karl Pruter. 1991. OCLC #30566285.
vi+43 p. ISBN 0-8095-6600-1 cloth $19.95; ISBN 0-912134-07-
0 paper $7.95.

F8.   *The Strange Partnership of George Alexander McGuire and
Marcus Garvey*, by Karl Pruter. 1986. 50 p. LC 86-17628.
OCLC #13945917. ISBN 0-89370-529-2 cloth $19.95; ISBN 0-
912134-08-9 paper $7.95.

F9.   *The Teachings of the Great Mystics*, by Karl Pruter. 1985. 118 p.
LC 85-13306. OCLC #12189247. ISBN 0-89370-595-0 cloth
$19.95; ISBN 0-912134-00-3 paper $9.95.

F10. *The Theology of Congregationalism*, by Karl Pruter. 1985. 100 p.
LC 85-12844. OCLC #12188605. ISBN 0-89370-597-7 cloth
$19.95; ISBN 0-912134-09-7 paper $9.95.

G.

STARMONT HOUSE, INC.
AND FAX COLLECTOR'S EDITIONS
(Acquired 1 March 1993)
ISBN prefixes 1-55742, 0-930261,
0-916732, 0-913960

G1. *A. Merritt*, by Ronald Foust. STARMONT READER'S GUIDE, Number 43. 1989. vi+104 p. LC 87-9927. OCLC #15520984. ISBN 0-930261-36-4 cloth $23; ISBN 0-930261-35-6 paper $13.

G2. *The Adventure Magazine Index*, by Richard J. Bleiler. 1990. 1085 p. in 2 v., 8.5 x 11". LC 90-10407. OCLC #22596095. ISBN 1-55742-189-7 cloth $150.

G3. *Alfred Bester*, by Carolyn Wendell. STARMONT READER'S GUIDE, Number 6. 1982. 72 p. LC 80-19655. OCLC #6555295. ISBN 0-916732-17-7 cloth $20; ISBN 0-916732-08-8 paper $10.

G4. *American Fantasy and Science Fiction*, by Marshall B. Tymn. 1979. xii+228 p. LC 76-55151. OCLC #5110737. ISBN 0-913960-23-3 cloth $30; ISBN 0-913960-15-2 paper $20.

G5. *Anne McCaffrey*, by Mary T. Brizzi. STARMONT READER'S GUIDE, Number 30. 1986. [viii]+95 p. LC 85-17160. OCLC #12313723. ISBN 0-930261-30-5 cloth $23; ISBN 0-930261-29-1 paper $13.

G6. *The Annotated Guide to Fantastic Adventures*, by Edward J. Gallagher. STARMONT REFERENCE GUIDES, Number 2. 1985. xxii+170 p. LC 84-16228. OCLC #11158826. ISBN 0-916732-71-1 cloth $27; ISBN 0-916732-70-3 paper $17.

BP 300, by Robert Reginald & Mary Wickizer Burgess

G7. *The Annotated Guide to Startling Stories*, by Leon Gammell. STARMONT REFERENCE GUIDES, Number 3. 1986. [iv]+90 p. LC 86-6012. OCLC #13665014. ISBN 0-930261-51-8 cloth $20; ISBN 0-930261-50-X paper $10.

G8. *The Annotated Guide to Stephen King: A Primary and Secondary Bibliography of the Works of America's Premier Horror Writer*, by Michael R. Collings. STARMONT REFERENCE GUIDES, Number 8. 1986. [vi]+176 p. LC 86-1854. OCLC #13122509. ISBN 0-930261-81-X cloth $27; ISBN 0-930261-80-1 paper $17.

G9. *The Annotated Guide to Unknown & Unknown Worlds*, by Stefan R. Dziemianowicz. Starmont Studies in Literary Criticism, Number 13. 1991. 212 p. LC 93-202547. OCLC #24384620. ISBN 1-55742-141-2 cloth $29; ISBN 1-55742-140-4 paper $19. See also **A245**.

G10. *The Annotated Index to The Thrill Book: Complete Indexes to and Descriptions of Everything Published in Street & Smith's The Thrill Book*, by Richard J. Bleiler. STARMONT REFERENCE GUIDES, Number 18. 1991. vii+256 p. LC 93-202656. OCLC #27445269. ISBN 1-55742-206-0 cloth $33; ISBN 1-55742-205-2 paper $23.

G11. *The Arkham House Companion: Fifty Years of Arkham House: A Bibliographical History and Collector's Price Guide to Arkham House/Mycroft & Moran, Including the Revised and Expanded Horrors and Unpleasantries*, by Sheldon Jaffery. STARMONT REFERENCE GUIDES, Number 9. 1989. xvi+184 p., 8.5. x 11". LC 89-31701. OCLC #19513013. ISBN 1-55742-005-X cloth $39; ISBN 1-55742-004-1 paper $29.

G12. *Arthur C. Clarke, Second Edition*, by Eric S. Rabkin. STARMONT READER'S GUIDE, Number 1. 1980. 80 p. LC 79-84709. OCLC #7914529. ISBN 0-916732-22-3 cloth $20; ISBN 0-916732-21-5 paper $10.

G13. *Black Forbidden Things: Cryptical Secrets from the "Crypt of Cthulhu"*, edited by Robert M. Price. STARMONT STUDIES IN LITERARY CRITICISM, Number 44. 1992. iv+200 p. LC 93-

201926. OCLC #27107352. ISBN 1-55742-249-4 cloth $29; ISBN 1-55742-248-6 paper $19.

G14. *Brian Aldiss*, by Michael R. Collings. STARMONT READER'S GUIDE, Number 28. 1986. [iv]+115 p. LC 85-17224. OCLC #12345360. ISBN 0-916732-99-1 cloth $23; ISBN 0-916732-74-6 paper $13.

G15. *A Casebook on The Stand*, edited by Tony Magistrale. STARMONT STUDIES IN LITERARY CRITICISM, Number 38. 1992. xii+210 p. LC 93-214779. OCLC #27409535. ISBN 1-55742-251-6 cloth $29; ISBN 1-55742-250-8 paper $19.

G16. *Charles Williams*, by Kathleen Spencer. STARMONT READER'S GUIDE, Number 25. 1986. 104 p. LC 86-5750. OCLC #13396289. ISBN 0-916732-80-0 cloth $23; ISBN 0-916732-79-7 paper $13.

G17. *Children's Fantasy*, by Francis J. Molson. STARMONT READER'S GUIDE, Number 33. 1989. [vi]+97 p. LC 87-10145. OCLC #15792652. ISBN 1-55742-015-7 cloth $23; ISBN 1-55742-014-9 paper $13.

G18. *Christopher Priest*, by Nicholas Ruddick. STARMONT READER'S GUIDE, Number 50. 1989. x+104 p. LC 88-16046. OCLC #18052004. ISBN 1-55742-110-2 cloth $23; ISBN 1-55742-109-9 paper $13.

G19. *Clark Ashton Smith*, by Steve Behrends. STARMONT READER'S GUIDE, Number 49. 1990. vi+112 p. LC 87-16034. OCLC #16128811. ISBN 0-930261-99-2 cloth $23; ISBN 0-930261-98-4 paper $13.

G20. *C.S. Lewis*, by Brian Murphy. STARMONT READER'S GUIDE, Number 14. 1983. 95 p. LC 82-7346. OCLC #8494310. ISBN 0-916732-38-X cloth $20; ISBN 0-916732-37-1 paper $10.

G21. *David Lindsay*, by Gary K. Wolfe. STARMONT READER'S GUIDE, Number 9. 1982. [ii]+64 p. LC 82-5563. OCLC #8387873. ISBN 0-916732-29-0 cloth $20; ISBN 0-916732-26-6 paper $10.

BP 300, by Robert Reginald & Mary Wickizer Burgess

G22. *The Devil's Notebook: Collected Epigrams and Pensées of Clark Ashton Smith*, compiled by Donald Sidney-Fryer and Don Herron. STARMONT POPULAR CULTURE STUDIES, Number 16. 1990. xv+82 p. LC 89-29636. OCLC #20671895. ISBN 1-55742-161-7 cloth $23; ISBN 1-55742-160-9 paper $13.

G23. *Discovering Classic Horror Fiction*, edited by Darrell Schweitzer. STARMONT STUDIES IN LITERARY CRITICISM, Number 27. 1992. vi+191 p. LC 89-11431. OCLC #19922928. ISBN 1-55742-085-8 cloth $29; ISBN 1-55472-084-X paper $19.

G24. *Discovering H.P. Lovecraft*, edited by Darrell Schweitzer. STARMONT STUDIES IN LITERARY CRITICISM, Number 6. 1987. xiv+153 p. LC 87-9923. OCLC #15520963. ISBN 0-916732-82-7 cloth $27; ISBN 0-916732-81-9 paper $17.

G25. *Discovering Modern Horror Fiction I*, edited by Darrell Schweitzer. STARMONT STUDIES IN LITERARY CRITICISM, Number 4. 1985. [iv]+156 p. LC 84-2763. OCLC #11469384. ISBN 0-916732-94-0 cloth $27; ISBN 0-916732-93-2 paper $17.

G26. *Discovering Modern Horror Fiction II*, edited by Darrell Schweitzer. STARMONT STUDIES IN LITERARY CRITICISM, Number 16. 1988. [iv]+169 p. LC 84-2763. OCLC #11469384. ISBN 0-930621-48-8 cloth $27; ISBN 0-930261-47-X paper $17 [ISBNs for the first volume appear on the back cover].

G27. *Discovering Stephen King*, edited by Darrell Schweitzer. STARMONT STUDIES IN LITERARY CRITICISM, Number 8. 1985. 219 p. LC 85-2821. OCLC #11867037. ISBN 0-930261-07-0 cloth $29; ISBN 0-930261-06-2 paper $19.

G28. *Double Trouble: A Bibliographic Chronicle of Ace Mystery Doubles*, by Sheldon Jaffery. STARMONT POPULAR CULTURE STUDIES, Number 11. 1992. xvi+150 p. LC 89-11447. OCLC #19923011. ISBN 1-55742-119-6 cloth $27; ISBN 1-55742-118-8 paper $17.

G29. *E.E. "Doc" Smith*, by Joe Sanders. STARMONT READER'S GUIDE, Number 24. 1986. [viii]+96 p. LC 85-30434. OCLC #13002734.

BP 300, by Robert Reginald & Mary Wickizer Burgess

ISBN 0-916732-73-8 cloth $23; ISBN 0-916732-72-X paper $13.

G30. *Fear to the World: Eleven Voices in a Chorus of Horror*, by Kevin E. Proulx. STARMONT STUDIES IN LITERARY CRITICISM, Number 35. 1992. x+243 p. LC 93-242564. OCLC #30547994. ISBN 1-55742-174-9 cloth $30; ISBN 1-55742-173-0 paper $20.

G31. *The Films of Stephen King*, by Michael R. Collings. STARMONT STUDIES IN LITERARY CRITICISM, Number 12. 1986. [vi]+201 p. LC 85-17192. OCLC #12313859. ISBN 0-930261-11-9 cloth $29; ISBN 0-930261-10-0 paper $19.

G32. *Frank Herbert*, by David M. Miller. STARMONT READER'S GUIDE, Number 5. 1980. 70 p. LC 80-20880. OCLC #6648869. ISBN 0-916732-07-X cloth $20; ISBN 0-916732-16-9 paper $10.

G33. *Frederik Pohl*, by Thomas D. Clareson. STARMONT READER'S GUIDE, Number 39. 1987. x+173 p. LC 86-14587. OCLC #14187180. ISBN 0-930261-34-8 cloth $27; ISBN 0-930261-33-X paper $17.

G34. *Fritz Leiber*, by Jeff Frane. STARMONT READER'S GUIDE, Number 8. 1980. 64 p. LC 80-22107. OCLC #6735549. ISBN 0-916732-02-9 cloth $20; ISBN 0-916732-10-X paper $10.

G35. *Future and Fantastic Worlds: A Bibliographical Retrospective of DAW Books (1972-1987)*, by Sheldon Jaffery. STARMONT REFERENCE GUIDES, Number 4. 1987. xiv+297 p. LC 87-9901. OCLC #15628385. ISBN 1-55742-003-3 cloth $35; ISBN 1-55742-002-5 paper $25.

G36. *A Gazeteer of the Hyborian World of Conan: Including Also the World of Kull and an Ethnogeographical Dictionary of the Principal Peoples of the Era, with Reference to The Starmont Map of the Hyborian World*, by Lee N. Falconer [i.e., Julian May]. 1977. xiv+119 p. LC 77-79065. OCLC #3480800. ISBN 0-916732-19-3 cloth $25; ISBN 0-916732-01-0 paper $15.

BP 300, by Robert Reginald & Mary Wickizer Burgess

G37. *Gene Wolfe*, by Joan Gordon. STARMONT READER'S GUIDE, Number 29. 1986. iv+116 p. LC 85-17163. OCLC #12313726. ISBN 0-930261-19-4 cloth $23; ISBN 0-930261-18-6 paper $13.

G38. *Hal Clement*, by Donald M. Hassler. STARMONT READER'S GUIDE, Number 11. 1982. [ii}+64 p. LC 82-5577. OCLC #8430780. ISBN 0-916732-30-4 cloth $20; ISBN 0-916732-27-4 paper $10.

G39. *H.G. Wells*, by Robert Crossley. STARMONT READER'S GUIDE, Number 19. 1986. 79 p. LC 84-2691. OCLC #10753288. ISBN 0-916732-51-7 cloth $20; ISBN 0-916732-50-9 paper $10.

G40. *The Horror of It All: Encrusted Gems from the "Crypt of Cthulhu,"* edited by Robert M. Price. STARMONT STUDIES IN LITERARY CRITICISM, Number 31. 1990. [iv]+199 p. LC 89-26171. OCLC #20722823. ISBN 1-55742-123-4 cloth $29; ISBN 1-55742-122-6 paper $19.

G41. *H.P. Lovecraft*, by S. T. Joshi. STARMONT READER'S GUIDE, Number 13. 1982. 83 p. LC 82-10236. OCLC #8533570. ISBN 0-916732-36-3 cloth $20; ISBN 0-916732-35-5 paper $10.

G42. *H.P. Lovecraft and the Cthulhu Mythos*, by Robert M. Price. STARMONT STUDIES IN LITERARY CRITICISM, Number 33. 1990. [iv]+170 p. LC 89-34791. OCLC #19846516. ISBN 1-55742-153-6 cloth $27; ISBN 1-55742-152-8 paper $17.

G43. *H.P. Lovecraft: The Decline of the West*, by S. T. Joshi. STARMONT STUDIES IN LITERARY CRITICISM, Number 37. 1990. viii+155 p., 8.5 x 11". LC 95-215015. OCLC #31410745. ISBN 1-55742-208-7 cloth $37; ISBN 1-55742-207-9 paper $27.

G44. *Ira Levin*, by Douglas Fowler. STARMONT READER'S GUIDE, Number 34. 1988. viii+87 p. LC 87-16033. OCLC #16128809. ISBN 0-930261-26-7 cloth $20; ISBN 0-930261-25-9 paper $10.

G45. *Isaac Asimov*, by Donald M. Hassler. STARMONT READER'S GUIDE, Number 40. 1991. iv+129 p. LC 86-14585. OCLC #14164772. ISBN 0-930261-32-1 cloth $25; ISBN 0-930261-31-

BP 300, by Robert Reginald & Mary Wickizer Burgess

3 paper $15. Winner of the 1993 J. Lloyd Eaton Award for Best Nonfiction Work of the Year.

G46. *It's Raining Corpses in Chinatown*, edited by Don Hutchison. STARMONT POPULAR CULTURE STUDIES, Number 9. 1991. xxxviii+169 p. LC 93-202000. OCLC #30571944. ISBN 1-55742-125-0 cloth $29; ISBN 1-55742-124-2 paper $19.

G47. *Jack London*, by Gorman Beauchamp. STARMONT READER'S GUIDE, Number 15. 1984. 96 p. LC 82-7345. OCLC #8494309. ISBN 0-916732-40-1 cloth $20; ISBN 0-916732-39-8 paper $10.

G48. *James Tiptree, Jr.*, by Mark Siegel. STARMONT READER'S GUIDE, Number 22. 1985. 89 p. LC 85-17159. OCLC #12313719. ISBN 0-916732-68-1 cloth $20; ISBN 0-916732-67-3 paper $10.

G49. *J.G. Ballard*, by Peter Brigg. STARMONT READER'S GUIDE, Number 26. 1985. 138 p. LC 85-2724. OCLC #11756103. ISBN 0-916732-84-3 cloth $25; ISBN 0-916732-83-5 paper $15.

G50. *Joe Haldeman*, by Joan Gordon. STARMONT READER'S GUIDE, Number 4. 1980. 64 p. LC 80-21388. OCLC #6707292. ISBN 0-916732-15-0 cloth $20; ISBN 0-916732-06-1 paper $10.

G51. *J.R.R. Tolkien*, by David Stevens and Carol D. Stevens. STARMONT READER'S GUIDE, Number 54. 1992. vi+178 p. LC 93-17850. OCLC #28112937. ISBN 1-55742-238-9 cloth $27; ISBN 1-55742-237-0 paper $17. See also **A167**.

G52. *Kurt Vonnegut*, by Donald E. Morse. STARMONT READER'S GUIDE, Number 61. 1992. iv+128 p. LC 93-201941. OCLC #26235434. ISBN 1-55742-219-2 cloth $25; ISBN 1-55742-220-6 paper $15.

G53. *Lewis Carroll*, by Beverly Lyon Clark. STARMONT READER'S GUIDE, Number 47. 1990. viii+96 p. LC 87-16032. OCLC #16095117. ISBN 1-55742-031-9 cloth $23; ISBN 1-55742-030-0 paper $13.

G54. *Lin Carter: A Look Behind His Imaginary Worlds*, by Robert M. Price. STARMONT STUDIES IN LITERARY CRITICISM, Number 36.

BP 300, by Robert Reginald & Mary Wickizer Burgess

1991. vi+172 p. LC 93-242547. OCLC #30703279. ISBN 1-55742-230-3 cloth $27; ISBN 1-55742-229-X paper $17.

G55. *Lovecraft: A Look Behind the Cthulhu Mythos: The Background of a Myth That Has Captured a Generation*, by Lin Carter. STARMONT POPULAR CULTURE STUDIES, Number 10. 1992. xxii+198 p. LC 94-156858. OCLC #31670126. ISBN 1-55742-253-2 cloth $29; ISBN 1-55742-252-4 paper $19.

G56. *The Lure of Adventure*, by Robert Kenneth Jones. STARMONT PULP AND DIME NOVEL STUDIES, Number 4. 1989. [iv]+80+[iv] p. LC 89-34753. OCLC #19921031. ISBN 1-55742-143-9 cloth $20; ISBN 1-55742-142-0 paper $10.

G57. *The Many Facets of Stephen King*, by Michael R. Collings. STARMONT STUDIES IN LITERARY CRITICISM, Number 11. 1985. [vi]+190 p. LC 85-12598. OCLC #12134907. ISBN 0-930261-15-1 cloth $29; ISBN 0-930261-14-3 paper $19.

G58. *Marion Zimmer Bradley*, by Rosemarie Arbur. STARMONT READER'S GUIDE, Number 27. 1985. [ii]+138 p. LC 85-2721. OCLC #11756096. ISBN 0-916732-96-7 cloth $25; ISBN 0-916732-95-9 paper $15.

G59. *Mary Shelley*, by Allene Stuart Phy. STARMONT READER'S GUIDE, Number 36. 1988. 124 p. LC 86-6502. OCLC #13361038. ISBN 0-930261-61-5 cloth $23; ISBN 0-930261-60-7 paper $13.

G60. *The Moral Voyages of Stephen King*, by Anthony Magistrale. STARMONT STUDIES IN LITERARY CRITICISM, Number 25. 1989. [iv]+vi+157 p. LC 88-1076. OCLC #17439492. ISBN 1-55742-071-8 cloth $27; ISBN 1-55742-070-X paper $17.

G61. *Olaf Stapledon*, by John Kinnaird. STARMONT READER'S GUIDE, Number 21. 1986. 107 p. LC 84-2656. OCLC #10726446. ISBN 0-916732-55-X cloth $23; ISBN 0-916732-54-1 paper $13.

G62. *Patterns of the Fantastic: Academic Programming at Chicon IV*, edited by Donald M. Hassler. STARMONT STUDIES IN LITERARY CRITICISM, Number 2. 1983. [vi}+105 p. LC 83-587. OCLC

BP 300, by Robert Reginald & Mary Wickizer Burgess

#9350556. ISBN 0-916732-63-0 cloth $23; ISBN 0-916732-62-2 paper $13.

G63. *Patterns of the Fantastic II: Academic Programming at Con-Stellation*, edited by Donald M. Hassler. STARMONT STUDIES IN LITERARY CRITICISM, Number 3. 1985. [vi]+90 p. LC 84-2683. OCLC #10753249. ISBN 0-916732-88-6 cloth $23; ISBN 0-916732-87-8 paper $13.

G64. *Peter Beagle*, by Kenneth J. Zahorski. STARMONT READER'S GUIDE, Number 44. 1988. [iv]+124 p. LC 87-9924. OCLC #15520976. ISBN 1-55742-009-2 cloth $23; ISBN 1-55742-008-4 paper $13.

G65. *Philip José Farmer*, by Mary T. Brizzi. STARMONT READER'S GUIDE, Number 3. 1980. [ii]+80 p. LC 79-17691. OCLC #5239882. ISBN 0-916732-14-2 cloth $20; ISBN 0-916732-05-3 paper $10.

G66. *Philip K. Dick*, by Hazel Pierce. STARMONT READER'S GUIDE, Number 12. 1982. 64 p. LC 82-6005. OCLC #8494810. ISBN 0-916732-34-7 cloth $20; ISBN 0-916732-33-9 paper $10.

G67. *Phoenix Renewed: The Survival and Mutation of Utopian Thought in North American Science Fiction, 1965-1982*, by Hoda M. Zaki. STARMONT STUDIES IN LITERARY CRITICISM, Number 22. 1988. [viii]+151 p. LC 87-9920. OCLC #15520957. ISBN 1-55742-007-6 cloth $25; ISBN 1-55742-006-8 paper $15. See also **A166**.

G68. *Piers Anthony*, by Michael R. Collings. STARMONT READER'S GUIDE, Number 20. 1983. 96 p. LC 83-2466. OCLC #10403955. ISBN 0-916732-53-3 cloth $20; ISBN 0-916732-52-5 $10.

G69. *The Pulp Magazine Index, First Series*, by Leonard A. Robbins. 1988. 2,152 p. in 3 v., 8.5 x 11". LC 88-20056. OCLC #18163536. LC 91-658651 (series). OCLC #25543703 (series). ISBN 1-55742-111-0 cloth (3-Volume set) $175.

BP 300, by Robert Reginald & Mary Wickizer Burgess

G70. *The Pulp Magazine Index, Second Series*, by Leonard A. Robbins. 1989. 583 p., 8.5 x 11". LC 89-34752. OCLC #19846295. ISBN 1-55742-162-5 cloth $80.

G71. *The Pulp Magazine Index, Third Series*, by Leonard A. Robbins. 1990. 639 p., 8.5 x 11". OCLC #22781709. ISBN 1-55742-204-4 cloth $80.

G72. *The Pulp Magazine Index, Fourth Series*, by Leonard A. Robbins. 1991. 567 p., 8.5 x 11". LC 88-20056. OCLC #24310142. ISBN 1-55742-241-9 cloth $80.

G73. *Pulp Man's Odyssey: The Hugh B. Cave Story*, by Audrey Parente. STARMONT POPULAR CULTURE STUDIES, Number 6. 1988. xiv+146 p. LC 87-26706. OCLC #16901251. ISBN 1-55742-039-4 cloth $25; ISBN 1-55742-038-6 paper $15.

G74. *Pulpmaster: The Theodore Roscoe Story*, by Audrey Parente. STARMONT POPULAR CULTURE STUDIES, Number 13. 1992. xvi+173 p. LC 93-202524. OCLC #27636680. ISBN 1-55742-170-6 cloth $27; ISBN 1-55742-169-2 paper $17.

G75. *Ramsey Campbell*, by Gary William Crawford. STARMONT READER'S GUIDE, Number 48. 1988. [vi]+74 p. LC 87-16030. OCLC #16095112. ISBN 1-55742-037-8 cloth $20; ISBN 1-55742-036-X paper $10.

G76. *Ray Bradbury*, by William F. Touponce. STARMONT READER'S GUIDE, Number 31. 1989. iv+110 p. LC 87-16031. OCLC #16128808. ISBN 0-930261-23-2 cloth $23; ISBN 0-930261-22-4 paper $13.

G77. *Robert Bloch*, by Randall D. Larson. STARMONT READER'S GUIDE, Number 37. 1986. [iv]+148 p. LC 86-5751. OCLC #13359474. ISBN 0-930261-59-3 cloth $25; ISBN 0-930261-58-5 paper $15.

G78. *The Robert Bloch Companion: Collected Interviews, 1969-1986*, by Robert Bloch, edited by Randall D. Larson. STARMONT STUDIES IN LITERARY CRITICISM, Number 32. 1989. [iv]+157 p.

BP 300, by Robert Reginald & Mary Wickizer Burgess

LC 89-26126. OCLC #20672312. ISBN 1-55742-147-1 cloth $27; ISBN 1-55742-146-3 paper $17.

G79. **Robert E. Howard**, by Marc A. Cerasini and Charles E. Hoffman. STARMONT READER'S GUIDE, Number 35. 1987. [vi]+156 p. LC 85-17161. OCLC #12313724. ISBN 0-930261-28-3 cloth $27; ISBN 0-930261-27-5 paper $17.

G80. **Robert Silverberg**, by Thomas D. Clareson. STARMONT READER'S GUIDE, Number 18. 1983. 96 p. LC 83-542. OCLC #9350514. ISBN 0-916732-48-7 cloth $20; ISBN 0-916732-47-9 $10.

G81. **Roger Zelazny**, by Carl B. Yoke. STARMONT READER'S GUIDE, Number 2. 1979. 111 p. LC 79-17107. OCLC #5170777. ISBN 0-916732-13-4 cloth $23; ISBN 0-916732-04-5 paper $13.

G82. **Samuel R. Delany**, by Jane Branham Weedman. STARMONT READER'S GUIDE, Number 10. 1982. [ii]+79 p. LC 82-5545. OCLC #8387740. ISBN 0-916732-28-2 cloth $20; ISBN 0-916732-25-8 paper $10.

G83. **Science Fiction: A Teacher's Guide and Resource Book**, edited by Marshall B. Tymn. STARMONT REFERENCE GUIDES, Number 5. 1988. x+140 p. LC 87-10143. OCLC #15792642. ISBN 1-55742-021-1 cloth $25; ISBN 1-55742-020-3 paper $15.

G84. **The Science Fiction Reference Book: A Comprehensive Handbook and Guide to the History, Literature, Scholarship, and Related Activities of the Science Fiction and Fantasy Fields**, edited by Marshall B. Tymn. 1981. viii+536 p. LC 80-28888. OCLC #7197464. ISBN 0-916732-49-5 cloth $49; ISBN 0-916732-24-X paper $39.

G85. **Shadowings: The Reader's Guide to Horror Fiction, 1981-1982**, edited by Douglas E. Winter. STARMONT STUDIES IN LITERARY CRITICISM, Number 1. 1983. x+148 p. LC 83-21326. OCLC #10046225. ISBN 0-916732-86-X cloth $25; ISBN 0-916732-85-1 paper $15.

G86. *Shanghai Year: A Westerner's Life in the New China*, by Peter Brigg. 1987. [x]+115 p. LC 87-1949. OCLC #15251301. ISBN 0-930261-88-7 cloth $23; ISBN 0-930261-89-5 paper $13.

G87. *"The Shining" Reader*, edited by Anthony Magistrale. STARMONT STUDIES IN LITERARY CRITICISM, Number 30. 1990. xii+220 p. LC 89-29631. OCLC #20671876. ISBN 1-55742-107-2 cloth $30; ISBN 1-55742-106-4 paper $20.

G88. *The Shorter Works of Stephen King*, by Michael R. Collings and David Engebretson. STARMONT STUDIES IN LITERARY CRITICISM, Number 9. 1985. [vi]+202 p. LC 85-2822. OCLC #11867040. ISBN 0-930261-03-8 cloth $29; ISBN 0-930261-02-X paper $19.

G89. *The Shudder Pulps: A History of the Weird Menace Magazines of the 1930s*, by Robert Kenneth Jones. 1974. xv+238 p. LC 74-82614. OCLC #1904925. ISBN 0-913960-04-7 cloth $30.

G90. *Stanislaw Lem*, by J. Madison Davis. STARMONT READER'S GUIDE, Number 32. 1990. x+116 p. LC 87-17646. OCLC #16129629. ISBN 1-55742-027-0 cloth $23; ISBN 1-55742-026-2 paper $13.

G91. *Stephen King as Richard Bachman*, by Michael R. Collings. STARMONT STUDIES IN LITERARY CRITICISM, Number 10. 1985. [vi]+168 p. LC 85-2832. OCLC #11917660. ISBN 0-930261-01-1 cloth $27; ISBN 0-930261-00-3 paper $17.

G92. *The Stephen King Phenomenon*, by Michael R. Collings. STARMONT STUDIES IN LITERARY CRITICISM, Number 14. 1987. 144 p. LC 85-17164. OCLC #12313727. ISBN 0-930261-13-5 cloth $25; ISBN 0-930261-12-7 paper $15.

G93. *Sudden Fear: The Horror and Dark Suspense Fiction of Dean R. Koontz*, edited by Bill Munster. STARMONT STUDIES IN LITERARY CRITICISM, Number 24. 1988. x+182 p. LC 88-1077. OCLC #17439493. ISBN 1-55742-025-4 cloth $27; ISBN 1-55742-024-6 $17.

BP 300, by Robert Reginald & Mary Wickizer Burgess

G94. *The Super Feds: A Facsimile Selection of Dynamic G-Man Stories from the 1930s*, edited by Don Hutchison. STARMONT POPULAR CULTURE STUDIES, Number 8. 1988. [viii]+158 p. LC 88-1078. OCLC #17439495. ISBN 1-55742-091-2 cloth $27; ISBN 1-55742-090-4 paper $17.

G95. *Suzy McKee Charnas, Octavia Butler, Joan D. Vinge*, by Marleen S. Barr, Ruth Salvaggio, Richard Law. STARMONT READER'S GUIDE, Number 23. 1986. 52+44+72 p. LC 85-2715. OCLC #11726651. ISBN 0-916732-92-4 $27; ISBN 0-916732-91-6 paper $17.

G96. *Theodore Sturgeon*, by Lahna Diskin. STARMONT READER'S GUIDE, Number 7. 1981. 72 p. LC 80-21423. OCLC #6666079. ISBN 0-916732-09-6 cloth $20; ISBN 0-916732-18-5 paper $10.

G97. *The Unseen King*, by Tyson Blue. STARMONT STUDIES IN LITERARY CRITICISM, Number 26. 1989. viii+200 p. LC 88-1074. OCLC #17439490. ISBN 1-55742-073-4 cloth $29; ISBN 1-55742-072-6 paper $19.

G98. *Urania's Daughters: A Checklist of Women Science-Fiction Writers, 1692-1982*, by Roger C. Schlobin. STARMONT REFERENCE GUIDES, Number 1. 1983. xiv+79 p. LC 83-2467. OCLC #10458506. ISBN 0-916732-57-6 cloth $20; ISBN 0-916732-56-8 paper $10.

G99. *The Western Pulp Hero: An Investigation into the Psyche of an American Legend*, by Nick Carr. STARMONT POPULAR CULTURE STUDIES, Number 3. 1989. 134 p., 8.5 x 11". LC 87-18370. OCLC #16275980. ISBN 1-55742-033-5 cloth $35; ISBN 1-55742-032-7 paper $25.

G100. *William Gibson*, by Lance Olsen. STARMONT READER'S GUIDE, Number 58. 1992. vii+131 p. LC 93-201910. OCLC #27254726. ISBN 1-55742-199-4 cloth $25; ISBN 1-55742-198-6 paper $15.

H.

MISCELLANEOUS PUBLICATIONS
ACQUIRED FROM VARIOUS PUBLISHERS
(with New Borgo ISBNs as Assigned)

H1. *Cumulative Paperback Index, 1939-1959: A Comprehensive Bibliographic Guide to 14,000 Mass-Market Paperback Books of 33 Publishers Issued Under 69 Imprints*, by R. Reginald and M. R. Burgess. 1973. xiii+362 p., 8.5 x 11". LC 73-6866. OCLC #622653. ISBN 0-89370-022-3 cloth $51.

Acquired from Gale Research Company.

H2. *Science Fiction and Fantasy Book Review, Nos. 1-13, 1979-1980*, edited by Neil Barron and R. Reginald. 1983. 164+32 p. LC 78-2211. ISBN 0-89370-624-8 cloth $33.

Includes original issues and photocopied replacements bound together in maroon or gray binding.

H3. *The Paperback Price Guide No. 2*, by Kevin B. Hancer and R. Reginald. 1982. xvii+390 p. LC 82-11790. OCLC #8626856. Illustrated with reproductions of paperback covers. ISBN 0-89370-745-7 cloth $27; ISBN 0-89370-899-2 paper $17.

Acquired from Harmony Books.

H4. *Things to Come: An Illustrated History of the Science Fiction Film*, by Douglas Menville and R. Reginald. 1983. 212 p. LC 83-8789. OCLC #9488376. Illustrated with motion picture stills. ISBN 0-89370-019-3 cloth $31.

Acquired from Times Books.

H5. *Futurevisions: The New Golden Age of the Science Fiction Film*, by Douglas Menville, R. Reginald, and Mary A. Burgess.

BP 300, **by Robert Reginald & Mary Wickizer Burgess**

1985. 192 p. LC 85-20098. OCLC #12613295. Illustrated with motion picture stills. ISBN 0-89370-681-7 cloth $31; ISBN 0-89370-699-X paper $21.

Acquired from Newcastle Publishing Co., Inc.

H6. ***The Mushroom Jungle: A History of Postwar Paperback Publishing,*** by Steve Holland. A Zeon Book. 1994. xii+196 p. Illustrated with reproductions of paperback covers. ISBN 0-8095-6013-5 cloth $35; ISBN 1-874113-01-7 paper $25.

Acquired from Zeon Books.

BP 300, by Robert Reginald & Mary Wickizer Burgess

SERIES INDEX

THE AUTOCEPHALOUS ORTHODOX CHURCHES
(ISSN 1059-1001)

1. *A Directory of Autocephalous Bishops of the Churches of the Apostolic Succession, Eighth Edition*, by Bishop Karl Pruter
2. *The Russian Orthodox Church Outside Russia: A History and Chronology*, by Rev. Father Alexey Young
3. *The Old Catholic Church: A History and Chronology, Second Edition*, by Karl Pruter
5. *The Ancient Church on New Shores: Antioch in North America*, by Archpriest Antony Gabriel

BIBLIOGRAPHIES OF MODERN AUTHORS
(ISSN 0749-470X)

1. *The Work of Colin Wilson: An Annotated Bibliography & Guide*, by Colin Stanley
2. *The Work of Jeffrey M. Elliot: An Annotated Bibliography & Guide*, by Boden Clarke
3. *The Work of Julian May: An Annotated Bibliography & Guide.*
4. *The Work of George Zebrowski: An Annotated Bibliography & Literary Guide, Third Edition*, by Jeffrey M. Elliot and R. Reginald
5. *The Work of Robert Reginald: An Annotated Bibliography & Guide, Second Edition*, by Michael Burgess
6. *The Work of Charles Beaumont: An Annotated Bibliography & Guide, Second Edition*, by William F. Nolan
7. *The Work of Katherine Kurtz: An Annotated Bibliography & Guide*, by Boden Clarke
8. *The Work of Reginald Bretnor: An Annotated Bibliography & Guide*, by Scott Alan Burgess
9. *The Work of Brian W. Aldiss: An Annotated Bibliography & Guide*, by Margaret Aldiss

BP 300, by Robert Reginald & Mary Wickizer Burgess

BLACK POLITICAL STUDIES
(ISSN 0891-9631)

BP 300, by Robert Reginald & Mary Wickizer Burgess

BORGO BIOVIEWS
(ISSN 0743-0628)

1. *Starclimber: The Literary Adventures and Autobiography of Raymond Z. Gallun*, by Raymond Z. Gallun with Jeffrey M. Elliot
2. *Adventures of a Freelancer: The Literary Exploits and Autobiography of Stanton A. Coblentz*, with Dr. Jeffrey M. Elliot
3. *Deathman Pass Me By: Two Years on Death Row*, by Philip Brasfield and Jeffrey M. Elliot
4. *Legends and Lovers: Fourteen Profiles*, by William F. Nolan
5. *Ah Julian! A Memoir of Julian Brodetsky*, by Leonard Wibberley
8. *Bibi Mkuba: My Experiences During Wartime in German East Africa*, by Ada Schnee, translated and edited by Sam E. Edelstein, Jr.
9. *Lemady: Episodes of a Writer's Life*, by Keith Roberts

BORGO CATALOGING GUIDES
(ISSN 0891-9615)

1. *A Guide to Science Fiction and Fantasy in the Library of Congress Classification Scheme, Second Edition*, by Michael Burgess
2. *Mystery and Detective Fiction in the Library of Congress Classification Scheme*, by Michael Burgess
3. *Western Fiction in the Library of Congress Classification Scheme*, by Michael Burgess and Beverly A. Ryan
4. *World War I: A Cataloging Reference Guide*, by Buckley Barry Barrett
5. *World War II: A Cataloging Reference Guide*, by Buckley Barry Barrett

BORGO FAMILY HISTORIES
(ISSN 0733-6764)

1. *The House of the Burgesses, Second Edition*, by Michael Burgess
2. *The Wickizer Annals*, by Mary Wickizer Burgess
5. *The Genealogical History of Providencia Island*, by J. Cordell Robinson

BORGO LAUREATE SERIES

BP 300, by Robert Reginald & Mary Wickizer Burgess

(ISSN 1082-3336)

1. *Numbery: Poems*, by Richard Mathews

BORGO LITERARY GUIDES
(ISSN 0891-9623)

1. *Reginald's Science Fiction and Fantasy Awards: A Comprehensive Guide to the Awards and Their Winners, Third Edition*, by Daryl F. Mallett and Robert Reginald
2. *The Jack Vance Lexicon: The Coined Words of Jack Vance from Ahulph to Zipangote*, by Dan Temianka
6. *Victorian Criticism of American Writers: A Guide to British Criticism of American Writers in the Leading British Periodicals of the Victorian Period, 1824-1900*, by Arnella K. Turner
7. *British Science Fiction Paperbacks and Magazines, 1949-1956: An Annotated Bibliography and Guide, Revised Edition*, by Philip Harbottle and Stephen Holland
8. *The Transylvanian Library: A Consumer's Guide to Vampire Fiction*, by Greg Cox
10. *BP 250: An Annotated Bibliography of the First 250 Publications of The Borgo Press*, by Robert Reginald and Mary A. Burgess

BORGO POLITICAL SCENARIOS
(ISSN 0278-9752)

1. *If J.F.K. Had Lived: A Political Scenario*, by R. Reginald and Jeffrey M. Elliot

BORGO REFERENCE GUIDES
(ISSN 0891-9607)

1. *Stalin: An Annotated Guide to Books in English*, by Marty Bloomberg & Buckley Barry Barrett
3. *The Presidential-Congressional Political Dictionary*, by Jeffrey M. Elliot and Sheikh R. Ali
4. *The Chinese Economy: A Bibliography of Works in English*, by Robert Goehlert and Antony C. Stamatoplos
5. *The State and Province Vital Records Guide*, by Michael Burgess, Mary A. Burgess, and Daryl F. Mallett

BP 300, by Robert Reginald & Mary Wickizer Burgess

6. *Eastern Europe: A Resource Guide: A Selected Bibliography on Social Sciences and Humanities,* by Suzanne D. Gyeszly
7. *The State and Local Government Political Dictionary,* by Jeffrey M. Elliot and Sheikh R. Ali

BROWNSTONE MYSTERY GUIDES
(ISSN 1055-6859)

1. *Hardboiled Burlesque: Raymond Chandler's Comic Style,* by Keith Newlin
2. *The New Hard-Boiled Dicks: Heroes for a New Urban Mythology, Second Edition,* by Robert E. Skinner
3. *John Nieminski: Somewhere a Roscoe,* by John Nieminski, edited by Ely Liebow and Art Scott
4. *Frederick Irving Anderson (1877-1947): A Biobibliography,* by Benjamin Franklin Fisher IV
5. *A Detective in Distress: Philip Marlowe's Domestic Dream,* by Gay Brewer
6. *Rex Stout: A Biography,* by John McAleer
8. *Mystery Voices: Interviews with British Crime Writers,* by Dale Salwak
9. *The Mystery Fancier: An Index to Volumes I-XIII, November 1976-Fall 1992,* by William F. Deeck
10. *Detective and Mystery Fiction: An International Bibliography of Second Sources, Second Edition,* by Walter Albert
11. *Polemical Pulps: The Martin Beck Novels of Maj Sjöwall and Per Wahlöö,* by J. Kenneth Van Dover
12. *Hard-Boiled Heretic: The Lew Archer Novels of Ross Macdonald,* by Mary S. Weinkauf
13. *Self-Portrait: Ceaselessly into the Past,* by Ross Macdonald, edited by Ralph B. Sipper
14. *Murder Most Poetic: The Mystery Novels of Ngaio Marsh,* by Mary S. Weinkauf
15. *Mary Roberts Rinehart, Mistress of Mystery,* by Frances H. Bachelder
16. *The Mystery Scene Movie Guide: A Personal Filmography of Modern Crime Pictures,* by Max Allan Collins
17. *Laughing Like Hell: The Harrowing Satires of Jim Thompson,* by Gay Brewer
18. *Chicago Ain't No Sissy Town!: The Regional Detective Fiction of Howard Browne,* by John A. Dinan

BP 300, by Robert Reginald & Mary Wickizer Burgess

19. *Centurions, Knights, and Other Cops: The Police Novels of Joseph Wambaugh,* by J. K. Van Dover

CLASSICS OF FANTASTIC LITERATURE

1. *Firefly: A Novel of the Far Future,* by Brian Stableford
2. *Sansato,* by William F. Temple

CLIPPER STUDIES IN THE THEATRE
(ISSN 0748-237X)

1. *The Theatrical Rambles of Mr. and Mrs. John Greene,* by Charles Durang
2. *Popular Amusements in Horse and Buggy America: An Anthology of Contemporaneous Essays,* edited by William L. Slout
3. *The Italian Theatre in San Francisco: Being a History of the Italian-Language Operatic, Dramatic, and Comedic Productions Presented in the San Francisco Bay Area Through the Depression Era, with Reminiscences of the Leading Players and Impresarios of the Times,* by Laurence Estavan
4. *Broadway Below the Sidewalk: Concert Saloons of Old New York,* by William L. Slout
5. *Ink from a Circus Press Agent: An Anthology of Circus History from the Pen of Charles H. Day,* by Charles H. Day, edited and with a Circus Personnel Reference Roster by William L. Slout
6. *An Annotated Narrative of Joe Blackburn's A Clown's Log,* by Joe Blackburn, edited by Charles H. Day
7. *The Trial of Dr. Jekyll: An Adaptation of Robert Louis Stevenson's "The Strange Case of Dr. Jekyll and Mr. Hyde": A Play in Two Acts,* by William L. Slout
9. *Amphitheatres and Circuses: A History from Their Earliest Date to 1861, with Sketches of Some of the Principal Performers,* by Col. T. Allston Brown, edited by William L. Slout
10. *Doors into the Play: A Few Practical Keys for Theatricians,* by Sydney H. Spayde with Douglas A. Mackey
12. *Old Gotham Theatricals: Selections from a Series, "Reminiscences of a Man about Town,"* by Col. Tom Picton, edited by William L. Slout
14. *Life Upon the Wicked Stage: A Visit to the American Theatre of the 1860s, 1870s, and 1880s as Seen in the Pages of the New York Clipper,* edited by William L. Slout

BP 300, by Robert Reginald & Mary Wickizer Burgess

16.   *Clowns and Cannons*: The American Circus During the Civil War, by William L. Slout
17.   *Grand Entrée*: The Birth of the Greatest Show on Earth, 1870-1875, by Stuart Thayer and William L. Slout
18.   *Olympians of the Sawdust Circle*: A Biographical Dictionary of the Nineteenth-Century American Circus, by William L. Slout

ESSAYS ON FANTASTIC LITERATURE
(ISSN 0891-9593)

1.   *It's Down the Slippery Cellar Stairs*, by R. A. Lafferty.
2.   *Blond Barbarians & Noble Savages*, by L. Sprague de Camp
3.   *Ray Bradbury: Dramatist*, Second Edition, by Ben P. Indick
4.   *Non-Literary Influences on Science Fiction*, by Algis Budrys
5.   *The Poison Maiden & the Great Bitch*, by Susan Wood
8.   *Geo. Alec Effinger*: From Entropy to Budayeen, by Ben P. Indick

GREAT ISSUES OF THE DAY
(ISSN 0270-7497)

1.   *The Future of the Space Program*; Large Corporations and Society: Discussions with 22 Science Fiction Writers, by Jeffrey M. Elliot
2.   *The Trilemma of World Oil Politics*, by Jeffrey M. Elliot and Sheikh R. Ali
3.   *Fidel by Fidel*: An Interview with Dr. Fidel Castro Ruz, President of the Republic of Cuba, by Rep. Mervyn M. Dymally and Jeffrey M. Elliot
4.   *To Kill or Not To Kill*: Thoughts on Capital Punishment, by Rep. William L. Clay, Sr.
5.   *The Coachella Valley Preserve*: The Struggle for a Desert Wetlands, by Yvonne Pacheco Tevis
6.   *Mexico and the United States, Neighbors in Crisis*: Proceedings from the Conference, Neighbors in Crisis, a Call for Joint Solutions, edited by Daniel G. Aldrich, Jr. and Lorenzo Mayer
7.   *"We, the People!"* Bay Area Activism in the 1960s: Three Case Studies, by Richard DeLuca

I.O. EVANS STUDIES IN THE PHILOSOPHY AND CRITICISM OF LITERATURE
(ISSN 0271-9061)

BP 300, by Robert Reginald & Mary Wickizer Burgess

BP 300, by Robert Reginald & Mary Wickizer Burgess

MALCOLM HULKE STUDIES IN CINEMA AND TELEVISION
(ISSN 0884-6944)

THE MILFORD SERIES: POPULAR WRITERS OF TODAY
(ISSN 0163-2469)

BP 300, by Robert Reginald & Mary Wickizer Burgess

BP 300, by Robert Reginald & Mary Wickizer Burgess

BP 300, by Robert Reginald & Mary Wickizer Burgess

SFRA STUDIES IN SCIENCE FICTION, FANTASY, AND HORROR
(ISSN 1069-4668)

BP 300, by Robert Reginald & Mary Wickizer Burgess

2.   *Imaginative Futures*: *Proceedings of the 1993 Science Fiction Research Association Conference*, edited by Milton T. Wolf and Daryl F. Mallett

ST. WILLIBRORD STUDIES IN PHILOSOPHY AND RELIGION
(ISSN 1059-8375)

1.   *One Day with God: A Guide to Retreats and the Contemplative Life, Revised Edition*, by Bishop Karl Pruter
2.   *The Catholic Priest: A Guide to Holy Orders*, by Bishop Karl Pruter
4.   *The Priest's Handbook, Second Edition*, by Karl Pruter
5.   *The Mystic Path*, by Karl Pruter

STOKVIS STUDIES IN HISTORICAL CHRONOLOGY AND THOUGHT
(ISSN 0270-5338)

1.   *Lords Temporal and Lords Spiritual: A Chronological Checklist of the Popes, Patriarchs, Katholikoi, and Independent Archbishops and Metropolitans of the Autocephalous and Autonomous Monarchical Churches of the Christian East and West, Second Edition, Revised and Expanded*, by Michael Burgess
2.   *Candle for Poland: 469 Days of Solidarity*, by Leszek Szymanski
3.   *Tempest in a Teapot: The Falkland Islands War*, by R. Reginald and Jeffrey M. Elliot
4.   *Across the Wide Missouri: The Diary of a Journey from Virginia to Missouri in 1819 and Back Again in 1822, with a Description of the City of Cincinnati*, by James Brown Campbell
5.   *Decisive Warfare: A Study in Military Theory*, by Reginald Bretnor
6.   *Of Force and Violence and Other Imponderables: Essays on War, Politics, and Government*, by Reginald Bretnor
8.   *Whaling Masters*, by the Federal Writers Project
9.   *Calendar of Coroners Rolls of the City of London, A.D. 1300-1378*, edited by Reginald R. Sharpe
10. *The Association Oath Rolls of the British Plantations [New York, Virginia, Etc.], A.D. 1696, Being a Contribution to Political History*, by William Gandy
11. *California Ranchos: Patented Private Land Grants Listed by County*, by Burgess McK. Shumway

BP 300, by Robert Reginald & Mary Wickizer Burgess

12. *The Egyptian Gods: A Handbook, Revised Edition*, by Alan W. Shorter, with a new bibliography by Bonnie L. Petry
13. *Monumental Inscriptions: Tombstones of the Island of Barbados, New Edition*, by Vere Langford Oliver
14. *More Monumental Inscriptions: Tombstones of the British West Indies*, by Vere Langford Oliver
15. *Politics Quaker Style: A History of the Quakers from 1624 to 1718*, by John H. Ferguson
16. *Merry Wheels and Spokes of Steel: A Social History of the Bicycle*, by Robert A. Smith
17. *Providencia Island: Its History and Its People*, by J. Cordell Robinson

STUDIES IN JUDAICA AND THE HOLOCAUST
(ISSN 0884-6952)

1. *The Jewish Holocaust: An Annotated Guide to Books in English, Second Edition*, by Marty Bloomberg and Buckley Barry Barrett
2. *Survivors: A Personal Story of the Holocaust*, by Jacob Biber
3. *A Voyage to America Ninety Years Ago: The Diary of a Bohemian Jew on His Voyage from Hamburg to New York in 1847*, by S. E. Rosenbaum, ed. by Guido Kisch, newly translated and with an introduction by Nathan Kravetz
5. *Risen from the Ashes: A Story of the Jewish Displaced Persons in the Aftermath of World War II, Being a Sequel to Survivors*, by Jacob Biber
6. *First Century Palestinian Judaism: A Bibliography*, by David Ray Bourquin
7. *Displaced German Scholars: A Guide to Academics in Peril in Nazi Germany During the 1930s*, introduced by Dr. Nathan Kravetz
8. *Into the Flames: The Life Story of a Righteous Gentile*, by Irene Gut Opdyke with Jeffrey M. Elliot
9. *A Triumph of the Spirit: Thirteen Stories of Holocaust Survivors, Second Edition*, edited by Jacob Biber
10. *Kansas and Me: Memories of a Jewish Childhood*, by Annette Peltz McComas
11. *Defying the Holocaust: A Diplomat's Report*, by Aba Gefen
12. *A Wayfarer in a World in Upheaval*, by Bernard L. Ginsburg
14. *Justyna's Diary: Jewish Resistance to the Nazis in Wartime Poland*, by Justyna (Gusta Dawidsohn Draenger), translated by

BP 300, by Robert Reginald & Mary Wickizer Burgess

Majka Shephard, edited and with an introduction by Nathan Kravetz

AUTHOR INDEX

BP 300, by Robert Reginald & Mary Wickizer Burgess

Falconer, Lee N., pseud.—SEE: May, Julian
Fanthorpe, Lionel, A74
Fanthorpe, Patricia, A74
Federal Writers Project, A85, A102
Ferguson, John H., A236
Ferres, Kay, A203
Fisher, Benjamin Franklin IV, C8
Foust, Ronald, G1
Fowler, Douglas, G44
Fox, Georgette S., A298
Frane, Jeff, G34
Free, William J., A195
Gabriel, Archpriest Antony, A258
Gallagher, Edward J., G6
Gallun, Raymond Z., A124
Gammell, Leon L., G7
Gandy, William, A151
García-Gómez, Jorge, B5
Gefen, Aba, A164
George, Isaac, E1
Ginsburg, Bernard L., A177
Goehlert, Robert, A234
Golden, Bruce, A2, A120
Gordon, Joan, G37, G50
Gunn, James, A138
Gurley, John Hansen, A172-A173
Gyeszly, Suzanne D., A202
Hall, Frances, A26
Hall, Hal W., A80, A86, A101, A130, A134-A136, A158, A178, A205
Hancer, Kevin B., H3
Harbottle, Philip, A142, A192, A231
Hassler, Donald M., G38, G45, G62-G63
Heelas, Paul, A95
Herron, Don, G22
Hewett, Jerry, A182
Hillig, Chuck, A113
Hoffman, Charles E., G79
Holland, Stephen, A142, A192, A231, H6
Hopkins, James, A90, A279
Hubin, Allen J., C1
Huidobro, Vicente, B5
Hutchison, Don, G46, G94
Indick, Ben P., A100, A163
Jaffery, Sheldon R., G11, G28, G35
Jones, Robert Kenneth, G56, G89
Joshi, S. T., A262, G41, G43
Justyna, A239
Kern, Gary, B1-B2, B4
Kimberlin, Scottie, A131, A191

BP 300, by Robert Reginald & Mary Wickizer Burgess

Skinner, Robert E., A228, C5
Slout, William L., A82, A154, A161, A194, A199, A210-A211, A222, A253, A271, A284, A293
Slusser, George Edgar, A1, A4, A7, A9-A10, A14-A15, A19
Smith, Clark Ashton, G22
Smith, Curtis C., A243
Smith, Robert A., A237
Spayde, Sydney H., A175
Spencer, Kathleen, G16
Stableford, Brian, A32, A44, A81, A201, A207, A219, A233, A288, A289
Stamatoplos, Anthony C., A234
Stanich, Ray, C2
Stanley, Colin, A96
Stephenson, Gregory, A273
Stevens, Carol D., A167, G51
Stevens, David, A167, G51
Stovel, Nora Foster, D2
Swanbeck, Jan, A80
Szymanski, Leszek, A50
Temianka, Dan, A218
Temple, William F., A299
Tevis, Yvonne Pacheco, A157, A160, A240
Thayer, Stuart, A284
Thompson, Judith, A95
Touponce, William F., A297, G76
Trimble, Robert G., A174, A216, A266
Turner, Arnella K., A119
Tymn, Marshall B., G4, G83-G84
Valera, Juan, A174
Van Dover, J. Kenneth, A121, A162, A241
Vance, Jack, A218
Wagner, Geoffrey, A16
Walton, Hanes Jr., A227
Warren, Alan, A187, D1
Webb, Lucas, A3
Weedman, Jane Branham, G82
Weinkauf, Mary S., A183, A206, A246
Wendall, Carolyn, G3
Westfahl, Gary, A247
Whibley, Charles, A283
Wibberley, Christopher, A144
Wibberley, Leonard, A21, A27, A88, A144
Wilgus, Neal, A260
Wilson, Colin, A28, A42, A97, A294
Winter, Douglas E., G85
Wolf, Milton T., A213
Wolfe, Gary K., G21
Wood, Martine, A229
Wood, Susan, A99

TITLE INDEX

A. Merritt (Ronald Foust), G1

Across the Wide Missouri: The Diary of A Journey from Virginia to Missouri in 1819 and Back Again in 1822, with a Description of the City of Cincinnati (James Brown Campbell, ed. by Mary Wickizer Burgess), A112

The Adventure Magazine Index (Richard J. Bleiler), G2

Adventures of a Freelancer: The Literary Exploits and Autobiography of Stanton A. Coblentz (Stanton A. Coblentz & Jeffrey M. Elliot, ed. by Scott Alan Burgess), A156

Against Time's Arrow: The High Crusade of Poul Anderson (Sandra Miesel), A24

Ah, Julian! A Memoir of Julian Brodetsky (Leonard Wibberley), A88

Aldiss Unbound: The Science Fiction of Brian W. Aldiss (Richard Mathews), A12

Alfred Bester (Carolyn Wendell), G3

Algebraic Fantasies and Realistic Romances: More Masters of Science Fiction (Brian Stableford), A207

Alistair MacLean: The Key Is Fear (Robert A. Lee, edited by Robert Reginald), A5

American Fantasy and Science Fiction (Marshall B. Tymn), G4

Amphitheatres and Circuses: A History from Their Earliest Date to 1861, with Sketches of Some of the Principal Performers (T. Allston Brown, ed. by William L. Slout), A194

The Ancient Church on New Shores: Antioch in North America (Archpriest Antony Gabriel), A258

Anne McCaffrey (Mary T. Brizzi), G5

The Annotated Guide to Fantastic Adventures (Edward J. Gallagher), G6

The Annotated Guide to Startling Stories (Leon Gammell), G7

The Annotated Guide to Stephen King: A Primary and Secondary Bibliography of the Works of America's Premier Horror Writer (Michael R. Collings), G8

The Annotated Guide to Unknown & Unknown Worlds (Stefan R. Dziemianowicz), G9

The Annotated Index to The Thrill Book: Complete Indexes to and Descriptions of Everything Published in Street & Smith's The Thrill Book (Richard J. Bleiler), G10

An Annotated Narrative of Joe Blackburn's A Clown's Log (Joe Blackburg, ed. by Charles H. Day & William L. Slout), A154

Anti-Posters: Soviet Icons in Reverse (Boris Mukhametshin), B3

Anti-Sartre, with an Essay on Camus (Colin Wilson), A42

The Arkham House Companion: Fifty Years of Arkham House: A Bibliographical History and Collector's Price Guide to Arkham House/Mycroft & Moran, Including the Revised and Expanded Horrors and Unpleasantries (Sheldon Jaffery), G11

The Armchair Detective, Volume One (ed. by Allen J. Hubin), C1

Arthur C. Clarke, Second Edition (Eric S. Rabkin), G12

BP 300, by Robert Reginald & Mary Wickizer Burgess

The Association Oath Rolls of the British Plantations [New York, Virginia, etc.], A.D. 1696: Being a Contribution to Political History (ed. by William Gandy), A151

At Wolfe's Door: The Nero Wolfe Novels of Rex Stout (J. Kenneth Van Dover), A121

The Attempted Assassination of John F. Kennedy: A Political Fantasy (Lucas Webb), A3

The Barstow Printer: A Personal Name and Subject Index to the Years 1910-1920 (Buckley Barry Barrett), A68

The Beach Boys: Southern California Pastoral (Bruce Golden), A2

The Beach Boys: Southern California Pastoral, Second Edition (Bruce Golden & Paul David Seldis), A120

Below the Iceberg: Anti-Sartre and Other Essays, Second Edition (Colin Wilson), A294

Beneath the Red Star: Studies on International Science Fiction (George Zebrowski, ed. by Pamela Sargent), A248

Beware of the Mouse (Leonard Wibberley), A21

Bibi Mkuba: My Experiences During Wartime in German East Africa (Ada Schnee, trans. and ed. by Sam E. Edelstein, additional editing by Barbara Ann Quarton), A223

Bishops Extraordinary (Karl Pruter), F1

Black Forbidden Things: Cryptical Secrets from the "Crypt of Cthulhu" (ed. by Robert M. Price), G13

Black Paradise: The Rastafarian Movement (Peter B. Clarke), A93

Black Paradise: The Rastafarian Movement, Revised Edition (Peter B. Clarke & Bonnie L. Petry), A179

Black Women at the United Nations: The Politics, a Theoretical Model, and the Documents (Hanes Walton Jr., ed. by Paul David Seldis & Mary A. Burgess), A227

Blond Barbarians & Noble Savages (L. Sprague de Camp), A75

BP 250: An Annotated Bibliography of the First 250 Publications of the Borgo Press, 1975-1996 (Robert Reginald & Mary A. Burgess), A255

The Bradbury Chronicles (George Edgar Slusser), A7

Brian Aldiss (Michael R. Collings), G14

British Science Fiction Paperbacks and Magazines, 1949-1956: An Annotated Bibliography and Guide (Philip Harbottle & Stephen Holland, ed. by Daryl F. Mallett & Michael Burgess), A192

British Science Fiction Paperbacks and Magazines, 1949-1956: An Annotated Bibliography and Guide, Revised Edition (Philip Harbottle & Stephen Holland, ed. by Daryl F. Mallett & Michael Burgess), A231

Broadway Below the Sidewalk: Concert Saloons of Old New York (ed. by William L. Slout), A199

Calendar of Coroners Rolls of the City of London, A.D. 1300-1378 (ed. by Reginald R. Sharpe), A214

California Ranchos: Patented Private Land Grants Listed by County (Burgess McK. Shumway, ed. by Michael and Mary Burgess), A92

Candle for Poland: 469 Days of Solidarity (Leszek Szymanski, ed. by R. Reginald), A50

The Cape of Don Francisco Torquemada (Benito Pérez Galdós, trans. by Robert G. Trimble), A266

A Casebook on The Stand (ed. by Tony Magistrale), G15

BP 300, by Robert Reginald & Mary Wickizer Burgess

The Catholic Priest: A Guide to Holy Orders (Karl Pruter, ed. by Paul David Seldis), A150

Cat'spaw Utopia: Albert K. Owen, the Adventurer of Topolobampo Bay, and the Last Great Utopian Scheme, Second Edition (Ray Reynolds), A269

Centurions, Knights, and Other Cops: The Police Novels of Joseph Wambaugh (J. K. Van Dover), A241

Chaos Burning on My Brow: Don Juan Valera in His Novels (Robert G. Trimble), A216

Charles Williams (Kathleen Spencer), G16

Chicago Ain't No Sissy Town! The Regional Detective Fiction of Howard Browne (John A. Dinan), A274

Children's Fantasy (Francis J. Molson), G17

The Chinese Economy: A Bibliography of Works in English (Robert Goehlert & Anthony C. Stamatoplos, ed. by Daryl F. Mallett, Mary A. Burgess, Xiwen Zhang), A234

Christopher Hampton: An Introduction to His Plays (William J. Free, ed. by Dale Salwak), A195

Christopher Isherwood: A World in Evening (Kay Ferres, ed. by Dale Salwak), A203

Christopher Priest (Nicholas Ruddick), G18

Chronology of the Death Valley Region in California, 1849-1949; and, Place Names of the Death Valley Region in California and Nevada, 1845-1947: An Index of the Events, Persons, and Publications Connected with Its History (T. S. Palmer), A105

Clark Ashton Smith (Steve Behrends), G19

A Clash of Symbols: The Triumph of James Blish (Brian Stableford), A32

The Classic Years of Robert A. Heinlein (George Edgar Slusser), A14

The Clockwork Universe of Anthony Burgess (Richard Mathews), A25

Clowns and Cannons: The American Circus During the Civil War (William L. Slout), A271

The Coachella Valley Preserve: The Struggle for a Desert Wetlands (Yvonne Pacheco Tevis & M. Louise Reynnells), A240

Codex Derynianus: Being a Comprehensive Guide to the Peoples, Places, & Things of the Derynye & the Human Worlds of the XI Kingdoms: Including Historyes of the Major & Minor States & the Occurrences Which Have Been of Most Importance to Them: With Compleat Biographyes of the Prominent Personages & Holy Saints of Gwynedd, Torenth, Meara, Bremagne, Mooryn, Howicce, Llannedd, The Connait, R'Kassi, Orsal & Tralia, Fallon, Byzantyun, The Forcinn Buffer States, & the Other Countryes of This Region from the Birth of Our Lord Jesus Christ unto Anno Domini 1126: Together with a Detail'd Chronological Historye of the Great Sovereign Kingdom of Gwynedd and All Her Neighbours: Also Including a Liturgical Calendar of the Saints of Gwynedd: With Many Lists of the Patriarchs, Primates, Kings, Princes, Dukes, Earls, Counts, & Other Nobles & Notables of These States: With Much True Opinions & Observations Regarding Same (Katherine Kurtz and Robert Reginald), A286

Colin Wilson: The Outsider and Beyond (Clifford P. Bendau), A29

Comic Inferno: The Satirical World of Robert Sheckley (Gregory Stephenson), A273

Conan's World and Robert E. Howard (Darrell Schweitzer), A22

Confessions of a Trekoholic: A New Look at The Next Generation (Hilary Palencar), A263

The Cranberry Tea Room Cookbook (Richard Martinez, ed. by Gloria Chavez), A143

BP 300, by Robert Reginald & Mary Wickizer Burgess

BP 300, by Robert Reginald & Mary Wickizer Burgess

BP 300, by Robert Reginald & Mary Wickizer Burgess

George Orwell's Guide Through Hell: A Psychological Study of 1984, Revised Edition (Robert Plank, ed. by Robert Reginald), A198

Ghetto, Shtetl, or Polis? The Jewish Community in the Writings of Karl Emil Franzos, Sholom Aleichem, and Shmuel Yosef Agnon (Miriam Roshwald), A277

Glorious Perversity: The Decline and Fall of Literary Decadence (Brian Stableford), A289

Grand Entrée: The Birth of the Greatest Show on Earth, 1870-1875 (Stuart Thayer and William L. Slout), A284

A Guide to Science Fiction & Fantasy in the Library of Congress Classification Scheme (Michael Burgess), A60

A Guide to Science Fiction and Fantasy in the Library of Congress Classification Scheme, Second Edition (Michael Burgess), A87

Hal Clement (Donald M. Hassler), G38

Hardboiled Burlesque: Raymond Chandler's Comic Style (Keith Newlin), C4

Hard-Boiled Heretic: The Lew Archer Novels of Ross Macdonald (Mary S. Weinkauf, ed. by Mary Wickizer Burgess), A183

Harlan Ellison: Unrepentant Harlequin (George Edgar Slusser), A9

Hasan (Piers Anthony), A13

The Haunted Man: The Strange Genius of David Lindsay (Colin Wilson), A28

Heroes and Incidents of the Mexican War (Isaac George), E1

H.G. Wells (Robert Crossley), G39

A History of the Old Catholic Church (Karl Pruter), F4

The Holy Grail Revealed: The Real Secret of Rennes-le-Château (Patricia & Lionel Fanthorpe, ed. by R. Reginald), A74

The Horror of It All: Encrusted Gems from the "Crypt of Cthulhu" (ed. by Robert M. Price), G40

The House of the Burgesses (M. R. Burgess), A52

The House of the Burgesses: Being a Genealogical History of William Burgess of Richmond (Later King George) County, Virginia, His Son, Edward Burgess of Stafford (Later King George) County, Virginia, with the Descendants in the Male Line of Edward's Sons: Garner Burgess of Fauquier County, Virginia, William Burgess of Stafford County, Virginia, Edward Burgess, Jr. of Fauquier County, Virginia, Moses Burgess of Orange County, Virginia, Reuben Burgess of Rowan (Later Davie) County, North Carolina, Second Edition, Revised and Expanded (Michael Burgess & Mary A. Burgess), A184

H.P. Lovecraft (S. T. Joshi), G41

H.P. Lovecraft and the Cthulhu Mythos (Robert M. Price), G42

H.P. Lovecraft: The Decline of the West (S. T. Joshi), G43

Hugo Gernsback, Father of Modern Science Fiction, with Essays on Frank Herbert and Bram Stoker (Mark Siegel), A89

If J.F.K. Had Lived: A Political Scenario (R. Reginald & Jeffrey M. Elliot), A49

Imaginative Futures: Proceedings of the 1993 Science Fiction Research Conference: June 17-19, 1993, Reno, Nevada (ed. by Milton T. Wolf & Daryl F. Mallett), A213

Ink from a Circus Press Agent: An Anthology of Circus History from the Pen of Charles H. Day (Charles H. Day, ed. and with a Circus Personnel Roster by William L. Slout), A211

Inside Science Fiction: Essays on Fantastic Literature (James Gunn), A138

Interviews with Britain's Angry Young Men: Literary Voices #2 (Dale Salwak), A58

233

BP 300, by Robert Reginald & Mary Wickizer Burgess

Into the Flames: The Life Story of a Righteous Gentile (Irene Gut Opdyke & Jeffrey M. Elliot, ed. by Mary A. Burgess), A139

Ira Levin (Douglas Fowler), G44

An Irony of Fate: The Fiction of William March (Abigail Ann Martin, ed. by Mary A. Burgess), A189

Isaac Asimov (Donald M. Hassler), G45

Islands in the Sky: The Space Station Theme in Science Fiction Literature (Gary Westfahl), A247

The Italian Theater in San Francisco: Being a History of the Italian-Language Operatic, Dramatic, and Comedic Productions Presented in the San Francisco Bay Area Through the Depression Era, with Reminiscences of the Leading Players and Impresarios of the Times (Lawrence Estavan, ed. by Mary A. Burgess), A126

It's Down the Slippery Cellar Stairs (R. A. Lafferty), A76

It's Down the Slippery Cellar Stairs: Essays and Speeches on Fantastic Literature, Second Edition, Revised and Expanded (R. A. Lafferty), A217

It's Raining Corpses in Chinatown (ed. by Don Hutchison), G46

Jack London (Gorman Beauchamp), G47

The Jack Vance Lexicon: The Coined Words of Jack Vance, from Ahulph to Zipangote (Jack Vance, ed. by Dan Temianka), A218

James Tiptree, Jr. (Mark Siegel), G48

Jerzy Kosinski: The Literature of Violation (Welch D. Everman), A122

The Jewish Holocaust: An Annotated Guide to Books in English (Marty Bloomberg), A128

The Jewish Holocaust: An Annotated Guide to Books in English, Second Edition, Revised and Expanded (Marty Bloomberg & Buckley Barry Barrett), A208

J.G. Ballard (Peter Brigg), G49

Joe Haldeman (Joan Gordon), G50

John D. MacDonald and the Colorful World of Travis McGee (Frank D. Campbell, Jr., ed. by Robert Reginald), A8

John Nieminski: Somewhere a Roscoe (John Nieminski, ed. by Ely Liebow & Art Scott), C7

J.R.R. Tolkien (David Stevens & Carol D. Stevens), G51

J.R.R. Tolkien: The Art of the Mythmaker, Revised Edition (David Stevens & Carol D. Stevens, ed. by Roger C. Schlobin), A167

Justyna's Diary: Jewish Resistance to the Nazis in Wartime Poland (Justyna, trans. by Majka Shephard, ed. by Nathan Kravetz), A239

Kansas and Me: Memories of a Jewish Childhood (Annette Peltz McComas, ed. by Nathan Kravetz), A212

Knight with Quill: Essays on British and European Literature and Littérateurs (Charles Whibley, ed. by Frederick Rankin MacFadden Jr.), A283

Kurt Vonnegut (Donald E. Morse), G52

Kurt Vonnegut: The Gospel from Outer Space; (or, Yes We Have No Nirvanas) (Clark Mayo), A11

Laughing Like Hell: The Harrowing Satires of Jim Thompson (Gay Brewer), A244

Legends and Lovers: Fourteen Profiles (William F. Nolan), A280

Lemady: Episodes of a Writer's Life (Keith Roberts), A275

Lewis Carroll (Beverly Lyon Clark), G53

Libido into Literature: The "Primera Época" of Benito Pérez Galdós (Clark M. Zlotchew, ed. by Daryl F. Mallett), A171

BP 300, by Robert Reginald & Mary Wickizer Burgess

The Life and Struggles of Negro Toilers (George Padmore), E2

Life Upon the Wicked Stage: A Visit to the American Theatre of the 1860s, 1870s, and 1880s as Seen in the Pages of the New York Clipper (ed. by William L. Slout), A253

Lightning from a Clear Sky: Tolkien, the Trilogy, and the Silmarillion (Richard Mathews), A20

Lin Carter: A Look Behind His Imaginary Worlds (Robert M. Price), G54

Literary Voices #1 (Jeffrey M. Elliot), A39

Literary Voices #2 (Dale Salwak), A58

The Little Kitchen Cookbook (Scottie Kimberlin), A131

The Little Kitchen Cookbook, Second Edition, Revised and Expanded (Scottie Kimberlin, ed. by Mary Wickizer Burgess), A191

Lords Temporal & Lords Spiritual: A Chronological Checklist of the Popes, Patriarchs, Katholikoi, and Independent Archbishops and Metropolitans of the Monarchical Autocephalous Churches of the Christian East and West (Boden Clarke), A66

Lords Temporal and Lords Spiritual: A Chronological Checklist of the Popes, Patriarchs, Katholikoi, and Independent Archbishops and Metropolitans of the Autocephalous and Autonomous Monarchical Churches of the Christian East and West, Second Edition, Revised and Expanded (Michael Burgess), A232

Lovecraft: A Look Behind the Cthulhu Mythos: The Background of a Myth That Has Captured a Generation (Lin Carter), G55

The Lure of Adventure (Robert Kenneth Jones), G56

The Mad Kokoschka: A Play in 3 Acts (Gary Kern), B2

The Magic Labyrinth of Philip José Farmer (Edgar L. Chapman), A61

The Magic That Works: John W. Campbell and the American Response to Technology (Albert I. Berger, ed. by Mary A. Burgess), A159

The Many Facets of Stephen King (Michael R. Collings), G57

Margaret Drabble, Symbolic Moralist (Nora Foster Stovel), D2

Marion Zimmer Bradley (Rosemarie Arbur), G58

Mary Roberts Rinehart, Mistress of Mystery (Frances H. Bachelder, ed. by Dale Salwak & Daryl F. Mallett), A168

Mary Shelley (Allene Stuart Phy), G59

Masters of Evil: A Viewer's Guide to Cinematic Archvillains (Georgette S. Fox), A298

Masters of Science Fiction: Essays on Six Science Fiction Authors (Brian Stableford), A44

Merry Wheels and Spokes of Steel: A Social History of the Bicycle (Robert A. Smith), A237

Mexico and the United States: Neighbors in Crisis: Proceedings from the Conference, Neighbors in Crisis, a Call for Joint Solutions (ed. by Daniel G. Aldrich Jr. & Lorenzo Mayer, additional anonymous editing by Yvonne Pacheco Tevis), A160

Misfortune (Gary Kern), B4

The Monumental Inscriptions in the Churches and Churchyards of the Island of Barbados, British West Indies (Vere Langford Oliver), A98

Monumental Inscriptions: Tombstones of the Island of Barbados, New Edition (Vere Langford Oliver), A209

More Monumental Inscriptions: Tombstones of the British West Indies (Vere Langford Oliver), A152

The Moral Voyages of Stephen King (Tony Magistrale), G60

BP 300, by Robert Reginald & Mary Wickizer Burgess

BP 300, by Robert Reginald & Mary Wickizer Burgess

BP 300, by Robert Reginald & Mary Wickizer Burgess

BP 300, by Robert Reginald & Mary Wickizer Burgess

The Science Fiction Reference Book: A Comprehensive Handbook and Guide to the History, Literature, Scholarship, and Related Activities of the Science Fiction and Fantasy Fields (ed. by Marshall B. Tymn), G84

Science Fiction Voices #1: Interviews with Science Fiction Writers (Darrell Schweitzer), A31

Science Fiction Voices #2: Interviews with Science Fiction Writers (Jeffrey M. Elliot), A35

Science Fiction Voices #3: Interviews with Science Fiction Writers (Jeffrey M. Elliot), A40

Science Fiction Voices #4: Interviews with Modern Science Fiction Authors (Jeffrey M. Elliot), A47

Science Fiction Voices #5: Interviews with American Science Fiction Writers of the Golden Age (Darrell Schweitzer), A45

Science Fiction Voices #6: Interviews with Pulp Magazine Writers and Editors—SEE: *Pulp Voices*

The Second Marxian Invasion: The Fiction of the Strugatsky Brothers (Stephen W. Potts), A123

Self-Portrait: Ceaselessly into the Past (Ross Macdonald, ed. by Ralph B. Sipper), A220

Sermons in Science Fiction: The Novels of S. Fowler Wright (Mary S. Weinkauf, ed. by Michael Burgess), A206

Seven by Seven: Interviews with American Science Fiction Writers of the West and Southwest (Neal Wilgus), A260

Sextet: Six Essays: On Turning Eighty, Reflections on the Death of Mishima, First Impressions of Greece, The Waters Reglitterized, Reflections on the Maurizius Case, Mother, China, and the World Beyond (Henry Miller), A225

Shadowings: The Reader's Guide to Horror Fiction, 1981-1982 (ed. by Douglas E. Winter), G85

Shamrocks and Sea Silver, and Other Illuminations (Leonard Wibberley, ed. by Christopher Wibberley & Paul David Seldis), A144

Shanghai Year: A Westerner's Life in the New China (Peter Brigg), G86

"The Shining" Reader (ed. by Tony Magistrale), G87

The Shorter Works of Stephen King (Michael R. Collings & David Engbretson), G88

The Shudder Pulps: A History of the Weird Menace Magazines of the 1930s (Robert Kenneth Jones), G89

Sir Henry (Robert Nathan), A34

Sleepless Nights in the Procrustean Bed: Essays (Harlan Ellison, ed. by Marty Clark), A59

The Sociology of Science Fiction (Brian Stableford), A81

The Sound of Detection: Ellery Queen's Adventures in Radio (Francis M. Nevins Jr. & Ray Stanich), C2

The Space Odysseys of Arthur C. Clarke (George Edgar Slusser), A19

Speaking of Horror: Interviews with Writers of the Supernatural (Darrell Schweitzer, ed. by Daryl F. Mallett), A197

Stalin: An Annotated Guide to Books in English (Marty Bloomberg & Buckley Barry Barrett, ed. by Michael Burgess & Paul David Seldis), A165

Stanislaw Lem (J. Madison Davis), G90

BP 300, by Robert Reginald & Mary Wickizer Burgess

BP 300, by Robert Reginald & Mary Wickizer Burgess

A Triumph of the Spirit: Thirteen Stories of Holocaust Survivors, Second Edition (ed. by Jacob Biber, additional editing by Mary A. Burges), A285

The Unseen King (Tyson Blue), G97

Up Your Asteroid! A Science Fiction Farce (C. Everett Cooper), A6

Urania's Daughters: A Checklist of Women Science-Fiction Writers, 1692-1982 (Roger C. Schlobin), G98

A Usual Lunacy (D. G. Compton), A23

Victorian Criticism of American Writers: A Guide to British Criticism of American Writers in the Leading British Periodicals of the Victorian Period, 1824-1900 (Arnella K. Turner), A119

Voices of the River Plate: Interviews with Writers of Argentina and Uruguay (Clark M. Zlotchew, ed. by Paul David Seldis), A215

A Voyage to America Ninety Years Ago: The Diary of a Bohemian Jew on His Voyage from Hamburg to New York in 1847 (S. E. Rosenbaum, ed. by Guido Kisch, trans. by Nathan Kravetz), A242

Vultures of the Void: A History of British Science Fiction Publishing, 1946-1956 (Philip Harbottle & Stephen Holland, ed. by Daryl F. Mallett), A142

The Way of the Heart: The Rajneesh Movement (Judith Thompson & Paul Heelas), A95

A Wayfarer in a World in Upheaval (Bernard L. Ginsburg, ed. by Nathan Kravetz & Daryl F. Mallett), A177

"We, the People!": Bay Area Activism in the 1960s: Three Case Studies (Richard DeLuca), A204

W.E.B. Du Bois: His Contributions to Pan-Africanism (Kwadwo O. Pobi-Asamani, ed. by Daryl F. Mallett), A185

Welcome to the Revolution: The Literary Legacy of Mack Reynolds (Curtis C. Smith, ed. by Roger C. Schlobin), A243

Western Fiction in the Library of Congress Classification Scheme (Michael Burgess & Beverly A. Ryan), A91

The Western Pulp Hero: An Investigation into the Psyche of an American Legend (Nick Carr), G99

Whaling Masters (Federal Writers Project), A85

What Are You Doing in My Universe? (Chuck Hillig), A113

The Wickizer Annals: Wickizer, Wickiser, Wickkiser, Wickkizer, Wickheiser (Mary Wickizer Burgess with M. R. Burgess), A53

Wilderness Visions: Science Fiction Westerns, Volume One (David Mogen), A48

Wilderness Visions: The Western Theme in Science Fiction Literature, Second Edition, Revised and Expanded (David Mogen, ed. by Daryl F. Mallett), A170

William Eastlake: High Desert Interlocutor (W. C. Bamberger, ed. by Mary A. Burgess & Paul David Seldis), A169

William Gibson (Lance Olson), G100

Windows of the Imagination: Essays on Fantastic Literature (Darrell Schweitzer), A295

The Wings of Madness: A Novel of Charles Baudelaire (Geoffrey Wagner), A16

The Woman in the Portrait: The Transfiguring Female in James Joyce's A Portrait of the Artist as a Young Man (Julienne H. Empric), A278

The Work of Brian W. Aldiss: An Annotated Bibliography & Guide (Margaret Aldiss, ed. by Boden Clarke), A140

BP 300, by Robert Reginald & Mary Wickizer Burgess

The Work of Bruce McAllister: An Annotated Bibliography & Guide (David Ray Bourquin), A67

The Work of Bruce McAllister: An Annotated Bibliography & Guide, Revised Edition (David Ray Bourquin), A70

The Work of Charles Beaumont: An Annotated Bibliography & Guide (William F. Nolan, ed. by R. Reginald), A71

The Work of Charles Beaumont: An Annotated Bibliography & Guide, Second Edition, Revised and Expanded (William F. Nolan, ed. by Boden Clarke), A116

The Work of Chad Oliver: An Annotated Bibliography & Guide (Hal W. Hall, ed. by Boden Clarke), A101

The Work of Colin Wilson: An Annotated Bibliography & Guide (Colin Stanley, ed. by Boden Clarke), A96

The Work of Dean Ing: An Annotated Bibliography & Guide (Scott Alan Burgess, ed. by Boden Clarke), A117

The Work of Elizabeth Chater: An Annotated Bibliography & Guide (Daryl F. Mallett & Annette Y. Mallett, ed. by Boden Clarke), A193

The Work of Gary Brandner: An Annotated Bibliography & Guide (Martine Wood, ed. by Boden Clarke & Daryl F. Mallett), A229

The Work of George Zebrowski: An Annotated Bibliography & Guide (Jeffrey M. Elliot & R. Reginald), A72

The Work of George Zebrowski: An Annotated Bibliography & Guide, Second Edition, Revised and Expanded (Jeffrey M. Elliot & Robert Reginald, ed. by Boden Clarke), A114

The Work of George Zebrowski: An Annotated Bibliography & Literary Guide, Third Edition, Revised and Expanded (Jeffrey M. Elliot & Robert Reginald, ed. by Boden Clarke), A249

The Work of Ian Watson: An Annotated Bibliography & Guide (Douglas A. Mackey, ed. by Boden Clarke), A103

The Work of Jack Dann: An Annotated Bibliography & Guide (Jeffrey M. Elliot, ed. by Boden Clarke), A111

The Work of Jack Vance: An Annotated Bibliography & Guide (Jerry Hewett & Daryl F. Mallett, ed. by Boden Clarke), A182

The Work of Jeffrey M. Elliot: An Annotated Bibliography & Guide (Boden Clarke), A62

The Work of Julian May: An Annotated Bibliography & Guide (Thaddeus Dikty & R. Reginald), A64

The Work of Katherine Kurtz: An Annotated Bibliography & Guide (Boden Clarke & Mary A. Burgess), A145

The Work of Louis L'Amour: An Annotated Bibliography & Guide (Hal W. Hall, ed. by Boden Clarke), A130

The Work of Pamela Sargent: An Annotated Bibliography & Guide (Jeffrey M. Elliot, ed. by Boden Clarke), A109

The Work of Pamela Sargent: An Annotated Bibliography & Literary Guide, Second Edition, Revised and Expanded (Jeffrey M. Elliot, ed. by Boden Clarke), A250

The Work of R. Reginald: An Annotated Bibliography & Guide (Michael Burgess & Jeffrey M. Elliot), A63

The Work of Reginald Bretnor: An Annotated Bibliography & Guide (Scott Alan Burgess, ed. by Boden Clarke), A104

BP 300, by Robert Reginald & Mary Wickizer Burgess

ABOUT THE AUTHORS

ROBERT REGINALD (Prof. Emeritus Michael Burgess) is the author of more than 100 published books for a dozen publishers, including the standard bibliographies of the mass market paperback and fantastic literature, the standard annotated critical guide to reference works on science fiction and fantasy, and the standard chronology and history of the Eastern Orthodox churches. He has also published three fantasy novels, two science fiction novels, an historical mystery, and a collection of stories, and is currently working on many new projects.

MARY WICKIZER BURGESS, a native Californian, has authored twenty-five books in her own right. She helped found The Borgo Press in 1975, and edited at least a hundred of its publications. She has also contributed numerous critical pieces to the Salem Press guides and other literary series.

9 780809 512065